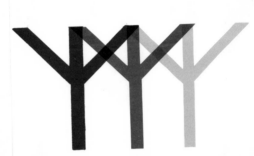

COST-EFFECTIVE SELF-SUFFICIENCY

or

The Middle-Class Peasant

COST-EFFECTIVE
SELF-SUFFICIENCY

or

The Middle-Class Peasant

Eve and Terence McLaughlin

David & Charles

Newton Abbot   London   North Pomfret (Vt)   Vancouver

British Library Cataloguing in Publication Data

McLaughlin, Eve
    Cost-effective self-sufficiency.
    1. Gardening – Great Britain
    I. Title   II. McLaughlin, Terence
    635   SB453.3.G7

    ISBN 0 7153 7474 5

Library of Congress Catalog Card Number: 77 91715

Set by HBM Typesetting Limited
Standish Street Chorley Lancashire
and printed in Great Britain
by Redwood Burn Limited, Trowbridge & Esher
for David & Charles (Publishers) Limited
Brunel House Newton Abbot Devon

Published in the United States of America
by David & Charles Inc
North Pomfret Vermont 05053 USA

Published in Canada
by Douglas David & Charles Limited
1875 Welch Street North Vancouver BC

Contents

Away From It All?

Are you tired of the rat race? Do you long to get away from it all—to sell up everything and buy a farm somewhere? Do you want to buck the money system and escape from the throwaway consumer economy? Do you sincerely want to be poor?

Consider the realities. Good, undeveloped farming land costs about £1,000 an acre, and if it is much less than that there is a good reason: it is too poor to support vegetable or animal life to any extent. A new tractor costs £5,000, a dear little pink pig for fattening about £50, and your lowing herd winding slowly o'er the lea represents, at £300 per dairy cow, the whole of most people's life savings, even non-accredited. You could pool your resources with a group of like-minded folk and form a commune, but when you think how difficult it is for just two people to live together in complete harmony, it seems asking for trouble to attempt it with twelve.

However, there is a compromise between remaining a discontented cog in the business machine and sinking your savings in a sea of mud. Stay put and develop your own patch. Make your garden, whether it is an estate, a backyard or simply a grow-bag on the patio, into a productive asset, instead of a recurring expense. Rather than working overtime to earn the money to buy convenience foods that are convenient only to the manufacturer, resign yourself to working less hard for other people, and start working for yourself. At least you have more chance of being appreciated.

Don't try to be entirely self-sufficient at first just for the sake of foolish consistency. If your friends point out that you are still dependent on the wicked commercial world for your clothes or cars or carpets, agree with them, and go on saving money on the things you *can* produce for yourself. As you get more adaptable, the range of these will widen all the time. Concentrate on food production first—this is, after all, the heaviest item of expense for most families—then on the saving of fuel and energy, or even home-production through solar or wind-power. If you can provide these essentials for yourself, you will find that a relatively small amount of paid work will keep you in clothes, transport, entertainment and other home comforts.

Of course, you may have to change some other aspects of your life. We have concentrated in this book on the use of land to grow the widest possible variety of vegetables because these will provide a perfectly adequate diet with little (or no) added meat and with the best utilisation of the space available. Rearing animals for meat is a dreadfully wasteful use of land. If your family's criterion of a proper meal is a large slab of meat with anaemic 'two veg' so subordinate as to go almost unnoticed, try to re-educate them.

We had only one motto for this book—Think Poor. Don't pay any attention to books or articles that tell you about gardening or wine-making or utilising solar energy, as if these are hobbies—a nice respectable way for the middle classes to use their spare time and a lot of their spare money. Don't buy gadgets that are really only toys. This is an unrespectable book, blatantly concerned with saving money, a mean, parsimonious book that—we are pleased to say—grudges every penny.

Now let us lead you up the garden.

The Realistic Alternative

Start right away, it doesn't involve moving house; you can go at your own pace and, if you get fed up with the whole idea, then at least you haven't burnt your boats behind you. In fact, in this way, you are very much less likely to get fed up.

The back gardens of Britain add up to around 5 million acres of cultivable land, yet most of them seem to consist, even in rural areas, of a scruffy lawn and a few measly herbaceous borders. If those gardens, or even part of them, were put down to vegetables, they could produce more, in proportion to size, than our arable farmers do on their vast acreages.

Farm and commercial horticultural planting is done at distances which allow for the ultimate height and spread of the various plants—you will often see this spacing quoted as correct for ordinary gardens. But, at home you do not plant a mass of carrots nine inches apart and harvest the lot at once. You plant at half that distance, and take every other one at intervals as young carrots when you want them, and let the rest mature. A commercial grower couldn't do that, so he loses half the potential of the planting space available.

In a garden, too, you can plant quick-growing crops in the gap between slow growers—which is called catch-cropping—and fill in any small spaces with a hand-ful of lettuces, or similar fast growers. The commercial man has to wait for a decent bit of space to be clear, if he does double-crop, since he can't sell half a dozen of anything separately.

So it is very difficult to say what size of garden you need to be self-sufficient. If you want a mixed diet, you will have to keep and kill some sort of animal, and these need much more space than crops. You can't really do much with grazing animals with less than about an acre of garden, since some of it will have to be fenced off for stock. Even then, you will have to buy in feed at times. Small animals or chickens need less space, but they do present certain problems in a suburb. If they are near the house, then they are probably near the neighbours' houses too, and there are bound to be complaints from the sort of people who like making complaints.

If you intend to live vegetarian, or to buy in any meat you want, then a much smaller space will do. The average family of four is reckoned to get a year's vegetables off a plot which measures 30 × 60ft (9 × 18m). But who is 'average'? If your available land is less than this, don't despair because your own requirements may be less too. The great beauty of domestic gardening is that the producer is also the consumer and can forecast very precisely what the family's needs are. If your teenage sons eat around half a hundredweight of potatoes a week, and there is a reasonably cheap source of supply locally, are you going to fill the plot with potatoes, or buy them and grow the pricier, fancy vegetables you would rather eat yourself? One thing to remember is that vegetables straight from the garden taste nicer, so more and more varieties, get eaten.

Even if you scarcely have a garden at all, it is possible to grow quite a lot in containers and odd corners. If you want to do better than that, are you keen enough to move to an older house with a larger garden in the same area? Builders of modern houses give the absolute minimum of land they can get away with, and often ruin it for cultivation for a year or so by stripping the topsoil. If you are stuck with a 'patio' house, you could probably rent an allotment.

One of the major snags of a modern estate development is that it is often land-scaped. This means that what should have been divided into individual, defensible space is open-plan grass in front of the houses which soon degenerates into a communal mudbath. If you are unlucky enough to have all your garden in front, the question arises as to whether you can claim it and fence it. If not, there is little point in growing things for the friendly neighbourhood vandals to flatten.

You may find that your efforts are hampered by the so-called 'amenity societies' —too often these consist of under-employed busybodies niggling away at the neighbours' slightly unusual projects while missing the major commercial eyesore down the road. Obviously, if you put up a pigsty in your front garden, you would risk offending 'amenities'. Pigs are clean, but keeping them so takes time. However, if your front garden is your only growing space, you will probably want to disguise the vegetable contents—and this is quite possible, by means of an 'edible herbaceous border'.

These suggestions and many other practical, money-saving ideas are examined in more detail in the following pages.

Tools and Accessories

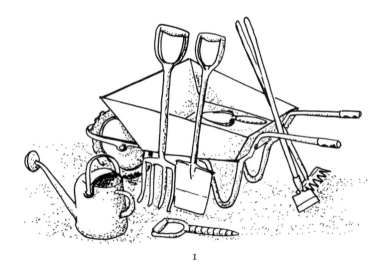

I

If you want to cultivate a vegetable garden, there are a certain number of basic tools you will have to buy (Figure 1). First come a good spade and fork. The spade —the one with the flat blade, not the curved-blade shovel used for muck-shifting— cuts edges, rough digs and scoops out trenches. The fork probes into the ground and breaks it into a workable tilth, letting nourishment down to the roots of plants. Both implements should be as solid and strong as possible, since they are in constant use in tough situations.

Select a tool which feels comfortable to your own hands when you hold it in a digging motion. Check, cautiously, that there are no sharp or rough edges on handle or shaft which could lacerate your skin. Once upon a time, there were tough, smooth ash shafts, which lasted a lifetime. Modern wood is inferior stuff, so go for a good strong metal tool. Don't be led astray by pretty paintwork, which wears off in no time, or plastic handles which snap at the first pressure. Pick a nice rounded handle, D shape for preference, though if you fancy a T shape buy it. Plastic covers on a steel handle are warmer to the touch on a chilly day, though they slip when wet.

If you are very small, you may find a fork with short tines easier to handle than a full-sized model. Any size of person will find one useful for top-forking bits of the ground in confined situations between growing crops. These border forks (sometimes called 'ladies' forks') are almost as expensive as the big ones, though.

Stainless steel tools will look smarter longer with less effort, but they are flimsy and may snap a tine under strain. Choose forged steel if you are serious about gardening (and saving money)—though it will rust unless the mud is cleaned off every time you finish work. This is a tedious chore at the end of a hard day, but, should you forget, washing the tools in vinegar will shift some rust and a proprietary cleaner, like Jenolite, the rest. Forged steel tools are cheaper—about £7 compared with £9–£14—and should last for years with care.

You will need a strong hand trowel for planting out, and a rake for taming the dug soil into smooth earth. The trowel will cost around £1–£1.50, and the rake might be anything from £3 to £6, according to paint and fancy shape. Again, pick what feels comfortable and tough to you and check for sharp projections first.

A hoe for weeding is also necessary. No two gardeners will ever agree about which kind is better—a push hoe or a draw hoe. A draw hoe has a curved neck and a blade roughly at right angles to the handle. It is used by bringing it down from above on to the weeds and chopping them vertically. The big danger is that the upstroke will clout any tallish plants adjacent and the down stroke can miss and slice into root vegetables or cut seedlings off in their prime. The push or Dutch hoe, which has a flat blade in line with the handle, is moved forward to cut off weeds below the surface. If your angle is too shallow or the pressure too feeble, part of the weed may be left in to grow again. However, it takes very little practice to become expert with it. We think the push hoe is a far more precise instrument and allows planting much closer than is safe with the draw hoe. On the other hand, the draw hoe is more adapted to earthing up potatoes. You pays your money— about £3–£4—and takes your choice.

The other basic tool is a dibber—a piece of wood for prodding tidy holes in the ground in which to plant potatoes, beans, small plants, etc. You make it yourself from the handle of an old fork or spade, with a comfortable D-shaped grip and tapered end—the abandoned corpse of a rusty tool would do. Or you can use a walking stick, a child's beach-spade handle, a garden cane or a strong stick with no spiky ends to jag your hand. You will find it useful to burn inch-divisions on the business end of the dibber.

Finally, you need wheels. A new wheelbarrow will cost between £12 and £25, according to size, strength and decorations. There is no denying that a strong metal barrow is handy for shifting heavy loads or loose earth, etc, besides allowing small children to participate harmlessly in the work. Alternatively, you can adapt an old pram or go-cart, or fix wheels to a box from the greengrocer, lined with plastic for carrying soggy stuff.

If you are starting from scratch, your outlay on tools can be cut dramatically by buying secondhand. Look out for local auctions, especially where the contents of big houses are being cleared. A full set of garden tools of good quality, with years of life in them, will often go cheap. Other useful, but not vital, items may be picked up the same way. A pair of shears, plus sharpening stone, helps with hedges and tough weeds,as well as awkward grass outcrops and edges. It even does crude pruning. Secateurs are the correct thing for pruning anything you value, like fruit trees and bushes, but it is worth waiting before buying. They are very often given away by gardening magazines as prizes for handy hints of the simplest sort and they are sure to appear on a list of birthday presents for anyone known to be taking an interest in gardening.

A watering can with a fine rose is a help with seed planting. If you possess trees, a wire rake with spring tines will remove the autumn leaves from lawn and beds without ripping holes in them, as the ordinary rake does. Leaves should not be wasted, and the right tool makes it easy to collect them from the street and other people's gardens (with permission).

Any sowing of seed in protected boxes and pots will necessitate a sieve. You might be able to make one from a wooden frame and wire netting, but the difficult bit is tucking all the sharp ends of wire safely out of the way.

There are certain accessories you will need, or want, to make gardening easier—depending on which kind of crops you choose to plant. Some of these necessities can be improvised and others are significantly cheaper to buy in bulk than in ones and twos. So you can either lay in sufficient to meet your own needs for years to come or share a bulk purchase with a group of neighbours.

If you grow peas, beans or any other tall, weak-stemmed crops, you will need stakes. Wood prunings from old trees, broom handles or scrap wood can be adapted for the purpose, but when these run out wood or bamboo canes must be bought. Wood in roofing-batten thickness, sometimes available secondhand, makes strong stakes and frames. Smooth canes are less rough on delicate plants, but string ties tend to slip down them more easily.

If you foresee much use of long canes—for runner beans, say—then study the prices as advertised by the big discount stores. You normally have to send away for a catalogue, so plan ahead. As an example, 100 medium-weight 4ft (1.2m) canes cost just over £4 and 100 7-footers for beans just under £9. By the ten they are more expensive, but still 40 per cent less than the cost per cane at ordinary shops.

A garden line is useful to keep your planting rows straight. It isn't the aesthetic appeal so much as knowing where it is safe to hoe before the seedlings are up. You can buy a commercial one, or make your own from string and sticks. If you grow many beans or raspberries, or any tall plant, a quantity of strong string or wire will be needed. And the cheapest way is to buy a roll of ex-army telephone wire— 200m cost about £4.

For minor tying-up jobs, you will need fillis—very soft twine for stringing up plants without cutting through the stems. The hairy string recovered from parcels will do as a substitute, but not thin hard cord with a sharp cutting edge. Torn-up rag, old bits of bandage or plaited wool scraps are better.

If your garden is plagued by birds—and they come from miles around at the first rumour of free food being provided—your seedlings must be protected from them. This particularly applies to peas, which need guards first and then support. The ideal thing for both jobs is wire netting in about 1½in (38mm) mesh. Unfortunately, it is expensive stuff. Farmers may throw away in ditches what look like great rolls of the stuff when improving their stock fencing. Keep an eye open for this, but be careful of any nasty lengths of rusty barbed wire in among the netting. This could give your hand an unpleasant injury—recycling is admirable, but not at the cost of tetanus.

You can improvise by protecting peas with a barricade of twigs, covering fruit with old lace curtains, or supporting beans on nylon net stiffened with inserted canes. But if you really feel the lack of wire netting, the cheapest way to buy it is from a discount house in 50m rolls at about 45p a metre for inch mesh. This compares well with shop prices, if you make a group purchase.

Plant pots are expensive, even with a discount for quantity. But every household has a lot of plastic containers—holding liquid detergent, shampoo, squash, yoghurt, soft margarine, etc—which can be washed and re-used for tender plants. Even egg boxes can be filled with earth for germinating seeds.

Detergent bottles should be cut in two places (Figure 2). The bottom makes a pot, with drainage holes pierced in the bottom. The middle section, placed on a lid or saucer and filled with earth, becomes a ring planter. The top makes a 'dark cover' for early germination and then a funnel for local watering. Transparent bottles, cut and upturned, become mini-greenhouses for delicate seedlings (Figure 3). The thinner sorts of plastic usually disintegrate in the sun after one season, but this doesn't matter, since they were free in the first place.

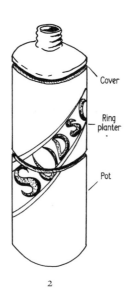

Cover

Ring
planter

Pot

2

3

Larger purpose-made pots, for tomatoes, are costly. Gallon squash containers, with the tops cut off, take quite a large plant and—if it is going to continue growing in a container—a plastic household bucket can be used; this is easily pierced with a hot skewer to make drainage holes at the base. Cheapest of all are buckets made of scrap plastic, often displayed as bait to lure you into a shop. These are handy for weeding and carrying small amounts of soil about.

Plastic trays for starting seeds germinating are valuable. Similar trays can be improvised from shallow wooden boxes, or cardboard ones covered in polythene with drainage holes pierced; polystyrene packaging, thrown away by shops, which has the added advantage of keeping the soil warm; a washing-up bowl with a hole in it; rusty baking tins, and waxed cartons. Some of these will have a limited life span, but they will have given some extra service.

4 Plant tin. Remove top completely, cut 3–6 triangular drainage holes in the bottom and drop the top inside, to rest on projecting points.

Even tin cans are re-usable. Detach the tops completely and hammer any jagged bits flat. Turn upside down and make four or six holes in the base with one of those triangular can piercers, leaving the points sticking up inside (Figure 4). Drop the lid in on top of these, which will give space for drainage. Fill with earth and plant up. When you want to get the plant out again, stick a skewer or knitting needle through the base holes and push the plant up on the lid.

Tumblers with chipped rims or wine glasses with snapped stems can be upturned over potted plants as mini-greenhouses. Obviously, you should put them somewhere in full view, so that no one tending the plants puts a hand down on the broken spike—preferably bind it with tape or cover with a blob of plasticine. Jam jars can be used the same way, but should be removed before the plant grows wider than the neck opening.

Polythene has a mass of uses in the garden, and is relatively cheap bought by the roll from manufacturers. However, an awful lot of it comes into the average house every week. Save polythene packaging of food and clothes and use it for covering pots or seed trays. Larger bags from the cleaners can be made into cloches of a sort. Heavily printed plastic can cover newly planted seeds—black plastic is even better, since it absorbs heat.

In general, don't throw away any packaging material before you have considered recycling it usefully in the garden. Most of it took a lot of our precious energy reserves to produce, and added a lot to the price of the original article. Getting extra mileage out of 'rubbish' is very satisfying—and think of the money it saves!

Machine-minder's Blues

The first comment of every armchair economist, as he looks out of his double-glazed window at a working garden, is that the home grower is seriously under-capitalised. Get some machinery, runs the argument. Install specialised buildings and automatic controls with flashing lights. Invest in elaborate watering systems and high-power spray equipment. And, if there is any room left in the garden after all this, get those undisciplined crops into neat lines, 3ft apart, so that the machines can plant, tend, water, weed, spray, pick, wash, and finally pop them into poly-thene bags so that they look almost as good as the shop varieties.

The machinery manufacturers are, as you might imagine, all in favour of this view. You can buy machines to dig, furrow, plough, trench, rake, hoe and earth-up—all reduced in size to garden proportions—and even such aids to gracious living as powered wheelbarrows, ride-on mowers, and automatic lawn-spikers that trundle around like some awful medieval weapon. No doubt, if you have all these, you can afford the time to go round the golf-course on your battery-powered trolley—and, after your heart-attack from lack of exercise, live the rest of your life with a battery-powered pacemaker. The fact is that most of these devices are merely toys for people who want to play farmers at the weekend, while others are useful, but for such a limited time that their cost cannot be justified in any real economic terms.

If you have more than 2–3 acres (1 hectare) under arable cultivation, not just pasture, you will need a small tractor, not only for planting and cultivating but for all the other jobs that go with this sort of area of land: ditching, hedging, bulldozing piles of compost around, and so on. If you want to use it for general carrying, even from your plot to your neighbour and back, you will need to license it before taking it on a public road.

If you have less than 2–3 acres of arable land but still need help, the answer may be a cultivator, which certainly takes a lot of the backache out of preparing the soil each year. Unless you are content just to scratch the surface of the soil, you need a machine with a 4–5hp engine; this will cost you around £300 new, or £170 reconditioned, for a reliable make with a range of accessories that fit. As one culti-vator advertisement puts it, 'One weekend can turn an overgrown wilderness into a mini market garden,' and this is true enough in its way. The problems come in deciding what your expensive pet is going to do for the other fifty-one weekends in the year.

The advertisements talk glibly about furrowing, weeding, raking, earthing-up potatoes . . . but wait until you try to do all these things with a machine that often feels like Boadicea's chariot with the steering gone. You can't weed by machine unless you leave room for it between rows, which entails a tremendous loss of productive ground. You can't earth up potatoes by machine—at least, we have never met anyone who could—without losing large numbers of tubers from the edge of the rows unless again you have your rows uneconomically wide apart. You usually end up by buying a rotary mower attachment for your cultivator, and using it to cut the grass for the rest of the year—employing a £300 machine to do the job of a £40 mower.

The best answer to this problem is to hire a cultivator for a week at the beginning of the season. This way you get the work done for about £15 a year, which is less than the interest on the capital cost of a cultivator, and someone else has the costs of housing and servicing the machine. You can get a 5hp cultivator into the back of a small hatch-back car, so saving delivery costs. Depending on the size of your plot, you might even be able to share a week's hire with a neighbour. The daily hire cost is about £5 and, as you can't depend on it not to rain on the day you have chosen, a week is a sensible period.

Of course, if you can buy a second-hand cultivator for around £60, this makes

5 Stirrup pump; second person needed to operate spray nozzle.

economic sense, because it will probably struggle on for another four years, possibly more. The feasibility of this idea will probably depend on your skill in reviving apparently dead internal combustion engines, as most people sell such machines cheap when they 'won't go'. Here is scope for all those teenagers who make weekends unbearable tinkering with motor cycles and old banger cars; a single-cylinder cultivator needs far less skill and know-how to get it going, but has quite a market value in the going state.

We quite like another garden machine, the compost shredder, but would not try to justify buying one at current market prices. Again, if you can acquire such a thing second-hand, or build it from scrap parts, it is useful. Ours was made from an old hammer-mill of doubtful parentage, and is driven by a home-made windmill (see page 242).

Spray equipment is necessary if you have full grown fruit trees, but need not be very elaborate. Most of the time you can use the cheapest kind of polythene hand spray—and a pair of steps, if necessary. Where there are more than one or two trees, you could invest in a stirrup-pump (Figure 5), obtainable from ex-government equipment suppliers for about £5. This is also useful for spraying tall banks of runner beans with water during the summer.

In general, don't imagine that machinery can be a substitute for care and thought. Where machines can actually save tedious manual work, use them—hire them if possible—but don't expect them to take over your responsibility for deciding exactly what has to be done. It is bad enough that the motor manufacturing industry suffers from this delusion, without it spreading to gardeners.

Starting a Garden From Scratch

On a new estate, you may be faced by a moonscape full of sordid deposits of builders' rubble and the junk thrown there by the local vandals. Before making a first-time garden, you will need to shift all this, but don't get rid of anything until you've pondered on it. Stones, broken bricks and blocks, mortar and even broken glass will come in handy for making the base of paths. Lengths of scrap wood will be useful for frames and plant supports. Even small pieces come in useful as fuel and rotten wood will compost.

Plastic containers—carefully relabelled—can be cut down to make planting pots or propagators. Even old large tins will serve as pots till they rust. Polystyrene food trays and packaging, polythene bags, bits of string, cardboard boxes—almost anything which people throw away can be turned to some use in the garden and may save you a great deal of money. The only discards are offensive-smelling or noxious articles and maybe glass, if this would endanger your children.

Having cleaned up the site, you are then probably possessed of an expanse of subsoil. It will hasten productivity if you can get a load of topsoil for it. On a new estate, the chances are that down the road the builders are still stripping topsoil from some other plot, which they then have to cart away and dump. A word with the boss may get you that topsoil more or less free. If not, you could advertise in the local paper. This might get you a load of soil on your front path at 8 am, but it will be worth the effort of shifting it.

In an older, neglected garden too there will be some of this junk clearing. Rusty water tanks are quite useful as compost containers or rubble holders till they finally fall to powder.

All the weeds can be put on the compost heap (see page 199). Twigs and branches won't compost without treatment, but will be useful for protecting and supporting peas and beans.

Existing flowers and small shrubs which are in the wrong place can normally be transplanted successfully, preferably out of their growing season. Autumn or spring, when the weather is dampish and the ground warmish, is best. Summer heat, winter cold or any sort of drought make things difficult. If necessary, soak the plant well before moving. The less time it spends out of the ground the better, to minimise the shock to the system.

First dig a large hole in the new place where you want your shrub to go, dumping the excavated soil on a plastic sheet or in buckets to save messing up the lawn and your feet. Then dig carefully round the transplant candidate, a good distance from the centre stem and outside the root run—poke around with a stick to find out where that ends. Then dig down below root level and lift the whole thing, with as much of the surrounding earth as possible. Edge the mass on to a plastic sheet or board and carry it to the new site. You will probably need a wheelbarrow or another pair of hands to accomplish this without dropping the lot halfway. Enlarge your new hole if necessary and replant at the original depth. If you need extra earth, take it from the original planting site—try to kid the transplant that its environment has not changed. Water well in and take the displaced earth to the original hole.

Larger shrubs and trees are a lot more chancy to shift, mainly because it is very hard to get them up with enough of their soil adhering. You may find in digging them out that one root appears to be going down to Australia. This is the tap root and in digging it out whole you may lose all the earth and break the fine root system higher up, which is more important. Therefore, if you meet this problem, scrape back the earth round this tap root and saw the villain through as low as possible. Try to keep the earth round the upper roots in place, with a sacking nappy.

Make sure your new hole is deep enough, cutting slots and channels to fit any big roots that stick out in odd directions. Put peat in the bottom of the hole, to retain moisture, sit your subject in place, very tenderly spreading the fine roots, which will take up nutrition fastest. If the shrub is rather tall, plant a stake with it, between the roots, and tamp the earth down hard round it. Fill up the hole with earth from the original site, and make sure there are no air pockets which will allow the roots to flop about when the wind shakes the top of the shrub. When the roots are well cushioned, heap more earth on top, a few inches above the level of the surrounding soil, and then tread the whole lot down firmly and tie the trunk to the stake.

Water while you are filling in, and soak afterwards. Be prepared to water every day for a week, and at intervals thereafter, when even more than a few days elapse without rain. If there is a hot spell, water over the leaves as well, since they will be giving out moisture faster than the unsettled roots will take it up.

If any hedges or trees round the boundary of the garden are so tall they seem to shadow the whole planting area, obviously something has to go. But don't just wade in and grub the lot up—they would take years to grow again if you made a mistake.

A tall privet hedge, so often found in town gardens of a certain age, takes most of the nourishment from the soil around it, in proportion to its height. A 10ft (3m) hedge robs the ground for 5ft on either side of it. But, is this villain hedge the only thing which stops Mrs Whatsit next door having a grandstand view of your garden from her bedroom window? Are you going to be happy working out there with her beady eyes boring into your back? Or, if a public path skirts your garden, is the hedge the only screen between the local schoolchildren and your ripening strawberries?

You could replace the hedge with a fence or wall, bearing in mind that the maximum legal height allowed for rear and side walls is 6ft 6in (2m) and for front walls, or any adjoining a public highway, about 3ft 3in (1m) with local variations. Close-board fencing will cost about £8 to £10 per 6ft (1.8m) run complete with fixings, and concrete block walling about the same. It is worth shopping around for quotations and availability, for the price of blocks varies a lot, usually by the number you order at one time. You will need rubble for foundations, which is an ideal way of disposing of your junk. Fencing is prettier, walling more durable— and the blocks can be rendered and painted. You could build a low wall with a short fence on top, to get the best of both worlds. We assume that you will do the work yourself, since it is simple enough for the average handyman. If you want it done for you, get a builder's quote and keep the smelling salts handy.

Don't creosote the fence if you intend to plant near it, but use a preservative non-toxic to plants. Remember that even fences and walls cast a shadow, and that the foundations of the wall project, making the 6–9in beside it useless for deep rooted plants.

Of course, you can only deal as you wish with a fence or hedge that is your own property. In towns, normally one side boundary is yours, the other your neighbour's. The deeds should have a mark showing who owns which side (see Figure 6). If not, ask a local resident in the road or take a look at any nearby fenced garden.

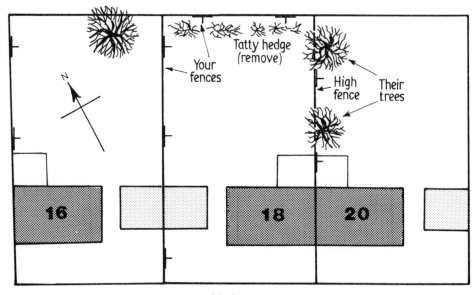

6 18, Avenue Road before operations commence.

The posts ought to be on the land of the person to whom the fence belongs. The same goes for any fence posts or wall piers you erect yourself. More often than not, it is the left-hand boundary, as you face the back of the garden, which is yours, but things get complicated at the corners of roads and with irregular street layouts. In case of doubt, try to come to an agreement with your neighbours before you start operations.

If there are hedges which cannot be removed, thin them or trim them to a better height. Privet which has gone all bare and leggy should be cut back really hard, and next growth season it will send out new shoots in close formation—much better as a barrier. If it is not your hedge, you are permitted to cut back any branches which overhang your property but only to the point where they cross the boundary. And the prunings technically belong to the owner of the hedge. The same applies to any fruit-tree branches which violate your air space. You may cut them, but not damage the tree in so doing, and the fruit is not yours. You mustn't spray other people's weeds either until they invade your land.

If you are left with a hedge to which you have done everything permissible and there is still a permanent shadow, don't despair, but use that side of the garden for your path and dump areas for rubble, compost and leaves. If you are stuck with hedges on both sides, plant shallow-rooted crops, like lettuce, near the hedge, and resign yourself to feeding the soil to replace what the hedge takes out.

One thing which may force you to keep hedges or even plant new ones is the attack from a prevailing wind, especially from north or east. Britain is a very windy country, and you may be glad of a windbreak to protect your small plants. Test the atmosphere near a gap in the hedge on a windy day, and imagine you are a tomato plant.

Oddly enough, walls and solid fences are less useful as windbreaks than apparently thin hedges. The wind hits any solid barrier, bounces up and comes down the other side with redoubled force. Hedges or open-weave fences filter the wind and take the sting away.

The ideal thing to plant, for windbreak, privacy and attractive appearance, is an evergreen hedge with height (no legal limits) but not too much thickness. Hedging conifers do very well, and can be green or gold or bluish. The fastest grower is probably *Cupressus lawsoniana*, available everywhere, but it is only fast *for an evergreen*. The catalogue illustrations show tiny little women dwarfed by huge, beautiful hedges, 6ft (1.8m) or more high. However, if you send for the amazing bargain offer of fifty for around £30 as advertised, you will receive wizened little things about 2ft high, which take four or five years to get to any decent height. In ten years, though, they look splendid and sturdy—if you can wait that long. You can buy really large container-grown trees, about 5ft (1.5m) high, from local garden centres, but they will cost around £3 each (or more in the season) and need care in their first year or two if they are to flourish.

Quickthorn is a lot cheaper, and deters small boys, but it is vicious to its owner. It is also not evergreen. Beech and hornbeam can be trained and trimmed to make a thin hedge of twisted twigs, and both will keep their brown leaves all winter if handled carefully when cut.

It is possible to do quite a lot with low hedges to keep the wind off the low-growing plants without blocking the sun. The Victorians used little box hedges round their vegetable plots, but mostly to conceal the utilitarian bits of the garden from the idle rich walking among the flowers. They are a bad idea, since they harbour pests. However, dwarf lavender and rosemary make neat little hedges, if trimmed from time to time, and both give a bonus crop for household use.

While you were clearing your garden, you will have been able to establish the patterns of sun and shade at different times of the day. With a compass or the map, find out where north is and, if possible, draw diagrams on a sunny day of where the maximum and minimum sun falls, in morning and afternoon. Any corner which never gets much light isn't going to ripen crops fast. The warmest spot is the place to be earmarked for the tomatoes. Note where the shadow of the house itself falls, and whether there is an accessible bit of south-facing wall. Mark the direction of the prevailing wind, and keep these diagrams by you when you are doing the detailed garden plan.

Soil testing

You will see a lot in books and magazines about acid and limy soils. Some plants hate one, some the other, and develop horrible ailments if planted in the wrong type of soil. How do you find out what kind of soil yours is? As a general rule, most town gardens are liable to be acid and those on chalk hills are likely to be limy. But this is varied by the kind of past treatment each has received, so you can test your individual garden soil to be sure.

Most people learn at school that litmus paper is turned red by acids and blue by alkalis or limy material. From any chemist who stocks wine-making apparatus, you can buy a sophisticated form of this called pH indicator paper, which shows not only if something is acid or limy, but how acid or limy. The whole pH scale runs from 1 (very acid) to 14 (very alkaline), but the papers generally available cover numbers 4 to 9, which is just the part of the scale you will need.

Collect samples of your soil when it is wet, from three, four or more different parts of the garden. Put each sample in a small jar and, if necessary, top up with distilled water until the soil has $\frac{1}{2}$ in (12.5mm) standing liquid on top. Tap water from some distant reservoir would falsify the results. Shake the sample vigorously, then leave it to separate again into mud and liquid.

Dip a piece of the pH paper in the liquid and match it up to the numbered colour chart which comes with the papers: 7 is neutral on the scale, so either 6 or 7 is fair to middling soil. If the sample registers 4 or 5, it is too acid; if it matches 8 or 9, it is too alkaline. If it is redder than 4 or bluer than 9, you have an acid bath or alkali desert there, not a garden. If only one sample registers too high or low, then there is probably some very local deposit of gunge. Try another sample a foot away from that one, or dig out the decaying car battery and destroy.

If your soil is noticeably acid, it will do no harm at all to add hydrated lime to it, and if it is noticeably limy, you will do no harm with compost, manure or sulphate of ammonia. However, don't be led into thinking there is a precise dose per square yard to be measured out with a fine scientific balance, even if you see this set out in a complicated table. Unless you tested every square foot of the garden separately, and then applied the prescribed dose to it from a dropper bottle, you could never cope with the local variations. One small area may have supported a greedy plant, and the next have been enriched by a natural fertiliser.

In fact, you won't go far wrong if you follow Grandfather's British Standard Measures—a little bit, a middling bit and a tidy bit.

If you are getting terrible results after a year of operation, with warped and stunted vegetables, then something may be deficient in the soil or you may have an infestation. Note down just what went wrong with each plant—yellowing leaves, coloured spots, wilting stems, etc. Read pages 209–13, or check up in one of the hundreds of books on garden ailments; ask the expert down the road; write to one of the excellent gardening magazines who offer free advice to readers. If the answer seems to lie in the soil, you can get it analysed for mineral deficiencies. We haven't found a good do-it-yourself kit sold commercially. A school or college laboratory might be interested; or the local Parks Department or Council Horticultural Adviser; or the Royal Horticultural Society, if you are a member; or an agricultural analytical chemist (yellow pages).

But, on the whole, if you treat the soil right and feed it compost, it will respond in a year or two. Whether it is acid or alkaline, the actual structure can be improved organically. Assess what breed of soil you have by the 'fist test'. Half an hour after a moderate rainfall, pick up a handful of soil and squeeze it in your fist. If it powders away between your fingers, then it is thin sandy stuff which won't retain water. If it clags all over your fingers, it's clayey, which will flood in winter and cake into blocks in summer. Pale, starved-looking stuff with whitish bits and a gritty feel is chalk marl, no better than sub-soil. Good soil is deep coloured—black, dark brown, or red in sandstone country—and it holds the print of your palm for a minute or two, then unfolds in decent-sized crumbs with plenty of fibrous matter in them. It's rather like squeezing a good home-made fruit cake.

If you haven't got good soil already, your object is to create it, by feeding in as much humus and nourishment as possible, ready for the demands the plants will make on it. It may take time to perfect, but every little helps, and you don't have to wait until perfection is reached. You may not get a brilliant harvest the first year, but there will be something to show for your labours and the promise of much more to come.

If you are making a new garden, especially one on poor soil, try to get the preparation done in autumn if you can, so that it is ready to plant up in spring. Even if the whole garden plan isn't worked out in detail, you have probably decided where the main plot comes, or the total area you are aiming to use.

Mark off with pegs and strings the area you intend to dig and slit along the edges with a spade. Pull up any large weeds and put them on the compost heap and strip off any grass. This is best done by cutting a slit, root deep, round three sides of a foot-square section, sliding a sharp spade under the flap and breaking back the piece. Pile the turf in a stack, face down, to rot quickly and re-use as humus.

When your plot is bare, you have to dig it over as deeply as possible. Correctly, it needs double digging, to loosen the soil for about 18in (45.7cm) (two spades, or spits) deep. Unless you are just after a quick return for a year or two, it is well worth double digging, but it is hard work, giving you aches in muscles you never had before. It will probably take an hour to dig 6ft (1.8m) square properly. This isn't so bad if you are working on a plot of only 12ft square total. This is four hours' digging at the same rate—call it five to allow for flagging energy. Then you can collapse with a virtuous feeling of duty done and possibly pounds off the waistline.

However, if virtue has no appeal, or you are dealing with a larger plot, a cultivator is the obvious answer. It is easy to handle and light enough for a delicate female to manage, and really rather fun. Most of them dig one spit deep, so you will have to shift the loose earth on the same principle as if you have done the digging, but this is as nothing compared with the full manual operation. If you come to the sub-soil—pale, gritty, inferior looking stuff, loosen it *in situ* to help drainage, but don't get it mixed up with the top layers.

As you go, put aside any large stones, preferably before they hit and blunt the cultivator blades. Also remove every scrap of couch grass. Its fat, white, unhealthy-looking roots spread everywhere, and any small bit left in the ground will multiply a hundred-fold and strangle your best plants. It is a nuisance to grub for it, but a lot easier than trying to get rid of it once the area is planted. The same applies to convolvulus, ground elder or any other perennial weeds.

If your plot is badly lacking in fibre-content, try burying small and thin-stemmed annual weeds, well down in layer two, as 'green manure' to rot there. Chop them up with the cultivator, if possible—and you can do the same with the removed thin turf. Don't try to chop thick-stemmed plants, because they will jam the machine. They are better off on the compost heap.

If you have access to any mature compost, strawy manure or well-rotted leaves, put a little between the two spits, where they will feed the soil ready for planting. If you need lime, then sprinkle it on top, or cover in lightly so it doesn't blow away. The average 'middling bit' of lime is 4oz (113g) or so per square yard. Don't, whatever you do, put in lime *and* fresh manure. They react together and give off ammonia into the air, which smells horrible and wastes all the goodness of both.

Especially in the case of clay soil, leave the dug ground rough and lumpy for the frost to break up. Try to keep the footballers off it, or the surface will form a hard pan and hold pools of water instead of letting it penetrate. There would be some benefit in actually sowing a winter-growing crop like rye or tares, as green manure, just to dig in when spring came to improve the texture of the soil. This depends on whether you can get seed.

Ordinarily, if you prepare the ground in autumn, all you will have to do in spring is remove any weeds—including the couch grass of which you shifted every scrap—maybe fork the top lightly and rake the bed to a nice smooth surface, ready for planting. The earth should break to a nice open texture with plenty of air spaces between the soil crumbs, to allow warmth and moisture to penetrate to the roots of the plants.

If you have to leave the preparation until spring, dig in the same way, though you will find the work much heavier with the ground full of winter rain. Don't try to work the soil when the ground is too wet, because it will compact into lumps beneath the surface and cause trouble to the young plants. Also be much more careful about adding natural fertilisers, since there will be no time for them to break down and spread through the soil. Some plants react very badly to freshly manured or limed areas, so check exactly what you are going to plant on a particular spot before adding anything. Probably you will need some form of artificial fertiliser to get things moving for this first year (see pages 187 – 98).

It is an advantage to start a compost heap (see page 199) early in the proceedings, so that you have somewhere to dump weeds as you strip them and also a place for kitchen waste during the winter.

It might seem logical to construct all the necessary paths and walks before you get busy with the planting season. This is sense in the case of boundary walls and paths which have only one possible position, next to a shadowing hedge. However, if you are new to the garden, and haven't seen just where the sun falls in summer, it might be as well to wait a while rather than running a path across what turns out to be the best tomato position. You can make a good temporary path from concrete paving blocks, laid on earth that has been tamped down level. Laying them on a bed of sand is rather better, but if you change your mind about the placing, getting the sand up again may be a problem.

By the end of your first season, you will have a better idea of what your final plan will be, whether you are going to build a greenhouse or frames, and any other ideas which may affect the layout of your path.

Grass paths between or round plots are easier to alter if you feel inclined, but remember to make them wide enough for your mower to run on, unless you sincerely enjoy crawling round with a pair of shears. Paths in the actual vegetable plots are only trodden earth and of minimum size. In a very wet period it may be necessary to put down stepping stones or boards to stop yourself sinking in as you work. You can get access to the back of a bed by mounting a board between two bricks or flower pots and doing a balancing act.

What Are You Going to Grow?

First comes the planning, which can be done largely in the cold days of winter—not the drawing of the diagram of *where* things will go, but deciding *what* you are going to grow.

The important thing is to decide what your family's preferences are. On the whole, if no one likes parsnips, it is probably a waste of time to plant them. If the dislike is based on a bad experience with some woody ones from a shop, then it's worth planting just a few to see whether the lovely fresh taste of them straight from the garden changes the family mind.

If you have teenage potato addicts, then you may devote a lot of space to growing them, or at least plant enough earlies under cloches to cover the gap when the old ones run out and new ones cost the earth. That is, if the lads remain as thin as rails. If you have a pudgy child, then maybe you will plant an alternative vegetable which is less fattening than the eternal chip.

If you entertain enough, you will probably want to grow early or exotic vegetables to astound your friends. However, to the non-gardener, *any* new vegetable fresh from the garden is exotic, compared with something from a tin or packet with all the flavour processed out of it.

Beware of over-production. Seeds look so tiny in a packet that it is very easy to plant too many at a time and land yourself with a lettuce mountain. There isn't an awful lot you can do to preserve lettuce and even the nicest salads pall after the fifteenth appearance in one week. When your lettuces and other vegetables have exhausted deserving friends and the Darby and Joan Club, and even the guinea pigs go on strike, you will resolve to sow in very small pinches next time. Ordinary surpluses can be mopped up by freezing or preserving, provided you catch them in time, before the produce is past its prime. Freeze the best, not the left-overs.

Allow for some crop losses from slugs or aphids. Controlling pests with chemical sprays, is feasible but uneconomic on the domestic scale, in general (see pages 207–16).

More difficult to plan for is the 'hungry gap' between the end of winter produce and the beginning of the new season's crop, in late May or June. Some root crops will stay in the ground through the winter, but there comes a time when they are frosted in or getting woody. It is then, about March, that you feel the need for something fresh, if only for the vitamin C content. Most of the possible vegetables belong to the brassica tribe—cabbage, cauliflower, sprouts, etc—some of which are cut-and-come-again plants. They take ages to grow, so they need garden space for a large proportion of the year. They are planted as seeds in early summer, transferred to a waiting bed as they grow and to their final wide spacing in autumn. The difficulty is finding space for parking in midsummer, when everything else is bursting out all over. If you want a lot of spring vegetables, allow for them in the overall plan.

It is perfectly easy, though, to grow lettuce all the year round, with slight glass protection, and a number of vegetables can be forced under cloches or in a greenhouse, though not in large quantities unless you have a whole lot of glass cover.

Now is the time to find out if other people down your street are thinking of growing vegetables this year. There are certain things you will all need—peat, polythene, pots, plants, seeds—and it is often possible to get a useful discount when buying in quantity. Leave time to write or phone to wholesalers for a quotation.

If you want an apple tree, but have limited space, your neighbour might be prepared to plant in his garden the necessary partner which will make it fertile (see page 131 on pollinators). Slightly different crops could be planned for each garden, so that a market and exchange for surpluses can be more easily found. But decide at the outset whether the exchange should be by simple quantity or not. A pound of carrots for a pound of parsnips, yes. But for a pound of asparagus? Beware of over-involvement, or you will find yourself giving away the tomatoes you wanted for your own lunch, or end up with nothing put by for the winter.

If you can restrain yourself, avoid growing for show. Maybe it would be fun to join the local horticultural society and carry off all the prizes in your first year, but it can't be reconciled with growing vegetables to improve your own standard of living or save money. Show vegetables are big, fat wallopers with little or no flavour left. To get them that way, you will have to feed and cosset the beasts all the time and this costs a packet in fertiliser, sprays and man-hours. You can't thin out any for eating because the very one cut off in its prime might have been the champion. By the time you harvest the reject monsters, they taste of old face flannels and have cost more per pound than anything in the shops.

If you are hell-bent on growing something for show, make it a marrow or pumpkin. Given average good soil—which you want for all plants—and plenty of water, they romp away without much effort and in such profusion that there are enough to eat young and still leave plenty to choose an exhibit from. Marrows of any advanced age are pretty dull vegetables cooked plain anyway, so being forced to turn your giants into curries or jam won't matter. Pumpkins also grow large without effort and are best mature. However, they have a distinctive flavour, which you either love or hate. It is a daunting prospect to find that you are the only member of the family prepared to eat a newly cut-open 42-pounder.

Planning Your Garden Layout

First, how much space are you actually prepared to put down to vegetables? What area is needed for the children to play in and how boisterous are they? Toddlers must be under your eye while you are working, so a sandpit is something to make room for. Footballers are a menace anywhere, so bar them from the breakable crops with a line of gooseberry bushes, which give as good as they get, or well-staked broad beans. A fruit cage makes quite a good pen for games players after the fruit is picked, which happens before the summer holidays.

Children enjoy lots of lurking places, and these are provided by any of the taller plants. Runner beans on a framework make a splendid den and double as a sheltered sitting out place for grandma. The clothes line needs to be sited where the vegetables won't get knocked over by the sheets or the sheets marked by the compost heap. A rotary line can be placed in the middle of a bed of low-growing plants, like herbs or roots. Washing hung out wet provides automatic watering in a dry summer.

If the garden is very small, look at some of the ideas on pages 140–2. A lot of vegetables look really decorative as they grow and an edible herbaceous border laid out with just a few flowers here and there would look far handsomer than a conventional one.

Decide on the best siting for a greenhouse or frames—these will prove a worthwhile investment if you have room for them (see page 219). Any sort of glass protection or plastic propagator needs space for storing or setting out where they will not be damaged or a hazard.

Where there is a wide-spreading tree in the garden, draw a circle on the ground to cover the area reached by the tips of the branches. Nothing much is going to grow in that circle, because the tree is extracting all the nourishment from the soil. Normal roots go deeper the farther they get from the trunk or stems (Figure 7a). Therefore, you can set plants with shallow roots above the outer tree roots, provided that, for a reasonable part of the day, the shade thrown by the branches is not too great. When trees have suffered from water shortage in their early years, the roots may have twisted up again in search of rain and can be seen or felt just below the surface (Figure 7b). In this case, nothing will grow even under the outer

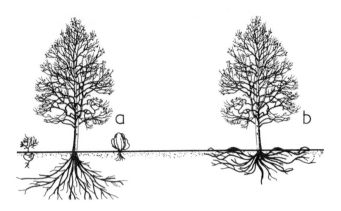

7 (a) Normal tree root pattern with plants round perimeter; (b) Tree starved of water in early years; no planting near it is possible.

perimeter of the branches, unless you pile earth on top of the soil surface.

Shade is a great problem in a garden. Plants need light, so any area permanently shaded by the house or any immovable object might as well be used for a path and storage of tools, pots and compost. If the shadow is caused by a hedge, you might be able to thin or shorten it a bit, to improve matters. If the culprit is a high wall, paint it brilliant white, to bounce back every scrap of light. It is surprising what a difference this makes to a gloomy semi-basement yard. If the back garden is a narrow strip completely overshadowed by the house, consider using the front garden for vegetables (see pages 140–2).

Half shade, where the light strikes through leaves, is enough for some plants, especially in summer. The strong midday sun penetrates the canopy, so there is plenty of heat and enough light. Lettuces do quite well near trees, though not directly next to the trunk where the roots compete; they do in fact prefer this to being out in full sun, which makes them limp and exhausted. You can grow very short carrots and baby round beet on the edge of a tree area, and winter-growing brassica, which are started in summer and spend a long period waiting for a home in the main plot, manage well in light shade, and thus save a lot of watering.

Most other plants like a lot of sun and planning a garden is largely a matter of sorting out priorities. Tomatoes will not perform at all unless they have the best sun and good shelter. If you mean to grow them out of doors you must pander to their tastes. All the frost-tender plants, like melons, cucumbers, marrows, French and runner beans, and sweet corn, must complete their growth cycle before the autumn bites, so they require a sunny place too. Onions need to finish with a coat of suntan if they are to keep well. Most root crops will manage with only reasonable sun once they are past the seedling stage, so they have to take the secondary positions. Peas are tough and tolerant, once they get their heads off the ground, and broad beans cope with all but severe frosts when they are young, besides making good screens for weaker vessels.

Tall plants, like runner beans, mustn't get between anything else and the sun, and should be located at the end or side of the garden, whichever most nearly faces south. Preferably all of them ought to face the sun, which means that, if you plant a double row, as is usual, the plants should be set out staggered, not directly facing each other. Tomatoes do best with the whole row facing south and like a bit of shelter from behind, so set them out in front of the bean rows, far enough away for them not to cast their own lesser shadow over the growing beans. You need access to both sides of the rows of tomatoes and beans, for tying up and regular picking, so there won't be much waste space, and some of that can be used as a waiting bed for winter brassica, which don't mind light shade.

Beans and tomatoes are best started off in boxes or pots under protection, and not set out till late May, so this desirable space can meanwhile be used for quick crops, like lettuces, or to start off other vegetables before transferring them to the main bed. After the first year, you will probably have winter brassica on part of the rows. If the garden is ready for planting in early spring the first year, you could sow summer cauliflower or cabbage at the back of the plot where the beans will grow in February to March and transplant them to the main plot in May. Don't sow them where the winter brassica will stand, because of the danger of transmitting club-root.

Early peas could go in the tomato bed in February under cloches, to be picked in late May. Strawberries at the front of this bed would benefit from the sun and not interfere with the growing tomatoes later on. Rhubarb planted behind the bean site would have finished its cropping before the beans are tall enough to shade it.

Once this sun spot is settled, any other very sunny areas can be allocated to cucumbers, sweet corn, wall fruit or anything which needs glass protection for part of its life to ripen at all.

Some plants have virtues. Peas and beans give back far more to the earth than they ever take from it, and can be planted anywhere which needs improvement for another crop. Carrots and onions discourage each other's pests, so do well together, and the feathery carrot foliage does not shade the onions too much if they are planted at right angles to the main sun path—running south (or south-east or west) to north. All the onion family are good policemen, so one or two spread around the plot, or next to wall fruit trees, will scare off pests, perhaps by confusing the scent.

By contrast, the potato is the baddy of the vegetable plot: frost-tender, fussy about having rich soil, a greedy feeder, robbing the ground of nutrients, and leaving only its undesirable offspring and a host of infectious diseases. The potato is best kept right away from its more valuable cousin, the tomato, or it will encourage the unpleasant ailment, blight.

All the cabbage tribe tend to suffer from club-root, though they do not pass it on to others. It is best to take precautions against this disease when setting out and never to plant brassicas in the same place twice if it can possibly be avoided. This is a good general rule: switch everything round next year, if you can, except the permanent beds, and feed those up to compensate. Even treasures like peas might as well spread their benevolence over as much of the garden as possible. This switching around is grandly called 'rotation of crops', but in a small garden with limited space it is more like a juggling act.

Planting plans

Figures 8a–f are some rough plans for such a garden, assuming morning shade from the house and a neighbour's high fence. This will be worse in spring than summer, when the overhead light is better, so all the early planting is concentrated on the sunniest side. As the light improves, the successional sowings, to mature a little later, can move across to the originally shaded side. Try to restrain yourself with those first sowings—a tiny amount of seed goes a long way if properly spaced—to avoid a massive crop early on followed by a blank in autumn.

With a larger amount of space available, you can lay down some more permanent planting, like fruit trees or bushes, asparagus or artichokes, according to taste. There is also a great deal more flexibility in the rotation of crops and the general layout of planting or recreational areas. Tea in the garden need not mean crouching in the middle of the onion bed.

Because the layout of a larger garden is more flexible, it might be a good idea to get used to it before planting up all of it. Fruit trees, once ordered, must be planted right away, and if you change your mind a year later about the siting it will set them back to move them again, nor is it an easy matter with a mature tree. Always allow for its ultimate height and spread, even if it is a pathetic little twiglet when it arrives (Figure 9).

Adapt your plans to your own family's requirements and cut out any planting or sowings which would produce a harvest while you are away on holiday. When you have decided how much space to allocate to any particular crop, check on pages 102 to 121 for the individual space requirement per plant of that type. This will tell you how many seeds to buy and sow. Most seeds will keep for another year, so store any half-used packets away in the dry.

Since the amount of produce you get out of the soil depends on the amount of nutrition in that soil, the more you can contribute towards it the better. This is done by collecting all your weeds and soft rubbish for compost, and importing horse or other manure, dead leaves, lawn mowings and any nutritious waste. If you have room, you can also grow green crops of nutritional value to the soil—comfrey, rye, *Tagetes minuta*, mustard—but the snag is that, except for winter rye, all these need to grow in summer and would occupy a plot which could be growing vegetables. This is worthwhile in the long term, since these crops not only make valuable green manure to be dug into the ground but also bring up nutrients from deep down and have anti-pest attributes. The excellent gardening books by Lawrence Hills give a detailed and enthusiastic guide to their virtues.

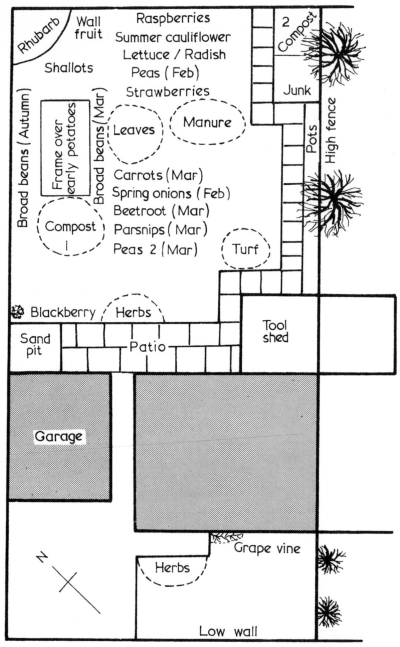

8 The Small Garden throughout the year. (a) *January to March*. Plot dug in autumn and heaps made for compost (1) including manure, turf and leaves then. Other manure (2) collected later and compost heap (2) started in spring. Broad beans (1) and rhubarb planted in autumn. WF = Wall trained peach, pear, apricot or apple. S = Strawberries. These, plus raspberries and giant blackberry, planted in autumn or spring will not crop this year. Early potatoes under frame or cloches. GV = Grape vine cutting planted Feb–March. Sh = Shallots planted in Jan–Feb. Make small successional sowings of root crops.

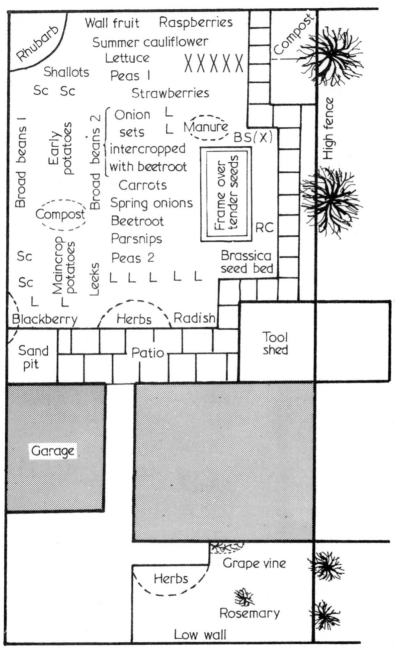

8 (b) *April to mid-May.* Use most of compost heap (i) and dig in rest on site. Plant onion sets inter-cropped with transplanted beetroot. Plant maincrop potatoes, under cloches if necessary .Transplant summer cauliflower from seed row to final positions (SC) and use up first lettuce row. XX = Erect bean framework in their place. Sow tender seeds under frame or cloches. Use up first peas (i) and erect tomato supports on site. RC = Red cabbage seeds sown. BSX = Sowing of brussels sprouts for Christmas use. Sow winter brassica including swedes in seed bed. Sow leeks in seed row. L = Catch crop lettuce: small regular sowings. Use some spring onions.

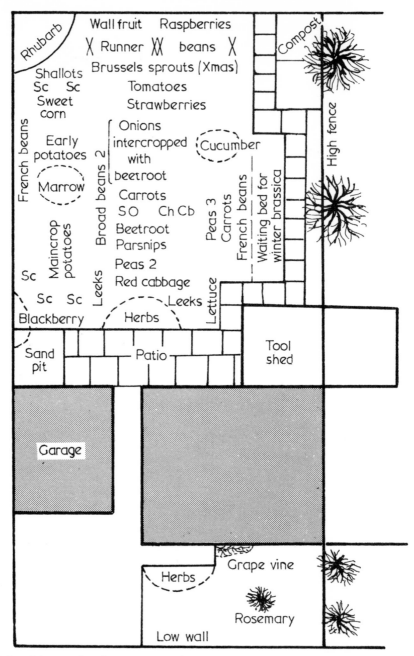

8 (c) *Late May to July.* Plant out runner beans and tomatoes. Transplant Christmas sprouts to waiting bed between them. Clear broad beans (1) and early potatoes (EP). Plant out tender crops from frame. Transplant leeks and red cabbage to final positions and winter brassica to waiting bed. Sow extra carrots etc and peas. BBY = Train blackberry along fence. Ch Cb = Chinese cabbage. SO = Spring onions. Use up these, and salad beet, lettuce and radishes. Sow lettuce in half shade from late May.

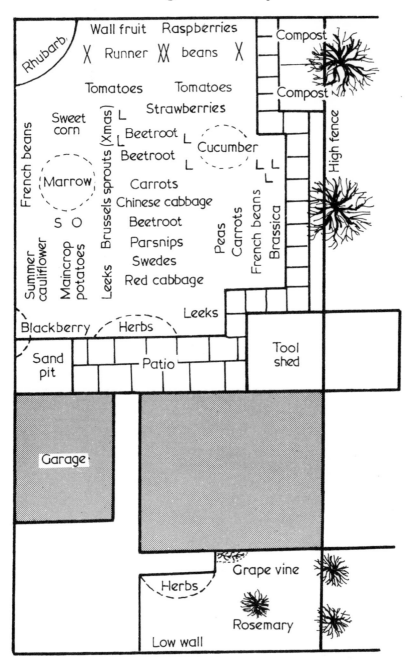

8 (d) *August to September*. Harvest onions, shallots, broad beans, salad crops, summer cauliflower and peas (2). Transplant swedes to pea site and Christmas sprouts to broad bean (2) site, leaving wires in place if garden is windy. Transplant other brassica as gaps arise in root crops. Earth up leeks and harvest all tender crops before first frost. Start compost heap (3). L = Catch crop lettuce. SO = Sow spring onions.

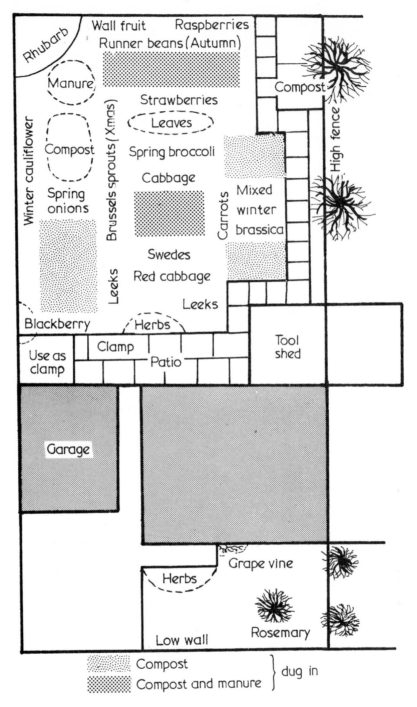

8 (e) *October to December.* Lift all roots and store in clamps. Plant out all brassica in final positions in firm earth. Harvest swedes and red cabbage in late autumn, leeks as needed. Dig in compost and manure where indicated in autumn and start collecting more, plus leaves, for spring.

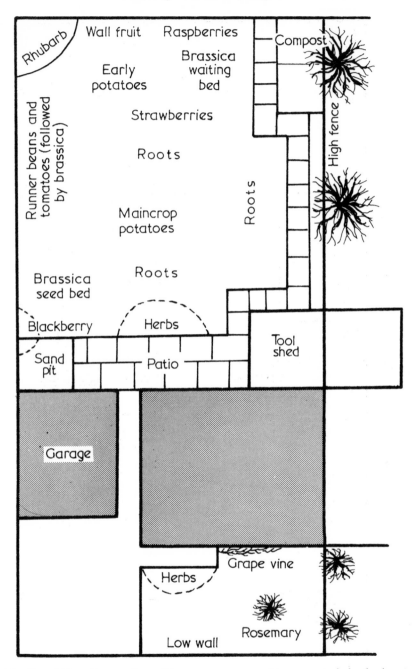

8 (f) *The Second Year*. Rotate all possible crops to new positions, particularly the brassica and potatoes. Some fruit will crop this year. Train vine rod up front of house.

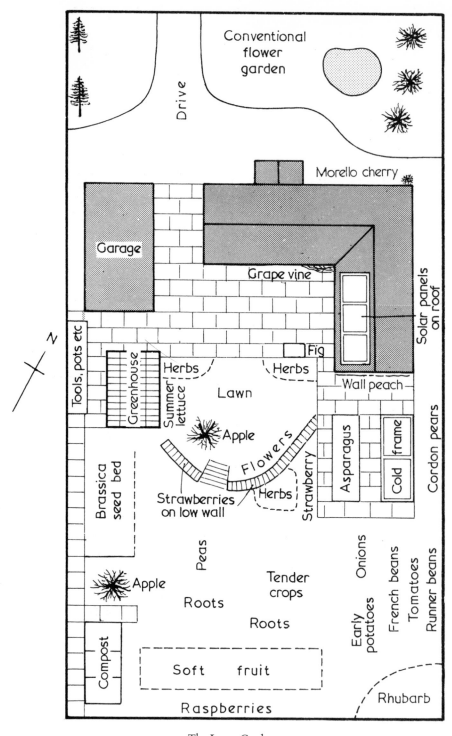

9 The Large Garden.

Prepare the earth for planting as far as you are able. If you can start in autumn, with completed plan, then all the right nutrients can be applied to all the right places. Even if you gave a reasonable general feeding then, not much special topping up will be needed in spring. Some crops, like potatoes, cucurbits, bush fruit, are greedy feeders that can take any amount of good stuff. Most crops would lap it up, but go wrong on the proceeds, producing a lot of leaves and no fruit, or big forked and split roots.

A little goodness does better for most crops than a lot. Tomatoes, for instance, do well on previously autumn-manured soil, or untouched soil which has had peas planted in it first. Give them both and they produce floppy, rampant stems and few tomatoes. If your soil looks middling, try it and see. Only the growth test will tell if it is in good heart. Do something about the texture of heavy clay, by incorporating peat or strawy compost, and about thin, starved chalk, again by feeding compost or decayed leaves. Otherwise, go ahead and plant and find out what you have there; don't spend pounds on chemicals to cure ailments which may not be present.

Draw out your planting plan in a notebook and write down each sowing, with date, type and variety. Make a note of any odd conditions of planting—warm, icy wind, thunderstorm next day, drought for a fortnight—which might affect the seeds. Add the date when the first seedlings show, and when most of them are through, with the rough proportion which germinated. Note the date of transplanting and keep a record of the crop-thinnings as well as ultimate harvest. Include any comments on pests or diseases which attacked the plant, and the family's reaction to the taste.

Planning ahead

You can cost up your profits on the crop by checking the price at local greengrocers on or about the day you gather your own produce, weighing and pricing yours. Decide if you are going to cost what you freeze at fresh or frozen food prices and similarly with any other forms of preservation, like jams, sauces, bottling and pickling.

The profits will look impressive, but to get a true picture, you will have to set against them all the costs involved in running the garden (see pages 250—3). To follow this plan, you will have to get into the habit of noting down all the expenditure—which is no bad thing anyway. At least you will know why you have got too much month at the end of your money and not vice versa.

When you come to planning the second year of planting, take into account what paid off and what didn't, what no one would eat or everyone wanted more of. You will be conditioned to some extent by the previous year's sowing. The cabbages and the potatoes must have a new home; the rest of the crops are better rotated, if possible. You will probably have some plants growing in the garden over the winter and well into spring, which will decide where the early sowings of hardy seeds don't go. If you can plan well ahead, then feed the extra manure and compost to the parts of the plot which need it particularly. The soil should get better and the work easier every year, as it becomes more automatic to do the right thing at the right time.

Allotment layout

If you are growing on an allotment, the problem of layout is different. There will probably be no large buildings or fences casting shade, so you can rely on better sun distribution to all parts of the plot. There may be a wind problem, if the site is open to flat land all round, or sited close to a very high block of flats which creates turbulence. In this case, low windbreak hedges may be a priority, and they can be made in edible bushes like rosemary.

If you are a newcomer, you will have no idea what was last planted on the plot. It may be possible to find out from a neighbouring allotment holder where the last man had his potatoes and cabbage, so you can avoid repeating these sites. All you can do otherwise is clear the site of weeds, lime it if necessary, except where the potatoes are to go, plant and hope for the best. Don't dose it with expensive chemicals it may not need. This makes your vegetables expensive and, unless you have security of tenure for a reasonable time, it may benefit the next holder more than you, or be bulldozed away to build a housing estate.

Allotment planting can be done on the rigid-straight-lines-all-going-the-same-way, compartmentalised style you see in very many gardening books. This looks a lot tidier than varying lines to suit crop and shade requirements. Take a line which faces as near south as possible, and set all the rows parallel, varying the heights of the crops, so that low always follows high; there should be enough light coming from all angles to develop the lot.

Onions, sweet corn and the brassica seed-bed are best planted in blocks, most of the roots in double rows. Potatoes are generally planted all in one place, several rows wide, but in blocks within those rows—a square of earlies at one end, then second earlies, then maincrop, so that the ground can be cleared in sections and given a chance to recover. Rotate the whole plot the following year.

It is wise to set the more attractive crops, like strawberries, tomatoes and cucumbers, away from the edge so that passers by cannot easily reach them. We have even lost pumpkins from our garden, which backs on to open farmland, but this fruit does demand a criminal parent to cook it. Most children steal what they can eat at once.

Seeds

Most vegetables can be raised from seed by most people, though in the north a gardener with no sort of sheltered growing area may have to buy in tomato plants to get the full benefit of the limited growing season. Onion sets are commonly bought for the same reason and most of the common plants, especially of the cabbage family, can be obtained in markets and garden shops, for people starting late in the season, but the initial cost will cut your profit to quite an extent.

Seeds are selected from good strong plants in one season to be sold the following winter, and the packets will be dated with both years. All seed has to conform to a certain standard of viability, so there is not point in paying extra for the seed of common vegetables. The expensive brands aren't better, they just cost more, usually because the firms sell fewer in total than the big boys. Sometimes, especially when you buy by post, there are fewer seeds in the packet too. This wouldn't matter if every seed you planted grew, since a few plants go a long way. But the ordinary grower isn't just dependent on fertile seed. What goes wrong may be his own fault, like lack of watering, or an act of God, like the cats having a fight in the garden and mowing down all the new seedlings.

What we need then is more seeds. And this is what we get from the standard packets available in any chain store, gardening shop or ironmonger. We counted the number of seeds in a standard packet of red cabbage, costing 15p. We lost count somewhere around 800—which is a whole lot of seed for your money. You certainly won't need that much in one year, even with patchy germination and frequent cat fights. Most seed will keep for several years, though the germination rate will drop as it gets older (see page 45). If you want to offset the cost in the first year, try sharing the seeds among a group; there will be plenty for everyone.

If you fancy growing exotic vegetables, it may be more difficult to get the seeds, and certainly more expensive. The biggest firms don't go in for exotics, so as to keep down their development costs and prices. The firms who do are taking a risk, since no one might fancy scorzonera or Chinese cabbage, and they want to get back their costs as soon as possible. Even so, if you want the added interest of growing something uncommon, the extra expense is not the main consideration. You can find out who stocks the offbeat seeds by sending for all the catalogues, or writing to a gardening magazine. It may mean getting seed by post, so think about it early in the season.

You will also see pelleted seeds on sale. They are individual seeds coated with clay or a mixture of nutrient and clay binder until they are the size of little pills. They are easier to handle, especially for anyone with arthritic fingers, and so can be spaced out mathematically to reduce overcrowding. As they grow, the binder falls away and the nutrients are there, available for each plant personally. However, some of the binders are so hard that the seeds sit there in their little jackets doing nothing for months. You will have to water them much more than normal, and sometimes even cut the coat open, which is a fiddly job and slows things up. They also cost more for less seed, but most of them will germinate if you are prepared to take the extra trouble.

Treated seed, sometimes pelleted, sometimes not, has been dosed with a stated chemical against a stated pest or disease. If you know, or are told, that some ailment is rampant in your area, buying treated seed may be worth the extra cost.

Some seeds are foil-wrapped, which is said to preserve their freshness and viability until the moment you open the pack. Since most seed lasts a fair time if kept dry, we remain unconvinced there is much advantage in this, except in damp areas where storage is more difficult even in shops.

Potato 'seed' consists of small potatoes, grown in Scotland or Ireland and imported so that they will not have been affected by any of the ailments afflicting local crops. Of recent years seed potatoes have been hideously expensive and not all of good quality. An alternative is to use old potatoes bought for the kitchen and which have started sprouting. They may fall victim to disease more easily, but they may not, in which case you have ten or a dozen good potatoes from what you might have had to throw away. It all depends on your spirit of adventure which you choose.

Certain seeds you buy, especially among the less common varieties, will be marked 'F1 Hybrid' on the packet and will probably cost more. These are cross-bred plants carefully developed for some particular characteristic—like size, large yield or unusual colour. You should get excellent results the first year, but it is no use saving the seed, as you can with most vegetables once you get going. F1 seed doesn't 'come true' but reverts to the characteristics of one of the parents, always the least desirable one.

Be wary also of varieties labelled 'Best for freezing'. More or less any vegetable will freeze reasonably well (see page 169). These seeds are more suitable for commercial frozen food manufacturers, because they ripen all at once over a very short period and keep the production lines rolling. Unless you are in a position to drop everything and turn your kitchen into a factory for a week or more and freeze, freeze, freeze, you will be better off with ordinary varieties, which ripen over a longer period.

Saved seed, whether from your own crops or bought food, can be tried. If you want to use your own, then leave a plant to ripen fully, but make sure it does not drop its seeds around the garden. Potatoes tend to hide in the earth and set themselves next year anyway, but they are such robbers of the soil that it is best not to have potatoes on the same spot for two years running. This means that the 'volunteers', as farmers call self-set potatoes, are liable to come up awkwardly in the middle of other crops. Even old peelings thrown out on the compost heap sometimes produce thriving plants.

Saving seed from bought vegetables is chancy. If you save exotics, like pepper seeds, or peach stones, they will probably turn out to be varieties which will only grow in tropical climates. However, people sometimes have remarkable results with orange pips, provided they have a sheltered south wall to grow them against. It is always worth trying anything like this which comes free, provided you don't spend more on bought fertiliser and heating than you ever would on the end product.

Viability of seeds

If you do not use all the seeds in a packet in the first season, fold it over, keep it in a cool, dry place and use the seeds in following seasons. Date the packet clearly, with the first sowing year. Damp or mouldy seed should be thrown away. Listed below are the average periods each seed will last, though some will deteriorate earlier, some later:

one year only—parsnips (butter and cream good for two) scorzonera, any F1 hybrids

two years—turnips, swedes, peas (some less), broad beans, French beans, runner beans, parsley, many herbs for preference, spinach

three years—leeks, carrots, mustard and cress

four years—lettuce, onion, radish, Chinese cabbage

five years—cabbage, cauliflower, broccoli, sprouts, kohl rabi, beetroot, spinach beet

six years—celery, celeriac

seven years—marrows, cucumbers, melons, edible gourds (but not if they dry out completely)

Sowing Calendar

All dates are approximate and should be varied according to the weather in any particular year.

sow = sow seed in the ground (*in situ*); plant = set out seedlings, offsets or bought-in plants; glass = any form of unheated protected sowing; heat = protected and given additional heat; south = southern or mild areas of the country; north = northern or chilly areas; (tomatoes) = unusual, early or late sowing for a special date or purpose; late = towards the end of the month if mild enough.

January

sow   Jerusalem artichokes (late)
plant   shallots
glass   spring onions
heat   potatoes in indoor boxes, (tomatoes for early greenhouse crop)

February

sow   Jerusalem artichokes, broad beans (south), lettuce (south), (onions), spring onions, parsnips (late), peas, salsify (south) scorzonera (south), summer spinach, (rhubarb seed)
plant   globe artichokes (late), shallots
glass   lettuce, potatoes in boxes. Also chit early potatoes
heat   onions, peppers (late), tomatoes for greenhouse

March

sow   broad beans, beet, (brussels sprouts for autumn), summer cabbage, carrots, summer cauliflower, land cress, kale, kohl rabi, leeks, lettuce, onions, spring onions for early summer, welsh onions, parsnips, peas, radish, and most herbs (except marjoram, balm, basil)

46

plant globe artichokes, asparagus crowns, early potatoes (south), pickling onions for June, rhubarb crowns, (tree onion)

glass cardoons (late), celeriac (late), celery (late), mustard and cress, peppers (late), early potatoes under cloche or in greenhouse, tomatoes. Also chit maincrop potatoes

heat celery, celeriac, indoor cucumbers (late)

April

sow asparagus, balm, broad beans for July, beet, brussels sprouts for Christmas, autumn cabbage, summer calabrese, carrots, autumn cauliflower, land cress, kale, kohl rabi, leeks, lettuce, marjoram, mustard and cress, onions, (spring onions for late summer), parsnips, peas, sugar peas, radish, spinach beet, (swedes), turnips

plant onion sets, pickling onion for late summer, early potatoes (north), maincrop potatoes (south). Bush fruits (early)

glass French beans, soya beans, runner beans, cardoons (early), celeriac (early), celery (early), courgettes, Japanese cucumbers, ridge cucumbers, marrows, melons, peppers, pumpkins, New Zealand spinach, sweet corn

heat aubergines; any of above in cold year

May

sow basil, French beans (late), haricot beans (late), soya beans, runner beans (late), beet, heading broccoli, winter cauliflower, sprouting broccoli for winter, brussels sprouts for Jan–Feb; carrots, cauliflower for Nov, winter cabbage, land cress, ridge cucumbers (late), kohl rabi, lettuce, marrows (late), Chinese mustard, mustard and cress, parsnips, peas, radish, Japanese radish, sweet corn (mid-late), spinach, swedes, turnips (both late, for August)

plant French beans (late), runner beans (late), soya beans (mid), cardoons, celeriac, celery (and bought plants), courgettes (late), leek plants, marrows (mid), potatoes, maincrop (north), pumpkins (late), sweet corn (late), tomato plants (late)

glass set out melons, indoor cucumbers, tomatoes in greenhouse bed, aubergines

June

sow French beans, runner beans, haricot beans, beet, winter cabbage, carrots, chicory, Chinese cabbage (cauliflower), ridge cucumber, endive, kohl rabi, lettuce, mustard and cress, Chinese mustard, radish, Japanese radish, winter savory, swedes for August

plant winter celery plants, tender beans, marrow, cucumber, melon in exceptional summer, sweet corn

glass aubergines, etc, to final growing position

July

sow   French beans, runner beans, haricot beans, beet, cabbage for late winter, Chinese cabbage, corn salad, endive, lettuce, peas, spring onions (north), Chinese mustard, mustard and cress, radish, Japanese radish, Spanish and China radish, winter spinach, swedes and turnips for winter

plant   winter celery plants

August

sow   (French beans, south), (beet, south), corn salad, land cress, endive, lettuce, mustard and cress, spring onions (south), radish, Spanish and China radish, winter spinach, swedes and turnips for winter

plant   strawberry plants, globe artichoke offsets

September

sow   corn salad, land cress, lettuce, mustard and cress, onions (south), radish, winter spinach

plant   bush fruits, strawberry plants, tree onions, Welsh onions

glass   onions (late, south), lettuce (late, north); all tender plants may need covering late

October

sow   (glass later) broad beans for May (south), cauliflower for May–June (south), lettuce

plant   tree onions, Welsh onions, tree fruits, autumn strawberries and raspberries

glass   lettuce (north), radish (north), spring onions (south)

November

sow   (glass later) broad beans (south)

plant   bush fruit in mild year

glass   lettuce (south)

December

sowings in heat or indoors only

Spring Planting

For most people, the garden year begins in spring—when the evenings are getting lighter and the air a bit softer and the trees are beginning to shoot.

If you did not manage to do your double digging in the autumn, get on with it as soon as you can, provided that the soil is not frosty or so wet that you sink more than a few inches. It is going to be a heavier job, with the winter rain still weighing down the soil, and you may have to compromise and dig single spit in most places, but deeper where you have decided to plant your root crops.

If you autumn-dug, then just strip off the weeds and, if your ground needs feeding, bury whatever goodies you can spare at one spit depth. Don't put fresh manure where you are going to plant the roots—they will get over-excited and coarse, like inexperienced drinkers at a rugby club. If you planted a green manure crop, dig it up, let it die off and then bury it a few days later. The digging should be easier this time, but on a heavy clay soil which has not been improved you will need to break up clods, and it is worth feeding in peat or wood-ash to lighten the texture.

When starting late, with no access yet to compost or manure, you will probably have to use artificial fertiliser for the first plantings. To economise, apply it topically —just to the rows where it is needed by what you are planting.

Assuming your ground is dug and fed, rake it flat, removing all the big stones and weed roots. Then tread over the surface to compact the soil and eliminate air pockets. On heavy clay which is not improved, don't tread but smooth with the back of the rake. Then rake the top inch loose again. This sounds crazy, but the top inch is where you plant the small seeds, and if the soil is all loose underneath, they could fall straight through and never surface again. They need a soft mattress and a fluffy cover on top, until they are big enough to dig down through the mattress.

February is about the earliest time for normal outdoor planting, and even then the soil is too wet and cold for small seeds. Two things which can always go in are large enough to take care of themselves: shallots and Jerusalem artichokes. Both are expensive compared with packets of seed, but once you have one, you have them for ever by leaving offsets in the ground to grow next year.

Shallots are first bought as offsets about the size of a young onion and reproduce themselves many times. Plant them 4in (10cm) apart with 9in (23cm) between rows, just sitting the bottom half in the soil. The top half projects and birds and cats love to hoick it out again, so cover the bulb with wire netting or spiky twigs until the roots take hold. The crop prefers soil which has previously been manured, but if you missed out in autumn let it take its chance, or dose with a little local fertiliser where the soil is very poor. Firm the earth round them so there are no pockets to hold freezing water against the bulb.

The other toughy, the Jerusalem artichoke, can be bought at the greengrocers. Plant any that are beginning to sprout. They do everything a potato does and have a much more interesting taste. The plants are a lot less fussy than potatoes and don't suffer from nasty infectious ailments. Give them a bit of compost, plant 6in (15cm) down and 18in (45cm) apart and they will do the rest. They can grow 6ft tall (nearly 2m), so plant them where they are a useful screen, not a nuisance.

Roots and pulses

Most of the other spring plants fall into two classes: roots and pulses. Roots like a deep-dug plot in order to grow straight. Carrots, parsnips, scorzonera, beet, salsify, etc, are roots proper, and swedes and turnips can be similarly grown in spring. Onions grown from seed, and the first sowing of the catch crops—lettuce and radishes—all go in now, and are treated in the same way, by sowing *in situ*—where they are to grow.

Having raked, trodden and raked again, set your garden line up where you intend to plant, twisting it tight with the stick. Cut a V-shaped indention with the hoe along the length of the line. The recommended planting depth—given on the seed packet and listed where it matters on pages 102–21—is mostly a rough guide. It may vary from $\frac{1}{8}$–$\frac{3}{4}$in (3–19mm), but don't fuss with a tape measure, guess.

Sowing small seeds

Take a pinch of seed from the packet and fold over the top before the rest spills. Sprinkle seed sparingly along the trench, aiming for one seed every 2in (5cm), which is practically impossible with small seeds. Beetroot have bigger seeds and can be planted straight away at 4in (10cm) intervals for round (globe) beet and 6in (15cm) for long beet. Then draw the earth from the side of the trench over the seed to the required depth and pat down firmly with the head of the rake.

Take away the line and mark the ends of the row with small sticks. Write the name, variety and date of planting on a label or bit of paper, place it in a small polythene bag, and secure the bag, upside down, to one of the sticks. This will help you to check what does well and what doesn't in your particular garden.

There is no 'right' date for planting any vegetable, because the weather is never the same two years running. Gardeners in the south can get going earlier than those in the north, but there are sheltered areas and windswept plains which affect planting. Town gardens, with the warmth spilling out over them from the houses, are ready sooner than a country garden backing on to open fields. You can ask the old chap in the local pub, watch what the neighbours do or use your common-sense. The results will be about the same.

As a rough guide, in an average year when things begin to move in early March, parsnips and onion family from seed go in then. Carrots are sown in late March to early April and beet a fortnight later. Even if you aren't sure, seed is so cheap that it is worth having a go with a small amount.

Once you have started sowing, repeat the operation at intervals of at least a fortnight or three weeks. The first sowings will produce some young vegetables ready for eating in roughly two or two and a half months. If you leave half or a third of this sowing to mature, it will produce the largest size of that vegetable to ripen in summer or early autumn for storing in clamps. The mid-season sowing will give you a succession of young vegetables during summer and the main crop for storage. The last sowings may or may not mature, according to the mildness of the autumn, but it is worth trying to extend the harvest season.

The number of sowings will depend on the amount of space at your disposal and your personal fondness for a particular vegetable. Almost certainly, when you are starting, the sight of empty space doing nothing will lead you to plant too much, and there will come a crisis when the brassica start demanding space which is chock full of roots. If this happens, any old deep container can be pressed into service to house the waiting plants, or you can pull more young vegetables and swap or freeze them small.

Radishes you can plant at any time from early March to fill a space but not hog it for long. A tiny pinch of seed between rows of slow-growing plants will be ready for eating in about a fortnight, as long as the plants get plenty of water. If radishes sit around in the ground, they will get old and woody, and encourage the dreaded club-root, since they are a member of the brassica tribe. Therefore, if you can't use them or give them away, pull them up and throw them on the compost heap before they cause trouble.

Lettuce grows almost as fast, but the seeds need warmer soil to germinate in. Cloche them or grow them in boxes under cover during March and let them out during April, according to the weather. Mature lettuce are tough and some kinds will stand the winter in most areas, so the planting season can go right on until October.

Both radishes and lettuce are used as catch crops, to make use of the gaps between slower-growing plants which will eventually need more space. They do not need a designated part of the plot, and one or two can fit into any tiny gap. This doesn't look so tidy, but it makes economic sense.

All these small-seeded plants have to be thinned out as they grow into seedlings. They can be transplanted, but this gets less easy as the season progresses to summer, especially when there is little rain. You may prefer to increase the original planting distances to the spacings given after first thinning, to save wastage and the labour of thinning. Old gardeners will regard this as heresy, but modern seeds generally germinate pretty well, given reasonable warmth and moisture, so there is no necessity to provide for the failure of half the seeds to grow. If you have doubts, plant a little clump of extra seeds at the end of your row ready to fill in the gaps—if they occur.

This technique pays off, particularly in the case of exotic and soft-stemmed vegetables. With exotics, you get very few for your money and, if you plant two seeds and discard one seedling, you are doing a favour to the manufacturer rather than yourself. Soft-stemmed plants, like the cucumber family and runner beans, bruise if handled much, as they must be to disentangle the roots of those which have been planted in bunches. Plant them as if you had faith that every one would grow, and you will mostly be repaid.

Peas and beans

The other major planting in spring is of the hardier pulses—early peas and broad beans. In some mild areas, broad beans can even be planted in November to stand the winter, but this has never worked for us, in a rather exposed garden. They don't like frost, but sometimes survive it if tucked up in leaves or earth.

Both have quite large seeds, which need to be planted more deeply, at 2in (5cm) or almost 3in (7.5cm). As they are easy to handle, they are planted in their final growing spacing. It isn't easy to guess distances down small dark holes, so it helps to have a dibber or cane marked at the required height.

A quick planting method, when time presses, gives moderate results. Just rake and firm the earth, then make holes on either side of the stretched line, in zigzag pattern, with each seed opposite a gap at 2in (5cm) deep, 3in (7.5cm) apart for peas and 6in (15cm) for beans. Cover in, firm the soil and mark the rows.

Much better, but needing more time, is to make a trench where the peas or beans are to grow. Mark out a space between lines 6in (15cm) apart for peas and 12in (30cm) for beans. Dig out a trench one spade deep, and fill the bottom half of the hole with compost, lawn mowings, rotted leaves or even kitchen waste destined for the compost heap. Sprinkle lime on top—which means no actual manure in the

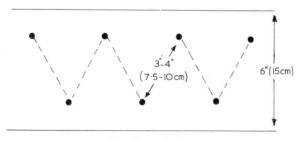

10 Peas planted in a shallow trench.

trench or they cancel out—and cover it with 2–3in (5–7.5cm) of the excavated earth. Tread down the mass firmly and water the trench.

Soak the peas or beans overnight before planting. Set peas out in the bottom of the trench in zigzag pattern (Figure 10) about 3–4in (7.5–10cm) apart in a double row. Cover with 2in (5cm) of earth and tread firmly. This should leave the surface of the planted area about an inch below the surface of the rest of the plot. This is useful if the weather turns dry, since they are thirsty creatures when growing pods. Set beans out in the same way, but 9in (22.5cm) apart; cover them with 2in (5cm) of soil, and firm. Keep the spare soil beside the bean trench and, if there is a sudden cold snap when the young leaves are showing, earth them up to just below the growing tip as frost protection.

Peas, though they look frail, are tougher than beans, but they do need protection from birds. You can keep them off with fences of short twigs, stuck in the ground beside the planting holes. A better method is to make pea guards out of wire netting, 3ft (90cm) wide and long enough to cover the row with a bit of tuck in at each end. Commercial guards are sold, or you can make these yourself. Balance a plank on a couple of buckets and place the centre of the wire netting on the plank. Bend the two sides down to make a flattened tent (Figure 11). Mount the tent over the rows of peas as soon as they are planted, and anchor sides and ends with canes at intervals.

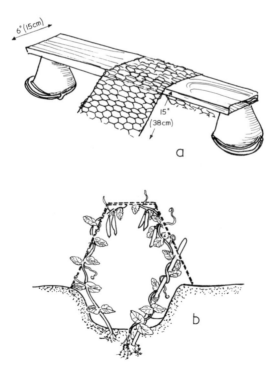

11 Pea guards. (a) Shaping wire netting over a plank—cut to length of row plus ends. (b) Set the guards over trench and anchor with sticks or canes at intervals.

Close the wire together at the ends of the rows. This netting also acts as a support for the plants as they grow up. The size of the mesh should be a compromise between what will keep out the birds and what will allow your fingers through to pick—about $1\frac{1}{2}$–2in (4–5cm).

Soya beans

If you want to try these, buy the seeds in a culinary packet, soak before planting in mid-April. Set out 9in (22.5cm) apart in a double row. You can gather the pods to cook, though they taste rather nasty. Otherwise let them ripen on the plant and use as dried beans for store. Soya beans are an excellent source of protein. They are also surprisingly hardy, withstanding late frosts, and appear to have no ailments.

We tried sowing the highly expensive seeds specially bred for northern climates and, for comparison, seeds taken from a very much cheaper packet bought for cooking from a health food shop. The cheap seeds germinated better and grew larger and sturdier plants. Neither, however, produced enough of a yield to justify the space they occupied in the garden over several months. We don't consider soya beans to be an economic plant for English gardens, which is a pity.

Onions

Onions can be grown from seeds planted *in situ*. It is useful to place rows of onions between other plants to discourage various pests. The maincrop can be planted in a rich bed of their own, with spring onions, or rarer varieties like tree and Welsh onions, dispersed among other crops. You can keep the latter going year after year from your own stock, just like shallots. Garlic is another onion tribe plant, best bought at the greengrocers and set out. You won't need many cloves to provide a plentiful supply for yourself and possibly for sale, since the crop is marketable.

Another onion relative is the leek, planted as seed in March 1in (2.5cm) deep, or bought in as plants later on. It develops slowly from seed, and needs gentle handling while it is young, so that the soft roots are not broken in transplanting.

Because onions from seed are sometimes very slow to get going, it is common practice to buy onion sets and plant these as an insurance in late March to April. The richer the bed which can be provided for all onions—except those for pickling —the better the yield will be. Plant the little sets like shallots, with their tops showing and, until they are settled in, protect them from tweaking birds with sticks laid on top or wire netting. If these are your only onions, plant them 4in (10cm) apart for thinning. If you have others to pull and use, and wish to grow these for store, plant them 6in (15cm) apart, and leave 12in (30cm) between the rows—here you can catch crop lettuce or grow beetroot, if the soil is good enough to support both crops.

Pickling onions don't mind poor soil, since they don't need to plump up. Plant them in April, fairly thickly, in short rows and they'll be mature by August.

Potatoes

The last of the spring crops is the potato. It is very sensitive to frost, so—except in the really mild south—it should not be planted until latish in April, unless the sowing is protected under glass or plastic.

In any other circumstances, it is best to delay outdoor planting and start the seed potatoes off in a frost-free light shed or room. Sit them in a box with the rose end upwards. This is the part of the potato with the eyes which eventually sprout. For generations good gardeners have divided up their seed potato into two or more parts, each with a growing eye, to increase the potential plants. Now farmers, who used to plant the whole seed potato, have cottoned on to this, and tests done by the Harper Adams Institute have proved that the yield is not decreased by this cutting up.

Potatoes which have run to seed in the rack make poor eating, but they will grow if planted out. If they have been in a bag, the shoots will be white and scraggy, not purplish like the proper seed potatoes, and they won't do as well, but you will get some return for nothing.

If you want early potatoes and the weather is still bad, you can grow them under glass or one or two at a time in a box of good earth, or a bucket, anywhere light and frost-free.

When they can be planted out, they will want a rich bed, with compost, manure or anything nourishing—except lime, which upsets their delicate skins. With a dibber, plant them 6–7in (15–17.5cm) deep, trying not to break off the shoots. The earlies are planted about 12in (30cm) apart with 18in (45cm) between the rows and maincrop 15in (37.5cm) apart with 2ft (60cm) between the rows. You can reduce by 6in (15cm) the distances between rows by planting quincunx fashion, and this gives you more plants on a smaller area (Figure 12). But don't do this unless you are pushed. The closer you get, the more the greedy beasts fight each other for the available nourishment, and this may reduce the total crop. If the weather turns frosty after the crop is planted, cover the shoots with sacking, newspaper or anything available, otherwise they will blacken and die. If you are caught out, leave the potatoes in. They will produce more shoots, but the crop will be lighter and later.

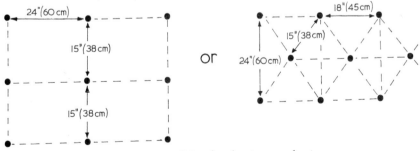

12 Potatoes—traditional and quincunx planting.

Weeding

As the young seedlings begin to appear, so do the weeds, generally looking much more vigorous. They must be removed, for they are competing for every scrap of nourishment in the soil. Hoe them down ruthlessly and put them on the compost heap where they can rot down and do some good in the future. If your lines are straight, pushing the Dutch hoe along beside the rows is easy. For weeds within the rows themselves, hand treatment is necessary. If you aren't too sure what the young seedlings should look like, study an illustration, and when in doubt await developments. Some seeds produce two totally uncharacteristic leaves before the familiar foliage appears. When you are sure which are the baddies, pull them out and use your fingers to firm back the soil round the seedlings.

Try to catch the weeds young, and never let them run to seed on the plot, for each seed will produce another weed. On the compost heap they dry and die, and the heat kills off future trouble. Deep-rooted weeds like plantain should be tackled when small, or they will need digging out with the trowel, which disturbs the surrounding soil.

Chemical weed-killers are an easy though expensive remedy. But be careful. Some just kill the foliage they are applied to, and all will be well if you keep them off the plants next door to them. Other weed-killers sink into the ground and destroy the whole weed, but they stay in the soil making it impossible to grow weeds *or plants* there for months. Make sure what you are doing before ruining the garden for a season (see pages 217–18).

Transplanting and thinning

Unless you have a really steady hand, too many plants will have emerged from the sowing. Thinning out is necessary to reduce them to numbers which will grow to maturity.

To do this, select a sturdy seedling at regular intervals and ease the others away from it, using a trowel to loosen the earth and taking care not to cut the plant or break the roots. Firm back the disturbed earth and water over.

Traditionally, the reject seedlings are thrown away, but those which look healthy and have unbroken roots and leaves can be saved for transplanting. Do this as soon as possible after lifting, on a damp, overcast day for best results, handling the seedlings as little as possible. Make a hole longer than the longest root, using a short cane for small plants and a dibber for the big ones. Slip the plant into the hole, making sure the roots are well disposed and shake down earth to fill the hole. Firm round the plant on the surface and water in if there is no rain to do it for you.

If the weather suddenly turns sunny, shade the transplants for a couple of days with plastic, cardboard, newspaper or a strategically placed flower-pot. Water well at night till they are settled in. Some will droop and die, but most should mature about a week or fortnight after the seedlings that were left undisturbed.

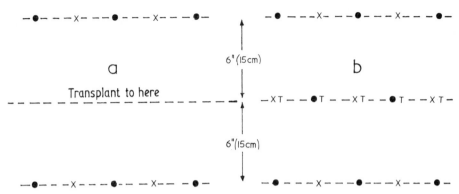

13 Carrots (a) original sowing after thinning (b) after transplanting. Thin all Xs, then XTs for eating small, leaving Os and OTs to mature.

Carrots

Where you have planted a double row of carrots, say, with 12in (30cm) between rows, thin them to 2in (5cm) apart. Set the surplus seedlings in a row down the middle of the two rows, where you have been taking a catch crop of radish. As the carrots grow larger, take every alternate one in the outer rows for eating young or freezing, then every alternate in the centre row. This leaves 4in (10cm) between each carrot and 6in (15cm) between rows (Figures 13a and b). This is fairly tight packing, but it should smother weeds. Keep the shoulders of the carrots covered or they tend to discolour and split at the top.

Parsnips

The same principle applies to other roots. Parsnips, with more spreading foliage, are planted in wider spacing, in rows 9in (22.5cm) apart. Thin the seedlings from 2in to 4in (5cm to 10cm), and move the spares to a separate row. Use alternate roots and leave the final spacing at 8in (20cm) apart in the rows.

If you want to grow really huge parsnips, make a hole 12in (30cm) deep—which is difficult unless your digging was very thorough—and almost fill it with a mixture of sand and sifted soil. Set the parsnip seedling in this, firm down and water well. Very large parsnips can go woody in the middle, but the variety 'Tender and True' will become huge and edible, if it has enough to drink while growing.

Beetroot

This needs slightly different treatment according to the variety and ultimate use. Each seed, like a cork granule, produces a clump of seedlings clinging very closely together. It is very difficult to get them apart without damaging the roots and sometimes even the stem, so these will have to be discarded right away as compost.

Some of the others will transplant successfully, providing they are kept damp at all times.

Having planted widely apart, as recommended, you will only have to select the best seedling in each bunch and remove the rest, carefully firming back the disturbed earth. But if you planted closer, whole bunches of seedlings must come out, so you will need to stagger the work over more than one day.

The long beet are generally grown on towards maturity like other root crops, with some half-grown ones pulled at intervals during the season. Your original rows should have been 8in (20cm) apart with 6in (15cm) between the plants. You can transplant suitable spares to any deep-dug part of the garden. They do rather well between well-spaced rows of onion sets. By the time the beet foliage is spreading out, the onions are harvested and can be replaced with lettuce, which like a little shade in summer.

Round beet can be grown on to maturity in the same way, in which case they need an ultimate 6–8in (15–20cm) to bulge into. Most people like to eat or pickle them young, at about 2in (5cm) diameter. If you intend to use all your globe beet this way, keep them planted at the original 4in (10cm) apart in rows 8in (20cm) apart, and transplant into the centre of the row opposite gaps in the outer rows.

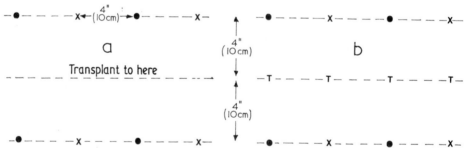

14 Round beet (a) original sowing after thinning (b) after transplanting. Use all Os, then all Xs, then all Ts as baby beet or alternatively use Xs, then Ts and leave Os to mature.

Use the outer rows first, by which time the inner will be ready. If you want to compromise—using some small, some large—plant at this 4in (10cm) overall spacing, and use every other one in the outer rows and every one in the centre row as babies, and let the rest, now 8in (20cm) apart, grow on to full size. They can get huge without going woody (Figures 14a and b).

Onions

Onions are harder to transplant because their soft stems tend to bruise. Spring onions are usually left unthinned, jostling each other till they are a sufficient size to pull for salads. Firm back the earth round the roots of those which remain.

Ordinary maincrop onions are transplanted as soon as they are big enough to handle. Apart from soft stems, they have fat roots which snap easily, so they should be carefully eased out with a trowel from well below and fingered as little as possible. Plant them 4in (10cm) apart, if you mean to use alternate ones young, and 6in (15cm) apart when growing on for store.

Once onions are growing, most of the bulb sits on top of the earth, but it is difficult to make it do so if you transplant it so high. Set each bulb sufficiently into the ground to make it firm, and press the earth well down beside it. As the transplants grow, they will raise themselves up to the right position.

They need plenty of water in the first six weeks or so, to help them increase in size. After that, they spend a while consolidating their gains, and then the tops droop, at which stage they are ready for the harvesting process (page 152).

Although onions will grow perfectly well in three ranks, like other vegetables, they are very handy as a policemen for other plants, warning off certain pests. For this reason, it is useful to plant your onions in single lines between other crops, like carrots and beet, but never where they can be overshadowed. They will not grow out of the sun.

Garlic

Garlic shares the policeman habits of onions, and a single plant—with 8in (20cm) clearance round it—strategically placed can do wonders. It also does a grand job in the fruit garden, putting the frighteners on peach leaf curl; it doesn't make the peaches taste of garlic, interesting as this innovation might be.

Leeks

Leeks need slightly different treatment, since they sit low down in the soil. When they are ready to transplant, cut a narrow trench about 3in (7.5cm) deep, piling the spare earth on each side. Make holes 3in (7.5cm) deep in the bottom of the trench with a dibber and slip in the leek seedlings. Sprinkle loose earth into the holes and between the well-spread roots and water it in, but don't firm round the top more than enough to steady the plants. As they grow, draw the spare earth into the trench and bank it up against the stems. This is to blanch the stems, and stop them getting coarse in flavour.

Leeks for show are put into huge holes drilled with a crowbar and packed with manure down below and fine potting compost at the top. The earthing is reinforced by anchoring slates along the sides of the heaps against the stems. These leeks can grow enormous, but they are strictly for astounding the lads at the pub, not for eating, since they taste of old dishcloths.

Earthing up potatoes

As the plants grow, earth them up by drawing soil against them with a hoe and

Keep trench clear
of weeds

15 Earthing up potatoes.

patting it firm. This is done in straight lines for conventional planting or diagonals for quincunx planting. The earthing will smother small weeds among the plants, but large ones should be removed by hand and the gangways between the ridges kept hoed clean. There are two reasons for earthing up. The first and most important is that the young potatoes grow close to the surface and, if they emerge above the soil, the sun turns the skin green. This isn't just unsightly—it shows the presence of the active poison, solanine, which can make people ill or even kill them. This is why you should never eat greened potatoes (Figure 15).

The second reason for earthing is that the potatoes on each plant develop at different rates, so some are ready while others are tiny. If you have to dig the whole plant to get the big ones, growth of the others is stopped. With a ridge, you can scrape away earth from the sides, take the big tubers and cover up again without shifting the plant root at all. The haulm, or foliage, will die off while the plant is still developing. When it is dry, lift the potatoes and destroy the old haulm by burning it or burying it in the middle of the compost heap, where the heat will destroy the many infections potatoes can spread.

Care of peas and beans

Peas need very little attention when growing, provided you train the tips of the stems through the netting from the first. Unless they are given encouragement to twine in the right direction, they will strangle the next plant instead. Peas need a lot of water to grow, which is easier to apply if you have set them in a trench. In a drought, soak the trench thoroughly, then cover it completely with a mulch of grass mowings, leaves, compost or peat, to stop evaporation. Ordinary short peas need 3ft (1m) canes and soft fillis to secure them at first. Tall peas are more trouble, needing 6ft (2m) canes and either wires or garden netting between each one. They are rather a nuisance in a small garden, and don't bear noticeably better than a good dwarf pea.

When they start to pod, be ready to pick every day. Pick whole pods of the

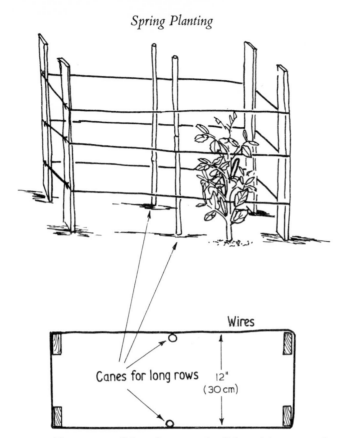

Wires

Canes for long rows 12"
(30 cm)

16 Broad beans. Use 5ft (1.5m) posts sunk 1ft (30cm) into ground.

French 'sugar peas' for eating. Ordinary peas are ready when you can feel peas in the pod. Keep picking a few and others will develop to replace them; if you leave the first peas to grow on, the plant will devote itself to the task and produce no more. Twist the pods off, don't tug the whole plant up.

When the crop is over the the plant turns yellow and dry, don't pull it all up, but chop off the roots and bottom inch of the stem and leave them in the ground, as a valuable source of nitrogen.

Broad beans are sturdy plants, but they grow moderately high—$3\frac{1}{2}$–4ft (1–1.2m) —and carry a lot of leaf and weight of pods, so they can be damaged by the wind. They are helped by individual canes or a framework of posts and wires. A single line of canes and wires is fair, but a double line of wires with a pair of stakes at each end will stand anything the winds care to do (Figure 16). When the beans are finished, the same framework can be left in position to hold up the brussels sprout plants over the winter.

If you planted in a trench, earth up each plant as it grows from the piles at the side. This shields the young plants from frost and helps the mature plant to take the weight of pods later.

Water well and mulch in dry weather (as described for peas). Pick the individual pods as they ripen. When growth has finished, cut off the roots and leave them in the ground to contribute nitrogen to the next crop.

Black fly is the great enemy of broad beans. It likes young growth, so 'stop' the plants by pinching out the top of the stem as soon as four clusters of flowers show. A derris spray will discourage the pests without harming the produce.

Protected Outdoor Planting

If the winter hangs on well into spring, it is not much use to attempt outdoor planting. The ground is fozen or soggy, so that if you walk on it the top wads together into a hard pan. The soil is cold, which retards germination, or in extreme cases, kills the seed. Even if the seed lives, it doesn't start moving until conditions are right, and will come up at the same time as a sowing made weeks later.

There are two basic problems: first, where the plant is hardy but the ground is not ready for it; second, where the plant is tender and the air temperature is too low. If you have a greenhouse or frames, the matter is easily solved (see pages 219–31). If you haven't any structural glass, things are less simple but not desperate.

Cold ground can be improved from below by incorporating horse manure (or other fresh manure) just under the planting layer. This heats up as it decomposes and warms the soil round it. If you live in a neighbourhood where little girls go around on ponies instead of chopper bikes, you should be able to find deposits of manure— although, not all plants appreciate fresh dung.

A strip of black polythene spread along the ground and held down with bricks, will warm the soil a little, since black absorbs heat and radiates it locally. The amount of heat is increased if you weight the plastic with odd sheets of glass or an old window frame. This may raise the temperature just enough for planting, but you have to keep it that way if the cold weather continues.

The simplest and cheapest form of protection is a polythene tunnel cloche, which you can make yourself from a length of polythene tubing and a few lengths of strong wire (see page 220). When you plant the seeds, they can be covered for the first few days with black polythene, for extra warmth, and then with transparent plastic, since they must have light to develop properly. In a windy garden, the edges of the tunnel must be anchored with stones or piled earth, which makes watering a complicated business. If possible, therefore, arrange some sort of watering device inside the tunnel—such as a leaky hose which can be fed from outside, or bits of slate or plastic along the edge to direct rain-water into the tunnel (see page 222).

An improvement on this home-made tunnel is a hard plastic cloche, which is a lot easier to handle for watering and to keep from blowing away—and also a lot more expensive. Here again you can make your own—from stiff plastic sheeting, as used for car-ports, etc. Bend it in a semi-circle and anchor with stakes or wires (see page 221). You must block off the ends, or the whole thing becomes a wind tunnel where nothing will survive.

All types of plastic cloches are on sale, some of which seem to be remarkably cheap. But be sure to buy plastic stated to be 'UVI' (ultra violet inhibited) or it will disintegrate after the first summer, due to the action of the sun. Some cloches are made in semi-translucent, doubled-walled plastic. In our experience, these just do not let through enough light for the plants to grow, and they are flimsy.

Glass cloches, which provide a better shelter than the thinner plastics, are more flexible as regards watering and less likely to blow away. But glass breaks if it is handled clumsily. And small children are as dangerous to glass cloches as glass cloches are dangerous to small children. Wired or plate glass is tougher, but it costs an astronomical amount, even compared with ordinary glass. If you do use glass cloches, remember to ask for horticultural glass, which is cheaper than window glass and normally comes in standard sizes to fit greenhouses.

Small seedlings often suffer damage from chill winds, even when they can take the ordinary air temperatures. A board or two propped up to act as a windbreak; a fence of flower pots, sticks or old bricks along the row, even cardboard or news-paper draped across the plants when there is a frost warning may all help to prevent a total loss.

If you can afford a greenhouse or can construct a frame (see page 225), half your problems are over. The soil is treated and mixed, and can be warmed readily in small lots. Most seeds will grow without any extra cover than the structure itself provides, in open boxes or in the bed of the frame. There are refinements, some of which can be employed outside a greenhouse or frame. Electrically heated pro-pagators are mini heated greenhouses; propagating trays with their own plastic covers are little cold greenhouses and a box with a bit of glass on top is an embryo cold frame. Seed trays can be lined up on a warm windowsill or along a sunny, south-facing house-wall, sheltered by a few panes of glass leaning at 45 degrees against the wall. Cats love this arrangement and tend to use the boxes as sofas, unless you block the access.

If you are growing seeds in boxes, pots or frames, it pays to take a little extra trouble and start them off in good soil. Ordinary garden soil has weed seeds and roots and spores of plant diseases lurking in it, which might kill your plants before they mature.

The traditional medium for planting in seed boxes is John Innes compost. This isn't compost as in 'compost heap', made from decomposed weeds and kitchen gunge, but compost meaning 'mixture'. There is a determined attempt to replace John Innes with the newer Levington compost, for reasons unknown to anyone but the manufacturers. Both are readily obtainable in bags from ironmongers and garden shops, and do a good job in growing seeds free of weeds.

If you are short of money but have time and patience, you can make your own John Innes-type mixture. The formula is: 2 parts good loam, sterilised; 1 part peat; 1 part sand, coarse. To each bushel of the mix add 1½oz superphosphate of lime; ¾oz ground limestone or chalk. The loam is the variable bit. Strictly speaking it should be good quality Kettering loam made by stacking and rotting down turves for six months or more. If you made a turf stack in autumn, there may be some usable loam inside it, but unless you live in Kettering the quality is as you find it. If it looks tolerable, it is worth trying.

Sterilise the sieved loam in a steamer—a perforated pot over a saucepan of boiling water—or more easily in a tin in the oven after a cooking session. You can, alternatively, leave the pan on an old-fashioned, uninsulated boiler top or balanced on a fierce central heating radiator. These indoor methods can be a very messy business if someone backs into the pan. Much less trouble would be to set up a solar dryer (see page 238) in the garden, which could be employed regularly to sterilise soil against the time when it was needed.

A decent bit of ordinary garden soil can be sieved to get out the stones and weed fragments, before mixing in the other ingredients—in the hope that the seeds will beat the weeds to it. This will mean a lot of hand weeding of boxes, but this isn't too difficult on a small scale. If the soil has some horrible disease, then you will lose your plants, so it is better to risk this with the cheaper seeds, not the expensive and sparse exotics.

The seeds can be grown in plastic trays, pots, old wooden boxes, plastic packaging or containers (see page 14). Drainage holes must be made in the bottom at regular intervals. If the box has wide slats at the base, which would allow your valuable compost to trickle through, line it with newspaper. This will rot away by the time the soil has compacted with the roots sufficiently to stay put.

Fill your box or pot to within an inch of the top, water the earth well with a fine-rosed can and firm it down with the flat of your hand. Then plant your seeds, at regular intervals of 1–2in (2.5–5cm) according to size. Very tiny seeds, like those of some herbs, are very difficult to separate; these can be mixed up with a little sand to spread them out a bit. Cover with compost to the required depth and pat the surface down again. Put a light-proof cover of black plastic or newspaper over the box or pot until germination starts, then remove it at once.

Small quantities of earth in a box or pot dry out a lot faster than in the garden, and there will be no natural rainfall to compensate, so you will have to keep watering. To reduce the need to water when the seeds are still loose and liable to be shifted, line the box with peat before the compost goes in; water the compost very well before sowing, and retain the moisture with black polythene until germination. Young seedlings can be watered from the top, with care, using a fine-rosed can held well away, or a little pot-plant watering-can with its thin spout pointed precisely between the rows of plants. A detergent squeeze bottle can be adapted for directional watering, or an old tin with tiny holes punched in the bottom can be held high over the box to simulate fine rain. The other important thing, apart from not flooding the plants out, is not to let blobs of water stand on the leaves when the sun shines brightly, or they will scorch and die.

Cold frames can be either used to house a collection of seed-boxes and pots, or filled with earth and treated like a gigantic seed-tray. When filling with earth, first put a few broken pots or stones in the bottom of the frame for drainage, add coarse compost—the garden sort, not John Innes—or leaves, to about half way up, then good soil. This should preferably be sterilised—which is possible if you have a solar dryer—but at least well raked and sieved to remove weed seeds and stones. The surface of this soil should be three-quarters of the way up the box. Top it with John Innes compost, 3in (7.5cm) deep, and firm. Plant your seeds, in rows 5in (12.5cm) apart, or in square blocks, marked off with labels. Sprinkle sand over the surface, close the frame and darken off the lid with black polythene or sacking until germination starts.

If the soil in the frame was well watered before planting, it should stay damp until the seeds are up and flourishing, after which fine sprays of water may be necessary. The lid will need to be opened during the day once the plants are growing, and eventually taken right off, though by that time the plants may be ready for setting out in the open garden, after hardening off (page 67).

If the seedlings in trays or pots have grown well but the outside atmosphere is still unsuitable they will have to be transplanted to larger, deeper boxes, and set farther apart, to prevent their growing weak and spindly or wilting altogether. Prepare the new box with the same sort of soil mix, and water well. Place it in the greenhouse well in advance, so that the seedling moves into a soil temperature it is used to. Water the seedlings well just before moving, to ensure that as much of the original soil as possible clings to the roots.

Ease the seedlings out of their box, a few at a time, working from underneath with a plastic label, lolly stick or old table fork. Never chop them apart from above with a trowel or half the roots will be damaged. Very gently edge one root system apart from the next seedling's and lay the separated plant on your hand or trowel. Don't pick it up between your fingers, as this would bruise the stem. Make a good-sized hole and slide the seedling in; let the roots spread and cover them in, firming the surface gently when the operation is complete. Shade the box for a day or two, and water between, not on, the plants.

To reduce the need for transplanting—which is a shock to the system—it is a good idea to plant direct into large boxes or individual pots any seeds you know will produce large seedlings. Marrows, cucumbers, sweet corn, runner beans, melons, all prefer this treatment. Use the same mixture and they will be happy in their pots until the roots begin to show through the base holes. If you stand the pots in a saucer, watering from below is simplified too.

Peat pots are sold everywhere for germination. The idea is that plant roots grow out through the peat sides as well as the base and the whole thing can be planted without any check. This works if the pots are kept really wet. If they dry out, it is very hard to get them damp again. The roots cannot then penetrate the sides;

Instead, they start twisting round the root ball inside the pot. The only solution is to turn out the whole plant and repot or set outside, hoping the roots will unwind again before they choke each other.

When the time approaches to set your plants out of doors, they must first be hardened off. Gradually reduce the amount of heat and protection they have been used to, so that the open air does not come as a shock. Wean them slowly, first removing any heat, then daytime covers, then night-time covers, moving them steadily from the greenhouse or warm place to a cool situation, then outside in shelter, and finally into the open garden.

Only when this hardening-off process is complete should they be shifted from box or pot to the ground. To remove a plant from a clay pot, damp the soil and tap the sides with a trowel; from a plastic pot, damp the soil and wiggle the bendy plastic. Spread your fingers wide across the top of the pot on either side of the plant stem but not touching it. Up-end the pot, and the whole plant should come out into your hand. If it sticks, poke a skewer or plant label into the base hole and push.

Set plants from a pot a little lower than the ground surface. This is especially important in the case of plants in peat pots, which must be buried in soil or the sides will dry out and stop water getting to the roots or rotting down the peat. All transplants need watering well until they are established.

If it turns suddenly cold, protect your set-out plants with plastic, newspaper or other cover. Single seedlings—as of marrows and cucumbers—can be covered by an up-ended flower pot or jam jar, but remember to take it off in the daytime.

Warm-weather Crops

Between late May and August, a wide range of crops can be grown out of doors without protection. First, there are various beans: dwarf French, climbing French, runner and haricot, and less common sorts which have much the same habits.

Beans

Dwarf French beans are the simplest to handle, and they are quite often planted *in situ*. Rake the soil over very thoroughly to a 3in (7.5cm) depth and turn it over, so that the warmth penetrates—beans sulk in chilly earth. They like land which has been well fed, but not recently, so incorporate compost low down or let it take its chance. Do not firm down after raking—the stem is soft and can't push hard against compacted soil.

Plant 2in (5cm) deep, 6in (15cm) apart with 12in (30cm) between rows; or in zigzag fashion with 9in (22.5cm) between individual plants. If you set them in a trench, 1in (2.5cm) deep, they can be watered more easily and mulched with a top dressing of lawn mowings or peat in time of drought. If there is a sudden chill after planting, cover the rows with a strip of black polythene for a few days, but remove it the moment there is any sign of activity.

Place spiky twigs or a netting over the rows to stop birds fishing for the seeds. Not all of them may germinate, so plant a few spares at the end of the rows and transplant when you are sure there is a gap. As soon as the seedlings are 3–4in (7.5–10cm) high, draw the earth up round the bottom of the stems and firm in, to help the plants stay upright when bearing.

These dwarfs do not normally need staking, but in a windy area support them with short pea sticks or twigs. Pick the pods regularly, as soon as they are big enough, to maintain the succession of cropping. When they finish, leave the roots in the soil to provide nitrogen for the next crop.

Haricot beans are selected varieties of French beans planted 6in (15cm) apart in a staggered row. Set up your line and plant beans on either side of it, clearing it by 1in (2.5cm). They are not gathered young but allowed to mature on the plant.

17 Wigwam: use 4, 6 or 8 poles.

When the plant has finished, pull it up, apart from the roots, and hang it on a nail or rack to dry out before picking out the dried beans for storage.

Tall beans are slightly different, because they need support. It is easier to set this in position first, since there is a lot of treading round involved. The simplest framework is a wigwam of three or four 6–8ft (1.8–2.4m) canes, tied at the top, with the base of the canes about 12in (30cm) apart. Set a bean at the foot of each cane, with some horizontal strings to help them. The snag about this arrangement is that heavy cropping plants jostle together at the top, tangling and reducing the yield (Figure 17).

A more common means of support is to set pairs of canes about 12in (30cm) apart, crossed near the tops, with other canes laid across the V to steady them. The two ends need staying with uprights. You can buy a commercial metal framework with a triangular frame and netting to hold the beans (Figure 18). In our windy garden, we have made a stronger frame of 2in (5cm) roofing batten, braced at 10ft (3m) intervals with uprights and covered with netting stiffened with canes every $2\frac{1}{2}$ft (75cm). This defies the gales which collapsed the ordinary framework of canes.

When the supports are safely in position and the soil trodden down hard against them, plant the seeds or young plants in a staggered double row, 10–12 in(25–30cm) apart, by the canes or along the nets. Normally, beans train themselves, but some may need guidance at first (Figure 19).

Water well, since the high bank of foliage loses a lot by transpiration. Spray a fine mist of water over the flowers to aid 'setting' of pods. Once the growth of the pods starts, you will need to pick daily. The produce from one packet of beans can be enormous. Freeze some as you go, not waiting for the tougher ones at the end of the season.

Climbing beans also grow well against a wall, on a single-sided net or wires anchored

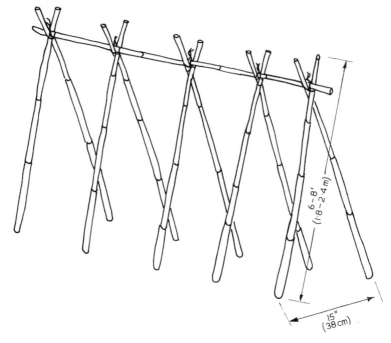

6–8'
(1·8–2·4 m)

15"
(38 cm)

18 Bean frame from lashed canes. Brace with uprights at ends and in centre of rows over 10ft (3m) long.

with metal 'vine eyes'. Being tall, both types of bean need to be at the end or side of the garden. The growth is very attractive, with bright orange or red flowers, and can be used as a living screen or sitting-out area in summer. They look good in the front garden too—the framework is very rapidly covered with leaves and beans. In both cases, when the plants are finished, leave the roots in the soil to release nitrogen, and compost the rest.

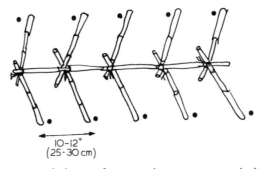

10–12"
(25–30 cm)

19 Staggered planting for runner beans to prevent shading.

Sweet corn

Maize is a tender plant and must not be put outside until the middle or end of May. It can then be planted in open ground but this doesn't leave it much time to ripen. It needs rich land—though not freshly manured or it will produce foliage instead of cobs.

Set the young plants out in a square, with 18in (45cm) between individuals. They will then give each other some shelter from the wind, and pollinate more easily than in a long row. Firm the ground well round the plants and repeat at intervals as they grow. Keep a flower pot or box ready to cover the plant if the weather turns cold even in late May.

The plant produces tassels of seeds at the top which should fall on the sheaths of coiled leaves below to pollinate. If necessary, encourage the process by inserting seeds in the sheath. The plants are greedy for water when the cobs are ripening and, unless you can satisfy this need, they are not worth growing.

Cucurbits

These include marrows, courgettes, cucumbers of all types, melons and pumpkins, as well as such fancy varieties as vegetable spaghetti and edible gourds. All of them react badly to the cold when they are young and shrivel at the first touch of frost. They are usually started in sheltered pots or boxes and not planted out until the danger of frost appears to be over.

Marrows can manage reasonably well on any but the poorest soils. Eaten small, in the form of courgettes—or as young marrows about 12in (30cm) long—they are more palatable. The great monsters reared for display at harvest festivals and shows are for impressing people, not eating—you would need an axe just to get through the skin.

Plant seeds about mid May, under jam jars or cloches, once the frosts are past. Otherwise raise under cover and plant out your seedlings in late May. In either case, set them in a circular depression, about 9in (22.5cm) in diameter, which will make watering easier. Plant bush marrows about 18in (45cm) apart—the ordinary trailing kinds need even more space. In fact, it is as well to keep marrows right out of the vegetable plot, since they will rampage across it, twining round any plant they meet. They do well in a separate bed of reasonable soil, and will trail up over a coal bunker or old tree stump, and will even climb a tree, given the chance.

Marrows need little aftercare, except weeding till they are big enough to smother opposition, and plenty of watering. Always remember to water round the stem, not over the leaves and fruit, as this could make blemishes. Just occasionally, they may need help with the first pollination (see under Melons, page 74) but in the ordinary way they manage perfectly well. The only problem is to stop them proliferating. If you have more than you could possibly want, pinch out the growing tip to stop them.

When the first frost is forecast, gather all the remaining marrows, big or small. Frost will blacken the plant and turn any fruit left on it mushy.

Pumpkins are just as easy to grow, but they become so big that they need even more space between plants. You can use them when they reach the size of footballs, but they are just as good as mature 40-pounders. They need a lot of water to flesh up and prefer fairly rich soil.

The fruits have rather soft skins when young; to prevent scratches it is best to cushion them on straw or a smooth tile while they are growing.

Cucumbers are rather more work. First, you must select an outdoor variety, particularly if you intend to grow tomatoes in your greenhouse, as the two don't mix. The outdoor cucumber looks coarser, but tastes just as good.

Secondly, if you start them in pots, as is usual, it is important not to let them get pot-bound—with the roots starting to twist round the soil ball. Cucumbers grow fast under cover and, once the roots show through the base holes of the pot, they must go out or into a larger pot right away.

They do benefit from rich soil. If you can, obtain some horse manure. Dump it on a vacant bit of garden, or on top of the compost heap for a few days to let the ammonia go off, then dig a hole a good 12in (30cm) deep and wide at the planting station. Put in a good ration of manure, add a bit of compost or rotted leaves, then top off with 2–3in (5–7.5cm) of earth.

Obviously, pick the sunniest place available, and use the spare earth to form a rampart round the pit, into which you plant your seedling. Each plant should be 18in (45cm) apart. If the weather turns chilly, shield it with a jam jar, or a pane of glass balanced across the earth rampart (Figure 20).

Cucumbers normally have male and female flowers, but if the males fertilise the females the fruit is bitter and twisted. Therefore, whenever you see a male flower, pinch it off before it makes trouble—they are the ones without the little fruitlet starting behind the flower. F1 varieties of seed have been bred to produce only female flowers. This is stated on the packet.

Growing cucumbers need a lot of water; run it into the pit but don't allow it to stand in a pool round the stem. They like a dampish atmosphere, so in dry weather

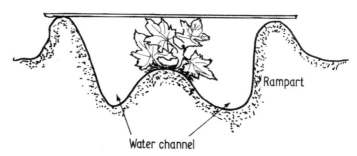

20 Cucumber seedling protected by rampart and glass cover. Keep water off the stem at all times.

give them a fine spray of tepid water at night. The leaves will scorch if they get large drops of water on them in hot sun.

Once cucumbers get going, they do very well in a good summer, and fruits will keep appearing all over, however fast you eat them. Support them on straw or old tiles to keep the slugs at bay. Frost will cut the plant down, so when the first one is forecast, go out and gather all the remaining fruit, otherwise it will go soggy and useless. A good cloche and a lot of straw packing may, however, save them for a week or so.

Japanese cucumbers, sold as exotics at high cost, look like indoor cucumbers but are darker and smoother-skinned than ridge types. They will grow out of doors in the most favourable circumstances only. Don't let them trail on the ground, but train them up fences. Alternatively, bend a length of Netlon or other stiff plastic trellis into a tunnel shape and train the plant over the top. The cucumbers will hang down inside and can be easily given extra protection if needed (Figure 21).

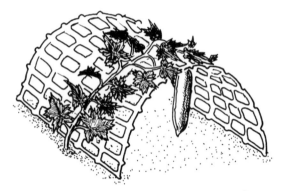

21 Japanese cucumber supported on plastic trellis.

Indoor cucumbers are longer, darker and smoother than the ridge varieties. They must grow under glass. Minimum shelter is a cold frame, in which they can be started, or planted out as seedlings, on a well-manured and composted bed. They will need covering at night, and at the beginning and end of their careers, but during the day and for the best part of the summer, the top can be removed or opened. One plant will fill a small frame easily. Spray the frame with tepid water from time to time and keep the soil as damp as possible but not soggy.

If you are growing tomatoes in a greenhouse and want to grow cucumbers there as well, things get difficult. Tomatoes like it warm and dry, cucumbers hot and wet. If you wall off a section of the house with plastic—rather like a curtained shower— you can keep just that area steamy. One cucumber, planted in a well-manured bed, or two in pots, will fill the whole space, trained up wires to the ceiling. More plants than that will produce too much fruit for any family, however keen. Those in pots will need feeding with fertiliser, and all of them will require mist spraying over the leaves on hot days and the removal of male flowers. Stop the tip of the plant when it hits the roof, and pinch out inconvenient side shoots. Some heat will be needed if the growing season is to be extended past the end of October.

You can grow cucumbers on hotbeds (page 231). For this, you will need a lot of manure—from a nearby farm or a whole string of ponies. Half a cubic yard or metre is about the minimum, plus leaves or compost and 12in (30cm) of soil. Fill a brick box, put a glass frame or window on top and let it rip. It smells to high heaven for a few days and the temperature will rise alarmingly—you may have to cool it with water. After hotting-up, it starts to decline to merely very warm, and this is the stage, at under 80 degrees, when the plants or seeds go in. Do this in February for seeds. They will grow fast and the soil will stay warm until the air temperature catches up. Proceed as for cold-frame cultivation.

Melons. The Canteloupe melon grows well in a cold frame or greenhouse and fairly well out of doors in the south or in a good summer. The other main type of melon will grow only in a heated greenhouse.

Don't give melons fresh manure, or they will run to lots of leaf and no fruit. They like a bit of compost, and good soil on top sieved to remove stones and weeds. Start the seeds off in pots while you prepare and warm up the bed—with black polythene if the sun does not cooperate. Two melons can go in a 6 × 4ft (1.8 × 1.2m) frame. In the greenhouse, if you have a bed at ground level, you can set one plant every 18in (45cm) square and give them a framework of canes and wires to climb.

Left to themselves, melons will not bother to reproduce, so they have to be encouraged, or rather, discouraged. As soon as three hairy leaves appear on side shoots, pinch out the plant's growing tip. It will respond by doubling up on the side shoots. When each new side shoot has three leaves, pinch out again. The plant will begin to feel threatened and therefore grows female flowers, with little lumps like baby melons behind them (Figure 22).

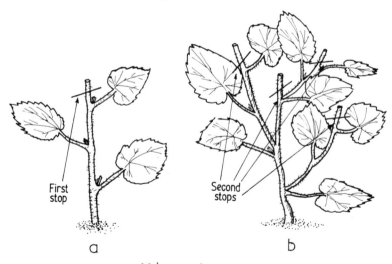

First stop

Second stops

a   b

22 Melon stopping: two stages.

As soon as there are enough—say, four per plant for large melons, six or eight for little ones—you will have to help again. The male flowers have pollen on their stamens, so either tap them towards the females, or pick off the male and dust the female flower with it. You will soon know if a 'set' has occurred, because the baby melons start to swell.

Once the plant is pregnant, feed it with plenty of water and general fertiliser or liquid manure. This should be poured on to the earth near the main stem, not touching it, and not on the leaves, which will blister if left wet under sunshine.

As the melons get bigger, they will need support. Tie the stems to the canes and wires regularly, and fix small nets under each fruit attached to the framework. Low-down melons can be supported on up-turned flower pots, which is the usual method for those grown in frames. In the greenhouse an alternative is to sling a whole fruit-net to the roof and loop it up at intervals round the growing melons, like a hammock. Make sure that no net is fastened tight, or the melons will warp to odd shapes. Slugs are very fond of melons, so to prevent grievous losses keep the plants surrounded with slug-bait.

The melons are ready when they begin to smell sweet. The stem end forms a slight callus round the neck and the other end feels slightly soft when you test it with your thumb. Don't leave them unpicked—they rob the plant and suddenly get overripe and rotten.

Before all the melons are ripe, the air temperature will drop, at least at night, below what they can stand. Close the greenhouse each day while the air is still warm, and keep it closed on chilly wet days. The frame light, which has been open daily through the summer and even at night for some of the time, must now be closed early. If necessary, in the event of a chill autumn, cover the frame with black polythene at night—it will pick up some warmth from the morning sun. Reduce watering as the weather gets cooler, but never let the earth dry out completely.

Tomatoes

Tomato seeds can be started in heat as early as January, but the plants are best grown on in a greenhouse. Plants intended for outdoor planting can be started in a cool greenhouse in late February to March and, after hardening off progressively (see page 67), planted out in late May or even June, when the frosts are past.

Outdoor growing

The growing season out of doors is very limited—three months in which to grow into a mature plant, produce fruit and ripen it—so the tomato needs all the help it can get. First, it must be placed in a really sunny and sheltered place. Second, it must have good soil, but not fresh nitrogen, which makes it put on leaves instead of fruit. Third, it needs support, since the fruit gets very heavy. Fourth, it needs adequate water.

The best site is one backed by a south-facing wall or fence. Failing this, runner beans, Jerusalem artichokes or, to an extent, gooseberry bushes serve very well as a windbreak or shelter.

Make a hole 12in (30cm) deep and about the same across and put in a good layer of compost and some wood ashes, if you have been shifting tree stumps, or useless prunings, as tomatoes need potash. If you haven't anything organic available, then feed with a dose of the natural chemical potassium sulphate. Part fill the hole with good earth and set the root ball of your plant well down into it, so that about 3in (7.5cm) of the lower stem is also buried. Strip off any leaves which grow this low. Mound the earth immediately round the stem and make a circular trough 2–3in (5–7.5cm) deep about 5–6in (12.5–15cm) away from the stem. This is for easy watering later in the season without upsetting the plant (Figure 23).

Set the stakes or canes firmly in before planting, 18in (45cm) apart in a straight line, or at slightly closer intervals in staggered rows where space is limited. Set every other plant 3in (7.5cm) forward of the planting line, but keep the individual distance between plants at 18in (45cm) or they will shade and rob each other.

As the tomato grows, it will need to be tied to the stake at intervals. Don't tie it tightly, since this will break the stem right away or bite into it as it thickens. A 2in (5cm) ring of space is best, with the string crossed between stem and stake to ensure

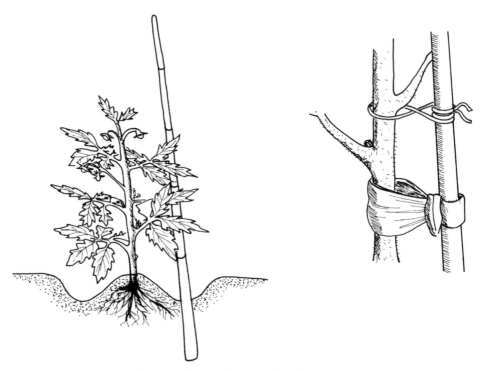

23 Tomato plant: setting out and positioning cane.
24 Two types of tie; keep them loose round the stem, tight round the cane.

security but freedom of movement (Figure 24). Elastic plant ties are available commercially, which can be copied by cutting strips from old bicycle tubes. Bits of rag or plastic or soft fillis or twine can be used. Avoid thin, hard string, which chews through the stem when the fruits put pressure on. Secure the stem 'under the arms' at leaf junctions, where it is less likely to slip.

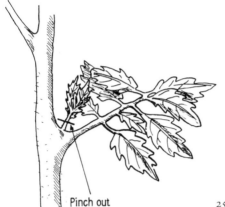

Pinch out 25 Side shoot removal.

Left to itself, the tomato will try to branch out, by producing a side shoot in the junction between leaf and stem. Pinch these out ruthlessly as soon as they appear (Figure 25). Frustrated, the plant will then turn to producing fruit trusses—little sprays of flowers which fall off and leave tiny fruit in their place. The number of these will vary according to the state of the weather. However far the plant has reached by the middle of July, pinch out the growing tip of the main stem. There are only six or seven weeks of good weather to go, and the plant will need all its energy to mature the fruits already started.

If a plant gets very heavy, help it with another short stake on the other side, and prop up any low-growing trusses of tomatoes on a bit of tile, straw or any old packaging material, to keep them off the ground and away from the slugs.

Apart from slugs, which should be regarded as enemy No 1 and destroyed on sight, tomatoes are liable to blight. This strikes late in the season, when they are full of fruit and promise. If the weather is warm and muggy in mid-July to August, you may expect trouble, so spray the plants with Bordeaux mixture (see page 214). Wash any sprayed tomatoes before using—the spray won't penetrate their skins.

You should be able to gather tomatoes from July, depending on the weather. If the trusses are very heavy, pick any fruit which is starting to blush—it will redden off the plant. Some people become addicted to fresh green tomatoes and have to be fought off in the interests of getting some red ones. It is worth braving the storm to drape plastic over the plants, as the fruit skins can be split by hail or heavy rain.

Tomato plants are on sale in May or June ready for planting. If they look healthy, treat them as you would your own stock, and water them well in.

Growing in containers

If you have no suitable ground, but a nice sheltered corner of the yard, tomatoes can be grown in pots. The larger the pot, the less trouble you will have with watering at the height of the season, but the more spare potting earth you will need to begin with. A 12in (30cm) diameter pot is about the minimum practical size for full growth.

Put broken pots or stones at the bottom of the continer, then a layer of coarse compost, leaves or peat, which will retain moisture. Fill up with good soil, prefer-ably sterilised, or a mixture of half John Innes compost and half soil. Set a bamboo cane firmly at one edge of the pot and then put in the young plant.

In any sort of container, it will need feeding with liquid manure, or any fertiliser recommended (see page 194) as soon as it produces a truss—at first once a week and, when it is heavy with fruit, twice a week. Never let the soil dry out, and pick off any broken or sick-looking leaves as soon as seen. Note the colour of those leaves and check (page 209) what deficiency needs correcting.

In a smallish pot, moisture will evaporate very fast. You may need to water the plant three times a day in high summer. If this is difficult, try standing the pot in a bowl of water during the day, but take it out if the soil gets soggy or dank. You might move the plants—being careful not to shake the trusses—to a spot less in the full sun for a while. As long as the air is warm, they will continue to grow.

Growing bags—plastic sacks of prepared compost and sometimes with added nutrients—are increasing in popularity. The bag lies on its side and the plants are grown through holes in the plastic. Two or, at a pinch, three plants can be grown per bag; they are treated in every way like pot-grown plants. They must be kept watered, and dosed with the liquid fertiliser usually supplied as part of the kit. This saves all the trouble of making up your own soil mixtures, but the cheapest cost £3 for four bags, and some three times as much, with seeds thrown in. After one using, the compost must be discarded; the mixture is good for the soil and can be put on the garden.

No tomato plant with a restricted root run, in a pot or any other container, will cope with more than four trusses of fruit out of doors. In pots smaller than 12in (30cm) across, two or three trusses will be enough. When this number have set, pinch out the growing point.

Towards the end of summer, they will need some protection, from a plastic cover at night or loosely tied-round newspaper. As soon as frost threatens, either move the plants inside to finish, or pick all the tomatoes, red or green, before they are damaged.

Under cover

Tomatoes grown in a cold frame can be protected more easily, provided they are not too tall for the lights to close. A plant can be finished under cover if the cane is removed and it is tipped on its side. It may be as well to grow a bush tomato—designed to grow low from the first. Fruit trusses will need padding with straw or packaging to keep them off the ground.

A tomato plant can be made to bush by taking out the growing point when three leaves are on the stem and letting lateral shoots develop. This is chancy, but worth trying if you particularly like the flavour of one of the climbing varieties. Don't stop a shoot when the weather is muggy—it encourages blight to take hold.

Tomatoes grown in a greenhouse, even without extra heat, have a longer growing period—by two or three months. We have picked fresh tomatoes at Christmas grown this way. The lean-to mini-greenhouses will do quite well for this purpose.

Greenhouse plants can be grown in pots on staging, in which case they must be watered and fed regularly, but can normally cope with six trusses of fruit before stopping. Wires from the roof will be needed to support them.

The ring culture method is popular with enthusiasts. The plants are placed in bottomless straight-sided pots, about 10in (25cm) in diameter, filled with potting compost. Sit the pots on a tray full of clinker and gravel. The plant throws out short roots within the ring and a second, longer system in the gravel. All the fertiliser goes into the rings and the plain water in the gravel. If you are keen on the idea, read it up in detail, since the prescribed quantities of this and that are complicated and the whole operation very time-consuming. It keeps grandfathers happy for hours.

In a Dutch light greenhouse, with glass to the ground, it is much simpler to grow the plants directly into a bed of soil. You can make this up on a solid floor by marking off a box with building blocks or bricks. Put in a drainage layer—of crocks, large stones or clinker—then coarse compost or leaves, and finally sieved soil mixed with peat and a bit of sand. Sterilise if you can, but weeding is easier on this scale. Plant the tomato seedlings diagonally 15in (37.5cm) apart. Fix canes, or run wires from the roof to short stakes in the ground. Cross wires at various heights fixed to the side of the greenhouse are useful too.

Treat the plants much the same as outdoor ones, removing side shoots as they appear and tying the stems loosely to the canes or wires as they grow. Don't stop the plants until they have filled all the space available—right up to the roof ridge, provided all the weight can be supported safely at maximum growth.

Under cover, tomato plants are less easily pollinated and may have trouble setting trusses of fruit. One way of helping them is to go in early in the morning, after a night-time closing of the greenhouse, and tap the canes or wires smartly, which should release a cloud of pollen and do the trick. Another method is mist-spraying the plants—ideally, squirt a fine jet of water from a hose at the roof, and let the mist fall on the tomatoes. Once the first trusses have set, they usually get the idea.

Tomatoes grown under cover need a lot of water, though the soil mustn't stay soggy round them. Always water round the roots. If the leaves ever droop, they may need the mist-spray treatment—done at night so no drops of water will catch the sun and burn the leaves. The fruit does not relish being splashed with water, so it is risky to set top trusses by mist-spraying.

Tomatoes like the air warm and dryish, but wilt if the heat is too fierce. Therefore greenhouse roofs are traditionally washed over with thin emulsion paint, whitewash, muddy water or 'special greenhouse shading compound' (whitewash) once the tomatoes have got going. Greenhouse blinds on rollers can be pulled up and down much more easily than the whitewash can be scraped off, but they are expensive. A fine net curtain can be lashed across the roof or a semi-opaque plastic lining fitted. The greenhouse could, of course, be sited in the first place beside a tree with summer foliage, which filters the amount of light when needed and obligingly drops its leaves as the heat of the sun lessens.

As the cold weather advances, all the shading must be removed and replaced with clear polythene as a barrier against heat loss. Soft polythene film is cheaper, but a semi-rigid sheet is a lot easier to fix, especially to a metal-framed greenhouse.

Always clear out any used soil from the greenhouse beds before the next season. Left in the house, it would incubate all kinds of pests and diseases, but spread around in the open garden the richness will improve the soil. Old potting earth should be emptied out in the same way, once it has been used.

Celery

Celery can be raised from seed in very sheltered conditions, or bought in as plants in May. It needs careful hardening off and, except in the sunny south-west, should not be planted out before late May or even June without a cloche.

Self-blanching celery is the summer variety, and is not frost-hardy at either end of its life. It should be planted in a 2in (5cm) deep trench cut with a hoe. The plants are set 9in (22.5cm) apart and packed round with enough soil to hold them firm—the spaces between them are left free to act as water holders and allow the passage of fertiliser to the earth. The soil in which they are planted should be rich, but not freshly manured. Incorporate some compost under the planting station, or dose the celery with liquid manure or superphosphate. Don't apply them within a day of each other.

In early August, start drawing the earth from the sides of the trench towards the stems, and fill in the gaps. The variety is reasonably self-blanching, but likes a little help at the end. If it is planted in a square block, 9in (22.5cm) between plants, the ones in the centre go much whiter than those outside. In mid-August, pull all the loose earth in between the plants and pile some extra soil round the outside of the block. Tuck straw or peat between the plants and, if you are really keen, wrap a strip of cardboard round the outside of the whole group. The celery will be ready for pulling in late August and should last till October, but if the frosts come early it must be lifted.

Ordinary celery is as delicate when starting but the mature plant will stand the winter, with protection. Make the trench at least 12in (30cm) wide and deep, and fill the bottom with compost, rotted leaves or lawn mowings—anything but fresh manure and pea/bean debris, which is too nitrogen-rich and makes the sticks coarse. Top with 4in (10cm) of soil—or 6in (15cm) on clay land which gets sodden in winter—and firm. In July set the small plants 12in (30cm) apart and add sufficient earth for them to stand firm. Fill the gaps with loose handfuls of compost or leaves, and dose with superphosphate unless the plot was well-manured in autumn.

Keep well watered, and dose later with liquid manure. In mid-August, draw a little earth towards the stems and over the compost, repeat a week later, and a week after that. While you are doing this, the stems of the plant should be bunched together, so that no earth gets into the centre. A collar of paper can be wrapped round the stems, held lightly with fillis string, to keep them clean. At the beginning of September, earth the plants right up to their top leaves, topping the soil with a good layer of peat and patting firm.

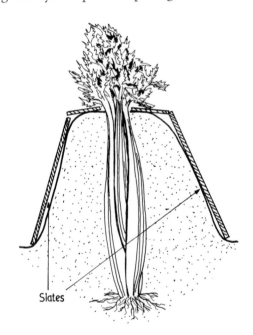

26 Celery: earthing up for blanching.

Cover the sides of these earthed-up mounds with old slates, sloping inwards like an inverted V. Shake more peat into the tops of the structure and cover the gaps between plants with bits of slate or stones to keep out water which might freeze. Don't lift the plants until you need to use the celery and it will last the winter (Figure 26).

If you live in a northern district, where frost is normal, the celery plus its earth can be lifted in early winter and set down again next to the house, or even in a shed; covered in tightly with its slates, it should be all right.

Chicory

Sow the seeds in good but not freshly manured soil in June. Thin to 12in (30cm) apart, if you are going to leave them in place, or 9in (22.5cm), if you are going to lift them (see below). The leaves can be used in salad, but are not a patch on lettuce; the roots you do not use. In September, cut off most of the leaves, ready for winter growing of chicons—the blanched chicory 'hearts'; this can be done in two ways.

You can leave the roots where they grew, and make an earth ridge above them, 5in (12.5cm) deep and secured in place by slates, as with celery. From December to January, the plant throws up more leaves—these are held together in a tight bunch like a lettuce heart by the pressure of the slates, and blanched whitish by the darkness. When you want them, take away a pair of slates and pull back the earth. Cut off the leaves—the chicon—just above the root, and cover up again with the ridge of earth for regrowth. Next time move the next pair of slates. Don't expose the root longer than you must.

Because this is a chilly business, some people prefer to lift the roots in autumn and store them in a shed or other frost-free place. If these are placed, a few at a time, upright in a box and very close together, covered by 5in (12.5cm) of mixed sand and soil, they will produce the chicons. These will appear faster if the roots are put under the staging in a warm greenhouse, but they will not be so crisp. The roots must be kept absolutely dark. Cut the chicons as soon as they surface in the box, and recover the roots with earth for re-growth. You should get chicons from about January.

Cardoons

Cardoons, a close relative of the globe artichoke, are grown more like celery. Start them under glass in late March to April and plant out in early May. Without glass, plant them in the open in early May, about 18in (45cm) apart.

They need a rich trench of soil, which can be prepared just as for celery. They must be extremely well watered through the summer, and fed with liquid manure at intervals. Tie them to a cane when they are about 12in (30cm) high. At all costs keep mud off them. This can be achieved by covering the surface of the soil with a pile of grass mowings, but don't let them rot to a close mat.

In late September, after letting the plants dry out thoroughly above ground, wrap them firmly in strong paper and then earth them up, as with celery or chicory. The stems will blanch in about six weeks ready for use like celery. Cardoons will not stand hard frost, so lift them in their wrappings and bring them in to a shed, making sure they are kept dark and the roots are packed round with earth or sand which is damp.

Endive

Endive is another blanching plant, but easier in cultivation. It is sown directly in the ground in late June, and should germinate extraordinarily fast. It likes reasonable soil, but not fresh manure or any pampering. It should not be sown in a trench, or it rots. A light cloche helps the seed to start well and can then be removed. When the seedlings are big enough to handle, set them out in a staggered double row, with about 10in (25cm) between plants.

Keep weeds and slugs away, and never let the plant dry out, though don't stand it in a puddle. From September, reduce watering, and in October cover plants with cloches to keep off the rain, as they must be dry before blanching. Set slug traps, or all the plants will be eaten. Tie the top leaves round with fillis.

Blanch just as many as you want at one time, by covering the required plants with peat and an up-ended large flower-pot or plastic bucket. At first the blanching will take about a week, but as the weather gets colder it will take two or three. Keep checking, because there is only a short period when they are blanched and perfect, then they rot.

The plants will stay out of doors in a certain amount of frost but die in hard winter, so either use all the crop by Christmas or lift part of it in autumn and re-plant in a cold frame. You can blanch several heads at once in a frame by putting matting on top to exclude light from a selected number, or make a thick paper cone and up-end it over one. The plants must not get wet or dirty at any stage, so be careful when cutting off the blanched heads in bad weather.

Chinese cabbage

Also known as Pei Tsai, Chinese cabbage is another strictly summer crop. It is far more like a lettuce than a cabbage. It needs warmth but can't take direct sun, so find a sheltered but not too shady corner. Sow directly into the ground in June or July—possibly August in the deep south. Thin to 6in (15cm) apart as soon as possible. Keep well watered—over the soil, not the leaves. Take half-grown specimens for kitchen use.

In the north, pick it all before the frosts come or cloche it over in October. In the south it will grow on to full maturity in November, or even December if left in the garden; but it must be watched closely, for there are only a few days between maturity and bolting.

It will not keep fresh for more than a matter of days after cutting—like a lettuce —so keep on thinning all the time. The last plants, standing in isolation, may need fillis tied round the leaves to stop them draggling in the mud.

Chinese mustard

A similar summer plant, to be grown in partial shade between about May and early

August, Chinese mustard likes good soil, and is a safer substitute for spinach. Sow *in situ* and thin as soon as possible to 6in (15cm) apart. Water well and use as soon as it reaches half-maturity. It is fully mature in about six weeks from sowing and after that it bolts—runs a stem up to flower—which makes it grow tough and rather unpleasant to eat. It will not stand frost at all.

Dandelions

Lastly, the humble dandelion, which grows as a weed, can be turned into an appetising salad vegetable. Pick the young leaves green, and up-end a flower pot over the stump to blanch the second growth; this tastes nutty and tangy.

Summer Planting for Winter Use

The major class of vegetables involved in summer planting are the brassicas—including cabbages, cauliflowers, brussels sprouts, broccoli, turnips and swedes. They will stand worse weather than most other vegetables and will come through the winter relatively unscathed. For this reason, most people do the sensible thing and grow them for winter use, when others are scarce.

They could, by carefully planned sowing, be available all the year round in one form or another, but unless you have a lot of space you will probably not aim for this. The big snag about brassicas in general is their long maturing period and the amount of room they take up. They need 2ft (60cm) or more between them, and their large leafy heads cast shadows over other plants during the major part of the good growing period.

Some varieties, especially summer cabbage and cauliflower, can be sown in spring like the root vegetables. We always grow a few swedes and cauliflower in spring because we like to have some ready in the summer. Pick your varieties with care—some need to be started in January to give them a long enough growing period. Most of the brassicas needed for summer use should be planted under shelter in January or February, or in the open in March. Brussels sprouts required for the autumn should go in during early April and the winter plants in May. Stagger the sowings by a month or so if you want to gather regularly from growing plants, or sow in larger groups if you intend to pick them all at once and store for later use.

Early summer sowing

Because of their long growing season, the seeds have to be started off in early summer, when space is short. Brassicas are therefore grown in seed beds, and kept there for as long as possible while young, to leave the main plot free for summer-ripening vegetables.

Much the same method is used for making a seed bed as for preparing the rest of the plot for sowing. Dig out all the weeds, lime the area and to discourage club-root (the major disease of cabbage-family plants) rake in thoroughly. Then firm the soil by treading, and loosen the surface again. Because the plants are going to remain in place, close packed, for a long time, it is really important to shift every scrap of weed root and seed you possibly can, by vigorous raking initially.

You don't want to encourage fast leggy growth, or to have to water every day in a hot summer, so try to place the seed bed out of the sun—anywhere unsuitable for your summer growers. To economise on space, plant the seeds in a block rather than in rows—though the better they can be set out at 2in (5.8cm) apart in any direction the better they will grow. This is a job which a patient, tidy-minded child can do—it takes ages and needs small fingers. If you haven't the patience, sprinkle the seeds over the block and hope that not too many come down in clumps or gaps. Cover ½in (12.5mm) deep and firm the soil well.

Don't let the ground dry out, particularly at germination and small-seedling stage. As the plants grow taller, a mulch of lawn mowings or peat tucked round them after the ground has been well watered will keep in the moisture.

Let them grow undisturbed—unless they clump—for as long as possible. When they start to jostle each other, they will have to be thinned out. Those which ripen in late summer to autumn can move into the main plot as soon as the early peas are done, but the rest, including all the winter stocks, must move to a waiting bed at greater distances apart—9in (22.5cm) if you can manage it. At any stage, brassica plants should be set very firmly in the ground, because they have a lot of top weight and catch the wind easily.

Planting out in autumn

As the summer crops are cleared, rake lightly over the top of the earth to remove dead leaves and decaying mulch which isn't quite ready to sink into the ground; but don't dig, since most brassicas like a firm soil. If their roots are not held tight, they flop about and produce blowsy plants.

Plant with a dibber or thick stick, and make a hole deep enough to take the roots without doubling, plus half or more of the stem, plus 2in (5cm). In that 2in (5cm) space, put a chunk of rhubarb leaf and leaf stem, as a precaution against club-root—rhubarb leaves are full of oxalic acid, which poisons the club-root virus. If you haven't any rhubarb, fill the bottom of the hole with horticultural naphthalene—available in country areas at least (old books will tell you to use moth balls, which used to be made of naphthalene; but nowadays they are mostly para-dichloro-benzene). Spinach past its prime is also full of oxalic acid, though we have no evidence as to its effectiveness if similarly used. In the absence of any of these, dust the soil round the roots of the plant with lime.

Lift the young plant with as much earth attached as possible—wet the soil well first—and sink it into the hole. Keep individual plantings about 2ft (60cm) apart. The tall plants—sprouting broccoli, heading broccoli (winter cauliflower) and brussels sprouts—may need provision for staking in windy gardens, since they carry a lot of top weight. Broad bean wires can be left in place for one of these crops.

Brussels sprouts

These can be planted out in mid-summer to crop from about October, or in September to crop by Christmas, or in October to crop at intervals during January to March.

Broccoli

Sprouting broccoli produces a stalk with a loose tassel of cauliflower-like florets. Planted in October, it crops in late January to March, with a few late starters running on into April. The purple variety looks very decorative as it grows, but disappointingly it cooks dark green. Heading broccoli (winter cauliflower) produces small cauliflower heads in February to April. Both these can be frozen if they come in a rush, to extend the season to cover the 'hungry gap'.

Cabbages

The various cabbages are slightly shorter, but need watching in case the plants tip sideways. The firm-ball sorts—red and white—are mostly planted out in late August to September and produce in early winter, though some will stagger production till spring. After that come the savoys, which are very hardy, stand the winter and crop in March and April. The leaves are floppy and crinkled and tend to cook soft.

Kale

Kale—the cabbage's poor relation—grows in any sort of hard winter, not even needing good soil, and is highly resistant to club-root. It crops from January and goes on till April or May, since leaves are pulled off a few at a time, not the whole plant. Though not to everyone's taste, it is a splendid standby when no other fresh food is available.

Radishes

Radishes, the baby of the brassica family, used as a catch crop are ready for eating within a fortnight of planting, but the Japanese, Spanish or China Rose types, planted in summer, can be grown for winter use. They need plenty of water all the time, since they grow large and would otherwise taste woody. They will reach maturity in the autumn. One goes a long way, so either restrict planting or pickle some of the crop. They will keep for a time in damp sand, like any other root crop, then wither away to nothing.

Autumn Planting

Apart from setting out the brassicas in the main plot (page 85), your major job of autumn planting will be to install any trees or fruit bushes you have ordered. Prepare the soil well by removing perennial weeds, add as much muck and compost as you can spare, and set the plant in firmly. The soil in autumn is still warm and the roots have a chance to take hold before winter stops growth. Stake any such trees or bushes firmly, and check from time to time that winds haven't rocked stake and plant loose, leaving a hole down which icy water can go.

Vegetables

Broad beans

Broad beans can be sown in sheltered gardens in November; they stand the winter as young plants which get going again in early spring. Don't plant them in the same place twice, since their valuable work of producing nitrogen should be spread around the plot. Don't set winter beans in a trench, since they might get water-logged, but earth them up almost to the tips to protect them from frost. If they survive, they will be so tough that the blackfly are scared off. In colder areas, plant in October and cover with a cloche, but don't forget to water from time to time.

Peas

In sheltered gardens a November sowing of peas will get off to a flying start in spring, but icy winds are their enemies. Sow an early like 'Feltham First'.

Lettuces

Lettuces sown in September stand a good chance of maturing in mildish winters.

Sown in October or November, lettuce will produce crops all through the winter in a cold greenhouse or frame, and possibly under a cloche. The variety 'All the Year Round' lives up to its name, with very slight protection.

Tree onion

This useful perennial isn't readily available, but snap it up if you see it. Plant it in the autumn, if you have any choice, though it will have to be put in at whatever time of year it arrives otherwise it will dry away to dust. You may get it as a handful of cocktail-size onions—which are planted 12in (30cm) apart, or by themselves. Or you may buy an older bulb, probably sold singly; this should go in at $2\frac{1}{2}$–3in (6–7.5cm) deep.

In the first year, it will just grow bigger, looking like an ordinary onion, but mark it so that someone does not dig it up and eat it. Leave it in and the following year it will throw up a stem, on which little bunches of tiny onions hang at intervals. The stem grows quite tall, and will need propping up, or the weight of the onions will snap it. Pick these tiny onions in autumn for use.

At the same time, the base bulb produces offsets, which will send up their own stems the next year, and so on. Left in, the clump becomes very congested in the third and subsequent years, so either eat some of the offsets, or lift and divide the clump in autumn. The original bulb gives up after five years, but by that time you will have younger plants to succeed it.

Welsh onion

Another rare plant, the Welsh onion is occasionally found as seeds. Sow in spring in a box, plant out into a nursery bed during the summer and transfer to its final position, 9in (22.5cm) apart, either in autumn or the next spring. Set the young seedlings well into the ground, about 2–3in (5–7.5cm), according to size. The most forward ones planted in autumn will produce a number of little offsets, like chives or spring onions, early in the year. Use some of these and save the others to start the process over again for next year. If possible, leave the continuation clump in the ground until autumn, before dividing the plant up, but do this at any time if they get too congested.

Long-term Producers

If you are reasonably sure of staying in the same house for some years, it is worth considering growing certain vegetables which show no return in the first year, but then bear increasingly for the next two, three or even twenty years.

These long-term producers will be living in the same soil for some years, therefore the better quarters you give them, the better results you will get. All of them do best if you prepare the site by digging out a whacking great hole and filling it with horse or cow manure, compost, rotted leaves, etc, and topping off with soil carefully sifted to exclude large stones, weed bits and insect pests. You can't overdo the food for perennial plants; if you haven't the means to do the job properly, either wait till next year or settle for inferior results. It isn't nearly as easy to add the food afterwards.

Globe artichokes

Globe artichokes are planted on a rich bed one spring for first use the next summer. March is early enough, unless the winter is very mild. They can be grown from seeds, under protection, but are normally bought as offsets and set in the ground with just the tip showing. If the weather turns chill, protect the tips with a bit of peat until the plants are established.

Globe artichokes are an acquired taste, so one plant may be enough for your family. Indeed, one plant may be enough for your garden, because it will eventually need a square yard of space. This will not be filled for the first two seasons, so initially you can plant other crops nearby.

The plant grows about 4ft (1.2m) high when mature, but for the first year it will be smaller. In an exceptional year, it may produce a head or two that same summer. Strictly, you shouldn't touch them for fear of weakening the plant, but if they look very vigorous sample not more than one-third of the total output, and leave the rest. The bit which is eaten is the fleshy flower head when young—left, it goes as tough as boot leather. Don't let them run to seed, but cut them off ruthlessly. In the second summer a whole mass of little heads will be produced. If you take the main head first, this will encourage the side shoots to produce more.

The plants are pretty hardy, but it is as well to protect them for the winter by packing earth, peat or old leaves round the stems, and removing it again when the milder weather comes. Chop off the foliage in November for compost and don't let the plants get waterlogged in winter, or they will rot.

A plant will go on producing for about four years, with luck, so in the third year take an offset from the bottom and start it growing again, as you have done with the first one, so that when mother dies, junior is ready to continue production.

When the old plant is on its last legs, you can take a different crop from it—chards. After gathering the heads, cut back the leaves to 6in (15cm) to produce new growths, or chards. When about 18in (45cm) high, wrap the whole thing up in paper, leaves, peat—anything to exclude all the light. In six weeks' time, the growths will have blanched and be ready for cooking. These chards aren't to everyone's taste, but it is interesting to try.

At all growing stages, globe artichokes need plenty of water, if the crop is not to be tough. In winter they shun it.

Rhubarb

Although rhubarb is a sort of fruit, it is usually planted in the vegetable plot and has more of the characteristics of a vegetable. Technically it could be raised from seed, but by far the simplest way is to plant a hunk of rhubarb root with a growing point, called a crown. Rhubarb owners are usually only too pleased to give a bit away, to try to keep a vigorous plant within bounds.

Dig an ample hole (on well-fed land) and spread out the roots, shaking soil well down round them. If you are planting more than one crown, keep them 2ft (60cm) or more apart—they will expand to fill any given quantity of space.

Don't take any of the sticks produced in the first year; in the second year be moderate, and after that you will be overwhelmed. Pull the sticks off the base with a twisting motion and take a few from each plant at a time. When you have pulled a stick, cut off the leaf and throw it straight on the compost heap. Never eat any of the leaf—it is poisonous to man and beast. It is also poisonous to club-root in brassicas so throw some rhubarb leaves in their planting holes in autumn.

After ten years or so, the oldest part of the plant stops producing. Either hack it out or take away crowns from it and plant elsewhere. Antique rhubarb is virtually indestructible. We have burnt fanged monsters on a fierce November 5th bonfire and they have reappeared, fresh and invigorated, from the ashes the following spring.

Rhubarb ripens naturally in early summer, but it can be advanced by about a month by forcing. This is quite simple. At Christmastime cover one plant with an old dustbin or bucket with a holey bottom. In severe weather, fill the container with leaves and a bit of compost and cover the top as well—this is easy with a dustbin lid. As soon as you spot any action, take out some of the packing so that the sticks will be a good colour. The forced plant will be no good for further rhubarb production

that year, but will recover the year after. Don't force the same plant twice running
or it will go sick.

Always cut off the central stem if it tries to flower, and feed the plants now and
then with a dressing of compost to keep them healthy.

Asparagus

Asparagus is the king of long-term plants. It gives no returns until it is three years
old, and then produces magnificently for up to about twenty years.

The bed does need careful preparation, because of the very long residence the
plant will have there. Every scrap of perennial weed must go, since it is very
difficult to get it out once the asparagus roots have filled the bed. Bury a good
helping of manure, compost, etc, and cover with 12in (30cm) of good earth.

The site must be reasonably sheltered, with a dwarf hedge—of rosemary,
possibly—to filter the wind. The crop is produced from April, and the tender shoots
are turned soggy by frost, so plant where it will be in the sun at that time and have
a supply of protective material ready.

Traditionally, asparagus beds are built up high. There is no need to do this,
unless the area is badly drained, which the plant cannot stand. The bed will get a
little higher each year anyway from additions made to it. If possible, separate the
bed from the ordinary vegetable plot with a strip of path, then the plants can have
the nourishment from the soil under that as well. At full maturity, the root system
can spread to 4ft (1.2m) apiece. The individual plants can be set 18in (45cm) apart,
with 9in (22.5cm) at least on the path side, so you can get sixteen plants on a bed
5 × 6ft (1.5 × 1.8m) (Figure 27).

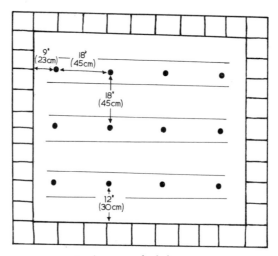

27 Asparagus bed: layout.

The plants can be raised from seed in a small bed and transferred into the asparagus bed two years later, or bought in as one- or two-year old crowns to save time. The one-year crowns settle in more easily, but the two-year ones flourish with just a little attention and produce the next year. 'Connover's Colossal' is an excellent variety commonly available, though you may have to accept whatever is around locally. Prepare the bed before you buy and don't open the bag until you are ready to plant.

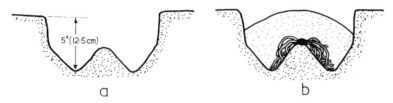

28 Asparagus (a) trench and mound (b) setting out young crown.

Cut a trench, about 9in (22.5cm) wide and 4–5in (10–12.5cm) deep, down the centre of the bed and along the two sides, and set the earth beside it. Then draw the point of a hoe down each side of each trench, to make a deep V-shaped indentation, which leaves a ridge of earth in the centre of each trench (Figure 28).

Take out one plant at a time, closing the bag again—they are very sensitive to drying winds, and if allowed to dry out at any stage, they wither away to nothing. Sit the centre of the crown on the ridge and let the roots dangle down each side. Cover the crown with damp earth to about 3in (7.5cm) and firm down; this will leave a mound of earth and a slit depression beside it, to channel the water down in summer. Complete the planting and covering of one crown before lifting out the next. Plentiful watering down the channels should send the roots downwards instead of poking out sideways into the space between the trenches. Sprinkle fish meal, agricultural salt, sodium nitrate or wood ash (or potassium sulphate) over the bed at intervals during this first summer and cover each dressing with a little earth from the spare trench soil. Firm it well down each time.

If your plants are one year old, take another crop, like carrots or baby beet, between the rows. Let the asparagus produce its crop of fern in late summer, but resist any cutting of this by flower-arranging addicts. When it dies down in October–November, cut it off and compost it.

With two-year-old plants, which have longer roots, pull a shallow dip between the trenches with a hoe, to stop the roots going sideways; pile the earth in ridges on the plants and grow a shallow-rooted crop, like lettuce, between the rows, in the half shade of the fern. Give the same feeds early in the season. You may get a few genuine asparagus sticks, but try not to cut them, for fear of weakening the plant. If you can't resist, sample no more than two and let the rest run to fern. When the fern dies, cut and compost it.

Flatten the ridges out every November and cover the whole bed with a good layer of rich compost or strawy manure, and top that again with a 2in (5cm) layer of dead leaves as a frost precaution.

In spring of the third year, brush off all the loose leaves and any strawy bits which have not decomposed, but keep them handy. Ridge up the three rows again, making a really deep dent down the two middles and the sides. Sprinkle on fish meal, at 4oz to the square yard, and wait for action. Cover with leaves in frost.

Soon, the spears of asparagus will start poking up through the ground, a few at first, then lots. Cut them with a sharp kitchen knife at the height you like them. Brush the earth back from the side of the ridge and select your spear. Cut away from the plant to avoid damaging the next little spear. You can break off the spear by twisting and pulling at the same time, which makes sure the next spear is unhurt. In either case, replace the earth till next day, when more will be ready. The speed of growth is fantastic, so keep eating. Freeze some as you go, before it gets large and coarse, or give it to friends who only know the restaurant variety, where size is preferred to flavour.

Don't take any more asparagus after early June the first year and mid-June later on. The production starts slacking off to warn you when to stop. Let the fern grow through the summer and cut it down when it dies in November, flattening the ridges and covering with 2in (5cm) of compost or manure plus leaves every year. In spring, clear the leaves, ridge up and stand by to gather asparagus. And so on for years and years, with increasing crops.

The only other attentions needed are removing annual weeds when seen; watering in spring with soot-water (old soot steeped in water for weeks), and scattering wood ash between the rows when any is going. The only pest seems to be asparagus beetle, little grey grubs appearing in summer. But they can be killed, just as people can, by applications of nicotine. Spray with a liquid made from old cigarette ends and water, but *not* until you have stopped cutting spears. Nicotine wash can damage your health as well as that of the asparagus beetle.

Female asparagus plants reproduce by throwing berries to the ground. If these take root between the rows, it is best to shift them to another bed, or they will complicate the ridging up in spring. They are also good trading currency when one or two years old.

Hops

At one time, hops were grown everywhere in England, except the north, and there is no reason why they should not be now, by anyone with a lot of space or an overriding thirst. The main commercial growing is done in Kent—the only likely source of the setts from which the plants are grown.

The chief problem in hop growing is the sheer size of the mature plant, which is a vine (called a bine) about 15ft (4.5cm) tall, needing light and air all the way up. The ideal support for the plant would be a windmill pylon, which it would clothe attractively. A post-and-wire framework, 15ft (4.5cm) tall, would be very difficult

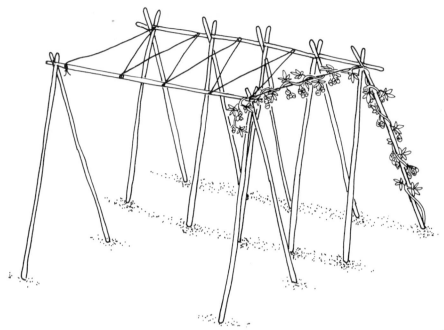

29 Hop arbour. Canes should be 8ft (2.6m) tall and set 6ft (1.8m) apart with joining wires or trellis at top.

to keep upright safely, so the best arrangement for a row of free-standing hop bines would be to erect a 6–8ft (1.8–2.4m) frame—as for runner beans—and train the remainder of the bines out over strong nets or wires to a second frame 6ft (1.8m) or so away. A redundant football goal would provide a basis for this set-up—it would make a cosy though strange-smelling arbour (Figure 29). Other possibilities include using an outdoor lamp-post and wires; a carport side and roof, or a trellis on a south-facing wall. The plant is quite elegant and unusual when growing, and would certainly make a talking point.

The sett is the base of an old bine, which is grown on in a nursery bed for the first year. Then it is planted out in spring, not closer than 5–6ft (1.5–1.8m) to any other bine. The soil must be quite rich, with manure and compost in a good hole in deep-dug land. The crown is set just below ground level. Great care must be taken in preparing a soil bed near a wall, for this is liable to be a shallow planting area unless a deep hole is excavated and refilled with good stuff.

There is only a little growth in the first year, but in the second the full height is reached and a crop is produced. Once moving, the hop rampages away like a grape-vine and needs the same tying in to wires and stopping of unfruitful or over-vigorous shoots (page 130). It may need spraying with Bordeaux mixture against mildew or soapy water against aphids in summer or autumn.

In late August or September, when the cones are dry and rustling, and smell hoppy, the hops are ready to gather. Take them piecemeal or cut down a whole stem and lay it on the ground for ease of stripping. Don't drag up the root of the bine, which grows again next year. The hops must be dried artificially and as soon as possible. This should really be done in a kiln, but it could be managed with an oven. Start at 100°F (37°C) slowly rising to 150°F (65°C) after four hours and then to 160°F (71°C), but no higher. Keep a draught going at intervals. (Take a look at some ready-dried hops, obtainable from wine-making suppliers, to help you check when the process is complete.) The hops will be brittle when they come out of the oven, and must be handled carefully. Leave them to cool down in an airy place, then pack in jars or tins for use (see beer recipe, page 179).

Undercover Plants

A few plants really need a greenhouse or a warm frame before you can grow them at all. Even in an exceptionally good summer, when they can stand outside for some time, they have to be started and finished under cover.

Exotics

Capsicums (red and green peppers) can be grown from seed. Start them early, in March at the latest, because they take ages to germinate. Place a plastic propagator or glass jar over your seed tray or pot. Transplant the seedling each time it outgrows its container until it is eventually in a 8–9in (20–22.5cm) diameter pot.

The plant must be kept damp but never soggy. Stand the pot in a saucer of water. The soil in the final pot must be rich—a mixture of John Innes and good compost or a little manure left to air for a day or two. Wait till late June before putting them outside and choose a very warm, sheltered corner. Bring them in again before the nights turn at all chill.

When the young peppers develop, they may need a little support from small canes to stop one fruit squashing another. Pick when green or wait until they turn red. When frost threatens, shelter them with an individual cover inside the greenhouse or pick all the fruit, otherwise they will turn mouldy. Their only pest seems to be green aphids, which retreat before a soapy water spray.

Chillis are grown similarly to peppers. They are picked and dried for use in soups and stews. Being very 'hot', not many will be needed.

Aubergines (egg plants) also need very similar treatment to peppers. Dose their final soil with dried blood as well. Aubergines are not really keen on being out of doors, except in really warm climates. Keep them well watered, but never let the soil puddle. As they ripen, the fruits will certainly need support, from nets attached to canes or an overhead hoop of wire. They too are upset by the first frost.

Orange and lemon trees can be started from pips and grow into neat little bushes which, in the very best circumstances, will produce tiny fruit. Although we know of one orange tree growing out of doors in Dorset, in a sheltered angle of a wall, in general these trees need a heated greenhouse. They need a large tub of good compost and soil; plenty of water in summer; freedom from frost, and warmth and light at all times. These are mainly fun plants, not serious croppers.

Coffee trees—the latest craze now being offered—cost around £20 for a young tree, or £3 for a baby seedling. They must be kept in a constant temperature of 65°F plus, and in a humid atmosphere, so a kitchen is suggested as the best site. It would take an estimated five years for you to get back 3lb of coffee, so it is not a productive proposition.

Easy growers

Bean sprouts, on the other hand, are very simple to grow and cheap to buy. A packet of mung beans can be obtained from a delicatessen or good grocer. Find a suitable covered container—a jam jar will do, or a plastic lunch-box or deep tray. The lid must be perforated or slightly raised—a cardboard-box lid works well for a tray. Line the base of the container with a piece of blotting paper and spread out the beans. More than one layer can be put into a jar, but don't fill more than one-tenth of it with beans.

Cover them with off-chill water and put in a warm, dark place. An airing-cupboard or a cupboard near the kitchen stove is ideal. Let them swell for twenty-four hours, then water them, twice a day, with tepid water, damping them thoroughly and running off the surplus each time. The beans will grow and grow, and are ready for eating in four or five days, depending on the temperature. Pull off and eat at the white-shoot stage—when they begin to grow their first leaves, they are past it. They can be eaten raw, or very lightly cooked, in spring rolls, chop suey and as a delightfully fresh accompaniment to any meal.

Mustard and cress can be grown indoors, very simply, and by children, on a tray, plate or saucer covered with a piece of damp flannel, hessian or polyurethane foam. Sprinkle up to half the area with a thin layer of cress seed. Three days later, spread the remainder with mustard seed. In a week's time, the little seedlings will be ready to eat; strip them off and start again.

Mustard and cress can also be grown on a tray of soil or a window box. Cover up the seeds as you sow them, and keep the cover on till the stems are 1in (2.5cm) high. When the crop is ready, use it all very quickly—the next day, it flops or coarsens, having no nutrients to sustain it.

If you want your crop to last a few days, or need more than a plateful, grow the same mixture on soil, which should be fine and well firmed. This can be done in a seed tray, with another upended over it to exclude light until the seedlings are 1in (2.5cm) tall. Unless it is kept indoors, wrap the double tray in polythene or put it in a greenhouse for warmth. The ideal temperature is between 50° and 60°F at all times. When the seedlings are ready, remove the covering tray and put back the polythene cover propped up on sticks. You will get about ten ¼lb punnets of mustard and cress off a standard seed tray. It will stand for about a week ripe.

The seeds can be grown out-of-doors in moderately mild weather, on a finely raked and firmed bed. Plant the seeds, with the cress always three days ahead of the mustard, on damp soil. Cover with a sheet of sacking or thick paper and top the whole thing with a black polythene cloche or a cardboard box painted black. This excludes light and absorbs the necessary heat. After the seedlings are 1in (2.5cm) high, take off the covers, but replace with a clear cloche if the weather is cool. This crop will be ready in about ten days, and will last about a week before it goes off. The quantity will vary with the box size.

Mustard and cress grown on soil must be kept wet, though not soggy. Water with a fine mist-spray, which can be improvised from a detergent squeeze bottle, or by using a hose with your thumb across the nozzle. Any wet soil tends to splat up into the crop and is very hard to shift. You can avoid this by planting the seed on a sheet of damp cloth on top of the soil. When the crop is ready, strip off the whole or part of the cloth plus mustard and cress, all clean. This saves skimming off the top layer of soil before re-planting, too, since all the debris comes off cleanly as well.

Mushrooms

Mushroom spawn is easy to come by, from garden shops and chain stores everywhere, but getting good results is not so easy. In their natural state, mushrooms grow wild in pasture fields with a short, close turf, grazed regularly for years, enriched by the droppings of cows, horses or sheep, or in woods with a lot of rotting vegetation lying about. Packets of spawn will enclose instructions which may imply you can copy this by lifting a square of lawn turf, stirring a bit of compost into the soil, planting the spawn and standing back to await results. If your lawn is an ex-pasture, with the right soil, this may work, but if not the spawn will just die.

You will get quite good results from buying a kit, which provides a packet of spawn and another of compost, sometimes even ready-mixed, in a plastic bucket. You add water, stand it in a warm place in the dark and, presto, up come the mushrooms. They do too, and very good and fresh they taste, but the quantity will only just cover the cost of the kit plus heat—though you do get a free bucket out of it. This is the only way for a flat dweller to grow the crop.

If you have more space and want to grow mushrooms in a fairly big way, you must have access to a lot of fresh manure and straw—and somewhere to keep it while it is in the smelly stage. You also need a dark or half-dark growing place, and either a brick box or trays for the compost. More or less any very rich compost will do—it is a matter of trying out what is readily available to you personally and judging the results. If it doesn't work, vary it; if it does, stick to it.

Mushrooms must have organic fertiliser, which could be any animal manure—cow isn't much good, but better than nothing; straw or decomposing wood, to provide the natural sugars, and calcium; they also like a touch of superphosphate and lime to protect them. They cannot use simple chemicals as such, so they need plenty of bacteria to break down all these ingredients into compost and this is encouraged by the fresh manure, which provides an ideal breeding ground.

You can make up all these ingredients into a simple hot-bed (see page 231) and sow the spawn in it when the temperature is falling. This will confine the operation to a single, manageable place, but it will not produce the maximum possible yield from the amount of valuable manure you have collected, and it will run out of steam in a matter of months instead of the greater part of a year.

If you are prepared to take more initial trouble for a much greater crop, first find out what you can collect together at the same time—odd bits acquired at intervals work at different rates and spoil the set-up. You will need a solid floor to work on, which can be cleaned down afterwards. A yard is ideal, but don't work too close to your—or the neighbour's—kitchen windows. Make arrangements with a local farmer or stable to deliver a load of manure, and get in a couple of bales of straw at the same time. One expert claims that wheat straw is the only one to use, because it has xylan, which converts to xylose in the heap. *All* straws have xylan, and most have more than wheat straw. If you want to be scientific, choose rye straw. Wood refuse has the same effect, so clean sawdust could be added, especially to cow manure.

The process of making the compost begins by spreading straw on the floor, wetting it thoroughly, adding a layer of manure, a layer of wet straw, and so on, until the whole thing is about 4ft (1.2m) high. Top with straw and bang the sides to shape it into a tidy heap. Keep it damp, but don't hose it loose. It will heat up, quite fiercely, and smell powerfully rich and farmyardy—this isn't nasty, just strong.

After about five days, pull down the heap, turn it over and pile it up again, with the former sides in the middle, so there is even fermentation. If the heap overheats enough to smoke, damp it down at any time, but don't drown it. Keep it moist but not soggy and cover it from heavy rain. Turn once or twice more, packing it well together each time. It will gradually turn into a uniform, brownish, pleasant-smelling compost or mixture, moist if squeezed but not dripping. After several heatings, its temperature starts to drop from 140°F to under 80°F and then it is ready for use, as quickly as possible. Add the calcium—in the form of nitro-chalk or real gypsum (not gypsum plaster from the builder), and stir it in.

Instead of using horse muck, you could make a heap of straw plus commercial activator plus dried blood, but this would cost more, not work as well and smell of old abbatoirs. You will do better with any sort of manure—pigeon, pig, chicken, even human, if you live in an isolated area.

You can check if the compost is ready, first by smelling it. If a urine/ammonia smell lingers, air it by spreading and re-heaping. Test the pH (see page 25) which should be neutral, about 7. More important, take the temperature, which should be 80°F or less, and falling. The whole process of preparing compost will take about a month.

Meanwhile, make the growing beds or trays. Ideally, the shed or room should be of solid material like rendered blocks or bricks, since the very humid atmosphere would soon rot wood. If the only available place is wooden, line it with polythene,

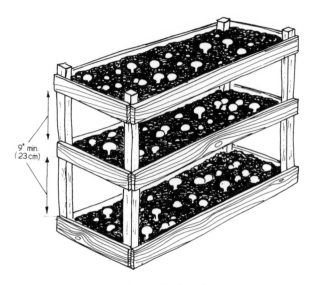

9" min.
(23 cm)

30 Mushroom bunks filled with compost

and paint with ship's varnish or several coats of gloss paint. At least, back the growing trays with plastic deflector curtains to keep the wet off the walls. You can build beds, 12in (30cm) deep and the length of your arm across, and set trays on staging or make triple bunk beds with about 9in (22.5cm) access space between each tier (Figure 30). Beds and bunks take less material to build, but trays are easier to fill and empty.

Fill each tray or bed with compost and firm it down well. If there seems to be a lot of moisture, add nitro-chalk. Plant the spawn, 2in (5cm) deep and about 6–8in (15–20cm) apart. Keep the atmosphere moist by covering the trays with damp newspaper and lightly spraying it if it dries out. The temperature should stay at about 60°F while the spawn is growing, so a small heater may be needed for a while. If this dries the air in the room, spray the walls, but never directly on to the compost at any time, or the spawn will rot.

Soon, in about a fortnight, the spawn will have spread little white mycelium threads all over the tray, under the compost. Little whitish patches show on the surface, which look like mould. This is reasonable—mushrooms are a sort of mould, which happens to be edible. At this point, remove the paper and case the beds, by covering the top with 1in (2.5cm) of sifted garden soil. Pat it firm and dust with lime. Preferably sterilise this soil; the crop is worth the effort. You can mix in a little peat and chalk too, which reduces the risk of the soil panning hard on the surface, and retains moisture.

Now relax and collect the mushrooms. You should not need any extra heat at all once the beds are cased, but if the air is very cold production will slow. Keep the casing moist but not soggy, preferably by watering where no mushrooms are visible. Ventilate well in summer and spray the walls to keep the air humid.

Vegetables: Cultural Summary

A = annual   B = biennial   P = perennial

Artichokes, globe   P   4–5 years   Details: page 90

soil	well composted, deep dug; well drained in winter
site	not in shade
height	4ft (1.2m), bushy
sow	offsets in March–April
plant	1 sq yd each (0.8sq m), crown just showing
culture	feed compost/manure in spring, water well in summer, cover with leaves in autumn/spring
harvest	heads from second summer, blanched chards in fourth-fifth year
propagate	offsets taken in third-fourth year

Artichokes, Jerusalem   A, but self-set easily   Details: page 50

soil	prefer rich, but tolerant of less
site	side or end of plot
height	5–6ft (1.5–1.8m)
sow	January–February *in situ*, tubers, 6in (15cm) deep
plant	18in (45cm) apart
culture	earth up on windy sites in summer; cut down in autumn
harvest	October on as needed. Leave rest in ground (or store in clamp)
propagate	small tubers left in ground will grow, or replant

Asparagus   P   lasts 15–25 years   Details: page 92

soil	rich, well dug, all weeds removed
site	open, sunny, well-drained, isolated bed

height	spears 6–8in (15–20cm) fern 2½–3ft (75–90cm)
sow	(a) seeds in April, 1in (2.5cm) deep; (b) one- or two-year crowns in March, 4in (10cm) deep, on ridges
plant	(b) 18in (45cm) apart, in rows; (a) transplant at one year to this distance
harvest	from third year of age, April to June each year
propagate	self-set seedlings transplanted to new site

Aubergines   very tender   Details: page 97

soil and site	potting compost plus a little manure in cool greenhouse, or very limited period outside in very warm place
sow	in peat pots or box in March to April under glass
plant	to 12in (30cm) pot as soon as large enough
culture	well watered but never soggy. Support fruit with canes and nets, reduce if too crowded
harvest	when purple, but either gather all before frost or enclose pot in mini-greenhouse with extra protection
store	freeze

Bean sprouts   very tender   Details: page 98

soil	none; water only
site	dark, warm cupboard
sow	jar or tray in water, handful of culinary mung beans
culture	add water at intervals
harvest	four days to a week after sowing, before leaves develop
store	freeze

Beans, broad   A   Details: page 61

soil	well composted, like potash
site	in trench 12in (30cm) wide below plot surface level
height	3–4ft (90cm–1.2m), stopped. Dwarf 12in (30cm)
sow	(a) Oct–Nov in south or under glass; (b) late Feb to March; (c) last sowing in late April. Seed beans, 2in (5cm) deep
plant	double row, staggered, individuals 9in (22.5cm) apart in trench
culture	(a) earth up and shelter in frost; (b, c) stop growth pre black fly attack; (a, b, c) support with canes or post and wires
harvest	pick pods regularly (a) from late May–June; (b) from July; (c) late August, Sept
store	frozen or dried, after shelling

Beans, French, dwarf   A   tender to frost   Details: page 68

soil	reasonable, plus potash
site	open, sunny in trench for watering
height	1–2ft (30–60cm) according to variety
sow	seed beans under glass in April, plant out in late May or outside in mid-May, 2in (5cm) deep. Successional sowings until mid July.
plant	6in (15cm) apart in rows 12in (30cm) apart or staggered double row, individuals 9in (22.5cm) apart in trench
culture	guard young seedlings. Water well, mulch in drought. Cover against late frost
harvest	pick pods regularly. Complete before frost
store	freeze, salt whole pods (or shell antiques for drying)

Beans, French, climbing   A   tender

as Beans, runner

Beans, French, haricot   A   tender   Details: page 68
as Beans, French, dwarf—but allow pods to mature on plant; store dried

Beans, runner   A   tender   Details: page 69

soil	well composted, potash added
site	open, sunny, not windswept, or single line against wall
height	6–8ft (1.8–2.4m)
sow	(a) under glass in April, transplanted late May to early June in open; (b) out of doors in mid-May under cloche, 2in (5cm) deep. Seed beans
plant	double row, individuals 10–12in (25–30cm) apart, zigzag spacing; single row against wall, 8in (20cm) plus from it. Set up framework of canes and/or wires first
culture	train round canes or wires at first. Keep well watered, mulch in drought, spray mist overhead to encourage set
harvest	pick pods regularly to encourage growth, from late July July
store	freeze, salt whole pods or shell antiques for drying

Beans, soya   A   half-hardy   Details: page 54

soil and site	as French beans (dwarf)
sow	under glass, April in pots, seed beans, ex culinary do best
plant	transplant in May, same distances as French beans (dwarf)

culture   as French beans (dwarf) and earth bushes on windy site
harvest   young pods (rather nasty) or leave to mature; poor yield experienced
store   dried ex pods

Beetroot   A   hardy   Details: page 51

soil   old compost, not freshly manured, deep dug for long beet
site   any, warm in spring
depth   6in (15cm) for round beet; up to 12in (30cm) for long beet
sow   seeds *in situ* in spring, late March to early April or fortnight earlier under cloches. $\frac{1}{2}$in (12.5cm) deep successional sowings end in July
plant   (a) long beet: 6in (15cm) apart in double row 8in (20cm) apart; (b) round beet: 4in (10cm) apart, double row 8in (20cm) apart
thin and
   transplant   (a) multiple growths to row on other site; (b) multiple growths to centre of rows, 4in (10cm) apart
thin (2)   alternate best in each row, opposite gaps, leaving final stations (a) 12in (30cm) (b) 8 in (20cm) apart
harvest   (a) half-grown thinnings to eat, mature to store; (b) baby beet at 2in (5cm) diameter, half-grown thinnings to eat, mature to store
store   pickle baby beet; freeze sliced or cubed; clamp mature roots. Will stay in ground till December

Broccoli, heading (winter cauliflower)   A   very hardy   Details: page 87

soil   old compost and nitrogen, very firm
site   open, not too windy
height $2\frac{1}{2}$–3ft (75–90cm), spreading
sow   seedbed in May, $\frac{1}{2}$in (12.5mm) deep
plant   in waiting bed 6in (15cm) plus apart in July
transplant   final station in autumn, 2ft (60cm) apart or more. May need staking in spring
culture   break leaf over maturing head to keep white
harvest   individual small heads from (February) March to May, central cabbage head. Cut as needed for use
store   freeze, pickle

Broccoli, sprouting   A and B   very hardy   Details: page 87

soil   old compost, very firm
site   open, not too windy
height   3ft (90cm), spreading

sow	(a) Calabrese (summer) in April in seed bed; (b) winter types in May in seed bed, $\frac{1}{2}$in (12.5mm) deep
plant	(a) 2ft (60cm) apart in late May; (b) waiting bed in July, 6in (15cm) apart
transplant	(b) to final stations 30in (75cm) apart in autumn
culture	may need staking in spring
harvest	(a) July–August; (b) regular picking of tassels of curds from standing plant, Feb–April. Finished when flowering starts. Note—purple broccoli cooks green
store	freeze

Brussels sprouts   B   very hardy   Details: page 87

soil	not too rich, very firm
site	open, not windy
height	2–2$\frac{1}{2}$ft (60–75cm), narrow but top-heavy
sow	(a) March in seedbed, may need cloche; (b) April–May in seedbed. $\frac{1}{2}$in (12.5mm) deep
plant	(a) (b) waiting bed in June–July 4–6in (10–15cm) apart
transplant	(a) final station as soon as space, July–August; (b) final station September–early October; (a, b) 2–2$\frac{1}{2}$ft (60–75cm) apart
culture	may need support—ex broad bean wires useful; net against birds
harvest	(a) from October; (b) from Nov–December. Ends about February. Pick as buttons mature, few from each plant
store	freeze

Cabbages, can be grown to mature at all times of the year by varying date of sowing; follow precise directions for variety bought)   fairly to very hardy

Details: page 87

soil	old composted, dose with anti–club–root substance
site	not where cabbage family stood last year
height	around 12in (30cm)
sow	seedbed in (a) early March for summer types; (b) April for autumn; (c) late April early May for winter, $\frac{1}{2}$in (12.5mm) deep. Successional sowings at monthly intervals for all types till July
plant	(a) summer types as soon as large enough to handle, double row, 15in (37.5cm) apart in zigzag spacing; (b) autumn types to waiting bed, 6in (15cm) apart in June; (c) winter types to waiting bed, 6in (15cm) apart in July–August–September
transplant	(b) in July–August; (c) in Sept–Oct to final stations 18–24in (45–60cm) apart, according to type

harvest	(a) late June–July; (b) mid-August–September; (c) November and through to March from successional sowing. Savoys sown in late May carry through till late April next year
store	leave in ground till needed. If whole plant is pulled and hung upside-down in cool place, will keep for limited period. Sauerkraut, pickle

Cardoons   half-hardy   Details: page 82

soil	rich, moist trench
site	sheltered in winter (or bring them in)
sow	seed under glass in late March–April, outside in May
plant	in early May, 18in (45cm) apart in trench
culture	water and feed well, wrap and earth up late September to blanch. Bring in before frost, in dark.
harvest	Six weeks after blanching commences
store	Use as needed; will keep in dark for limited period

Carrots   A   hardy root   Details: page 57

soil	not freshly manured, deep dug
site	warm in spring, then coolish
size	4–6in (10–15cm) in depth, stump-rooted; 7–10in (17.5–25cm) normal
sow	seeds *in situ*, late March–April. Successional sowings till June. $\frac{1}{2}$in (12.5mm) deep
plant	initially about 2in (5cm) apart, in double row, 12in (30cm) between rows. Plant next to onions
thin and transplant	any multiple seedlings, to centre of double row at 2in (5cm) spacing
thin (2)	alternate young carrots in each row, opposite gap in adjacent row to 4in (10cm) apart
harvest	thinnings of half-mature carrots from late May–June onwards. Lift all crop in autumn to defeat pests
store	clamp in sand. Freeze thinnings whole or mature sliced

Cauliflowers (summer)   not very hardy

soil	rich, manured
site	sunny, sheltered
height	10–12in (25–30cm) round head

sow	(a) autumn under cloches for over-wintering in mild districts; (b) March for summer; (c) successional sowings till May for autumn
plant	(a) plant out or uncover in mid-March; (b) plant out in May; (c) plant out when 6–8 weeks old. 2–2½ ft (60–75cm) apart
culture	shade from hot sun by breaking leaf over head
harvest	(a) late May–late June; (b) August–September; (c) September–November. Frost spoils the curd, so collect or cover with cloche
store	freeze, pickle. Limited period in cool shed

Celeriac   half-hardy

soil	rich, composted
site	sunny
sow	under glass in late March–April
plant	12in (30cm) apart in late May, shallowly
culture	destroy all suckers and side shoots. Earth up in October
harvest	November. Stems as inferior celery in October
store	leave in ground in very mild districts or clamp roots in sand

Celery   tender   Details: page 81

soil	rich, deep dug, composted, not freshly manured
site	sunny, sheltered, well drained in winter, in shallow trench or square depression
height	15–20in (37.5–50cm)
sow	summer type (a) seeds in heat in late March; (b) seeds under glass April; (c) plants outside in late May. Winter type (a) in heat in early March (b) under glass in early April (c) plants in late June–July
plant out	summer types in late May in square block, 9in (22.5cm) apart for individuals. Winter types (a, b) early July, single row in trench 12in (30cm) apart. Second row in similar trench 12–15in (30–37.5cm) away
culture	summer type: fill gaps with straw or earth as it grows; wrap in straw or paper round outside of blocks, early August to aid blanch. Winter type: wrap each one, earth up progressively from mid-August; earth up completely and cover with slates in September
harvest	summer type: late August to early October; winter type: lift as required late October to January
store	bring in to shed whole plant plus earth and slates in November. Won't freeze unless cooked

Chicory   half-hardy   Details: page 82

soil	good, not freshly manured
site	any (if lifted), well drained, sheltered (if left)
sow	seeds in June *in situ*
plant or thin	to 9in (22.5cm) (lifted) or 12in (30cm) (left in)
culture	(left in): cut off leaves in September, make earth ridge over, slate cover, for blanching; (lifted): dig up, place upright in box, cover with earth in dark place
harvest	uncover and use as needed, keep rest of chicons dark. Use from about January. Recover plant for regrowth

Chinese cabbage   Frost-tender   Details: page 83

soil	good, not fresh manure, apparently free of club-root
site	sheltered, not in full sun (like lettuce)
sow	late June, early July, small amounts in succession
plant	double row, 6in (15cm) apart in staggered rows
culture	must be kept watered or will bolt, shade in very hot spell. When large, tie leaves round with fillis
harvest	take thinning alternately, cut and use as needed; ends Nov–Dec
store	won't keep, except day or two in water, not refrigerator

Chinese mustard   slightly tender   Details: page 83

soil	good, not fresh manured
site	sheltered, not in full sun
sow	May–July for succession
plant	individuals 6in (15cm) apart
culture	water well, dose with dried blood when 4 weeks old, grow fast or it will bolt
harvest	thin as required; use up within 7–8 weeks of planting
store	won't

Corn salad (lamb's lettuce)   fairly hardy

soil	reasonable
site	sunny, sheltered, well-drained
sow	July–early September, late September in south
plant	4in (10cm) apart
culture	keep watered in summer for fast growing. Cover with cloche from late October
harvest	pick odd leaves as needed, never all from one plant

store   not really, but can be covered with flower pot to blanch, extend-
                   ing life a little

Courgettes

see marrows

Cress, American or land   P   hardy

soil   not fussy, but must be moist or cress nasty
site   out of sun, north border
sow   March, April (May–July), August, September (avoid summer
                   sowings unless shady site)
plant   6in (15cm) apart
harvest   handfuls or whole plant ad lib. Cover with cloche against frost to
                   preserve taste

Cress, mustard and   tender   Details: page 98

Indoors or in warm place outside

Cress, water

needs gently flowing stream (see *Watercress Growing* (HMSO))

Cucumbers, indoor   very tender

soil   very rich, deep layer of manure
site   cool greenhouse border, curtained off from tomatoes
sow   in heat, in pots, in March
plant   (in very large pot) into greenhouse border or very large box in
                   April–May
culture   train up wire supports; keep well watered and mist-sprayed at all
                   times. Stop plant when it reaches roof; pinch out shoots after
                   sufficient fruits have set. Remove all male flowers. Shade from sun
harvest   as ready; will not stand frost which affects greenhouse
store   pickle

Cucumbers, ridge   frost tender   Details: page 72

soil   very rich, fresh manure, moist
site   sunny, sheltered, south-facing best
sow   under glass in April or outside in late May–June

plant	in round pit, with small mound round stem to fend off water
culture	keep watered; remove male flowers; stop when sufficient fruits on each stem. Support fruit on straw, etc
harvest	as needed, picking young to maintain succession of fruit. Remove all before first frost
store	pickle or limited life in cool place

[Ridge cucumbers can be grown under cloches or in frames which extends growing season by about two months]

Cucumbers, Japanese   frost tender   Details: page 73

as ridge cucumbers, but train over plastic trellis to keep off ground; alternatively, up fence, but tie carefully

Endive   wet sensitive, slightly tender   Details: page 83

soil	reasonable, no fresh manure
site	sunny, well drained, but moist in summer
sow	late June *in situ*, small successional sowings under cloche if cool
plant	10in (25cm) apart for individuals; double row
culture	reduce watering in September; cover with cloche in October. Tie leaves up. Cover with pot to blanch as required for use
harvest	1–3 weeks after blanching commences. Use at once when ready

[Can be moved into frame or shed to finish off and blanch]

Garlic

as shallots (see also under Herbs, page 126)

Kale   very hardy, even in north   Details: page 87

as broccoli

sow	April or later in south, in seedbed
plant out	in autumn
harvest	cut top first, then few leaves at a time from each plant. Lasts well through spring. Tough when old.
store	not necessary; leave in ground until tired of it

Kohl rabi   hardy

soil	reasonable, not too wet
site	not fussy
sow	any time, March–June, small sowings for succession

plant	6in (15cm) apart *in situ*
harvest	thin alternate plants young. Don't let it get big and coarse
store	not for long, in shed in dark

Leeks   hardy   Details: page 59

soil	reasonable will do; rich soil makes enormous tasteless crop for shows
site	sheltered in winter. Cut trench 3in (7.5cm) deep
sow	early March–late April from seed; plants in late April
plant	transplant in late May–August, in 3in (7.5cm) holes at bottom of trenches, shaking earth round them only. 6–9in apart (15–22.5cm). Spread roots out well
culture	earth up progressively to base of leaves, to blanch and improve taste
harvest	lift as required for use, November–April
store	in frosty winters, lift and store some in cool place or heel in earth against house wall

Lettuce   fairly tender to fairly hardy according to variety

soil	plenty of humus, well raked to fine tilth
site	not in full sun, not waterlogged. Catch crop
sow	small successional sowings from March/April to August. February or September sowings of some varieties under glass. At any time in heat. (a) in boxes under glass, February–March; (b) out of doors, from March (south) late March–April (north) to August; (c) September–October in boxes outside for planting under glass in October–November
plant out	4in (10cm) initially in double staggered row 6in (15cm) apart. Use alternate plants as thinnings. Hearting lettuce may be planted at 6in (15cm) stations and not thinned till mature
culture	keep watered and shade from hot sun or they bolt. Late sowings out of doors need cloche cover by October. Set out September-planted seedlings under cover at same time, pre-frost; do not over-water these
harvest	thinnings ad lib; rest as they mature in 4–6 weeks. Summer varieties, except 'Webbs' Wonderful', bolt if not gathered. Autumn-sown from December to February/March. 'All the Year Round' stands without bolting
store	won't, so keep sowings small or eat fast

Marrows/courgettes   tender   Details: page 71

soil	fairly rich, but too much manure encourages large, tough fruit
site	sunny, moist but not waterlogged
sow	under glass in April; in pots or out of doors in late May, 1in (2.5cm) deep
plant	in pit, with soil round stem and watering trench beside
culture	pinch out ends when enough fruit set, train stems in convenient direction. Can climb trees, fences, so check free space for fruit and support if necessary. Water very well
harvest	young for best taste and texture. Courgettes 4–6in (10–15cm); eating marrows not above 12in (30cm). Will grow throughout season
store	in cool but frost-proof place. Jams, chutneys

Melons   very tender   Details: page 74

soil	good, composted, not manured
site	greenhouse bed, frame, limited outdoor in best of summers and/or deep south
type	cantaloupe varieties only; honeydews need heat
sow	in pots under glass in April
plant	into bed or large box or frame in late May; in frame, each needs sq yd; in bed, 18in (45cm) apart to be trained up wires
culture	stop twice (see text). Pollinate flowers. Support fruit. Fight slugs
harvest	at cricket-ball size in July–August. Will die at first frost unless protected and heated, so gather fruit
store	very limited period fresh. Jam after that

Mushrooms   medium tender   Details: page 99

soil and site	outside, in good quality loam plus manure under turf (very chancy). On hot bed. In covered structure (shed, cellar or bunker) containing very rich compost incorporating lot of manure
sow	on prepared bed (see text) spawn or brick of mushroom
plant	evenly spread, in dark or under cover
culture	keep sprayed with water and warm. Uncover when they first show
harvest	about 6–8 weeks after show
store	dried; frozen, pickled

Onions, maincrop   fairly hardy   Details: page 54

[good flavour: 'Bedfordshire Champion', 'Gt. Zittau'; mild: 'Ailsa Craig']

soil	rich, pre-composted, plenty of humus, dose with salt and soot before planting. Well raked and firmed
site	prefer own bed. Or intercrop with carrots. Must have good sun to mature
sow	(a) January in heat for early and monster sizes; (b) seeds *in situ*, late February to March; (c) late March in north; (d) sets in late March–April; (d) in mild areas, in September under cloches or in frame. $\frac{1}{2}$in (12.5mm) deep
plant	single rows, 4in (10cm) apart for thinning. Beds either 4in (10cm) as above or 6in (15cm) to mature together. Rows 9in (22.5cm) apart, or 12in (30cm) intercropped with lettuce or beet. (d) 6ins (15cm) apart in any direction
culture	protect young seedlings and sets with guards or spiky twigs till firm in ground. Water well until growth stops—about early June—then sparingly
harvest	raise from ground and dry off in sun (on netting if wet season) in August
store	ropes, nets, etc, hung in airy, dry place. Pickles, chutney, dried

Onions, pickling   Details: page 54

soil	not too good, well raked and firmed
site	dryish, sunny, will intercrop with anything
sow	seeds in March, April
plant	2in (5cm) deep, double or treble row
culture	do not thin, even if crowded
harvest	all at once, late June, July or early August, according to planting date
store	pickle

Onions, spring   hardy   Details: page 58

('White Lisbon')

soil	reasonable, old composted, well raked and firmed
site	intercrop with carrots, not in shade, not wet in winter
sow	(a) late July–August, seeds; (b) seeds in February (under cloche in north; (c) successional sowings in March, April if liked for summer and autumn

plant	(a) spaced 2in (5cm) apart to fit cloche space; (b, c) 2–3in (5–7.5cm) apart, single rows between carrots in double rows. Tighter spacing if eaten very thin
culture	(a) cloches or frames to cover during whole of winter; (b, c) do not transplant, thin for use
harvest	regular thinnings of alternate plants; majority ready (a) March–May; (b) June; (c) July–autumn
store	won't, fresh. Pickle, chutney

Onions, tree   hardy   P (rare)   Details: page 89

soil	good, composted
site	solo or pair; grows 4ft (1.2cm) tall. Not wet in winter
sow	offsets in autumn, 1in (2.5cm) deep, or mature bulb 2in (5cm) deep in spring, as available
plant	12in (30cm) apart minimum
culture	feed compost in autumn. Stake when bearing
life	about 5 years, divide or plant offsets from third year
harvest	nothing first year; bunches of cocktail onions on stems from second year. Some offsets to root may be eaten, or left to produce more stems
store	pickle

Onions, Welsh   (rare)   Details: page 89

soil	as shallots
site	as shallots
sow	seed in spring in box; or offsets in autumn—no known commercial source
plant out	in autumn or spring, 3in (7.5cm) deep for seedlings or offsets; 9in (22.5cm) apart
harvest	produces bunches of spring onions very early in spring. Replant some of these as offsets each year
store	pickle, chutney; but mostly used fresh

Parsnips   hardy   roots   Details: page 57

soil	reasonable, not freshly manured; deep or very deep-dug
site	not fussy
sow	seed *in situ*, February (south) to March (north) onwards
plant	2in (5cm) in double row × 9in (22.5cm) apart; thin to 4in (10cm) and transplant to new row

culture	water well when young. Keep shoulders of root covered with earth or mulch to prevent damage
harvest	thin alternate roots at half mature; grow rest on to autumn
store	in clamp in sand, Oct–Nov. Will stay in ground but liable to pest attack and woodiness

Peas   hardy   Details: page 52

soil	well composted, moisture retaining, left improved
site	not fussy. Trench planting best
height	dwarf: 1–2ft (30–60cm); sugar peas: 3–4ft (90cm–1.2m); tall: 5–6ft (1.5–1.8m). All thin, weak stems
sow	*in situ*, 2in (5cm) deep. Dwarf early February–March (earliest 'Feltham First', 'Kelvedon Wonder') and in succession to July; sugar and tall peas in April.
plant	in trench (or holes) double row, 3–4in (7.5–10cm) apart for individuals; or triple row, same spacing, quincunx planting
culture	cover with wire guards/supports from first or spiky twigs, then canes. Train to supports to keep off ground. Water well when pods developing
harvest	pick pods regularly to ensure succession. Sugar peas picked young to eat whole. Peas for drying left to mature (which stops succession)
store	freeze or dry

Peppers, sweet and *chilli*   very tender   Details: page 97

soil	good potting soil, with humus but good drainage
site	in greenhouse. Temporary growing outside in very sunny, sheltered place possible, but must start and finish inside. Chilli peppers more tender
sow	in heat in February; in pots under glass, with extra shelter, in March—or April, but if so, stop bush at 8in (20cm)
plant out	into final pots as soon as large enough and place in full sun
culture	keep well watered but not soggy. Ensure fruits have room to grow freely, support if necessary. Reduce water as weather cools
harvest	late August till frosts, gather green or red. Will not stand slightest frost, so enclose or add local heat; or pick before frost
store	freeze, pickle. Dry chillis

Potatoes   frost tender   Details: page 55

soil	very rich, compost plus manure, well dug in, no lime, left impoverished
site	sunny, sheltered; never same place twice
sow	seed potatoes, chitted indoors in trays in light place from Feb (earlies), late March (maincrop), till they sprout well. Kitchen rejects not good, but do something
plant out	6–7in (15–17.5cm) deep in blocks. Earliest 12in (30cm) apart; 18in (45cm) between rows. Maincrop 15in (37.5cm) apart, 24in (60cm) between rows; closer if planted in quincunx. Dates vary: earliest, from beginning March (very south) to April (risky, north); maincrop, April (south) to May (north). Cut all chitted tubers in half before planting
culture	if frost threatens, cover with cloches, sack, etc. Spray for blight in July. Ridge up with earth before tubers develop. Never let light reach tubers
harvest	ripe tubers lifted as they occur, few from each plant. When exhausted, lift and burn or deep-compost haulms. Complete lifting before frost
store	in clamps in sand, straw, etc. Frozen chips

Pumpkins   tender   Details: page 72

soil	good, well composted, moisture retaining
site	sunny, open, ideally separate space
sow	in pots under glass in April
plant out	mid to late May, on small mound with watering trench 24–30in (60–75cm) square for each
culture	very well watered when growing fruit. Check to keep within bounds. Place straw or tile under fruits
harvest	from football size, to encourage others. All fruit to be collected before frost
store	in nets or on slatted trays in airy place for some months. Keep dry. Jam, chutney

Radishes   hardy   Details: page 51

soil	not at all fussy
site	sunny for first sowings, then anywhere. Catch crop
sow	any time under glass, but normally (a) round type: small pinches of seed at intervals from March to early September; (b) Japanese long root: late March to July in succession; (c) Spanish and China Rose: July to August $\frac{1}{2}$in (12.5mm) deep

plant	(a) set at 2in (5cm), thin to 4in (10cm); (b) set at 3in (7.5cm), thin to 6in (15cm); (c) set at 6in (15cm). Normally single rows, if doubled, leave 9in (22.5cm) between
culture	keep watered in drought
harvest	(a) use thinnings half-mature, rest as soon as ready within 14 days of planting. Throw away old woody specimens; b) in 2–3 months from planting; (c) in October–November
store	(a) not really worth it; could pickle; (b) and (c) in box of peat. Can be left in ground but get woody and liable to pest attack. Chutneys

Rhubarb   hardy perennial   Details: page 91

soil	deep-dug, rich, compost and manure
site	sunny corner, permanent placing
spread	will shade 2ft square (60cm) each
sow	(seeds under glass in spring for planting out next year). Normally, crown (root plus shoot) offset in late spring, set in ground, shoot just showing
plant	allow 2ft (60cm) at least between individuals
culture	feed with liquid manure in summer after pulling stops. Compost leaves in autumn or use against club-root in brassicas. Cut off flowering stalks as they appear. Divide clumps when old and discard very ancient section
harvest	not in first year, little second year, then for maximum 3 months per year. Twist stalks to pull. NB: Leaves are poisonous; old sticks nauseous and may be slightly toxic too
store	bottle, jam, freeze, wine

Salsify   very hardy

as for parsnips if required as roots

culture	leave all or some in ground after autumn, or cover completely with leaves, earth, etc, till March
harvest	remove cover and gather young leaves as 'asparagus spinach' in late March–April
store	roots in clamps, otherwise left in ground till required

Scorzonera   hardy root

as parsnip, except:

sow	in late March, 2in (5cm) apart

plant	as soon as large enough to handle. Make deep dibber holes and fill with mixture of sand and fine soil, about 9–10in (22.5–25cm) deep
harvest	in October, lifting carefully. Can be left in ground to grow on in spring if wished
store	clamp in sand, if lifted; use from ground, if not

Shallots   hardy   Details: page 49

soil	good, composted, previously manured
site	not waterlogged, not shady
sow	offsets at first, then saved shallots, set with top showing above soil, in February (January in south)
plant	4in (10cm) apart, 9in (22.5cm) between rows; protect with spiky twigs until roots are settled in, or wire-netting guards
culture and harvest	when foliage dies down (about July), lift and leave to dry on ground (or take in out of rain). Set aside some bulbs as offsets for next year
store	on trays, in nets, in airy frost-free place; or as pickles

Spinach   hardy, poisonous

soil	rich, composted, plenty of humus
site	not waterlogged for winter spinach
sow	(a) summer type in February, 1in (2.5cm) deep, succession in March, May; (b) winter type in August–September; (c) spinach beet in late spring and mid-summer; (d) New Zealand spinach in April under glass
plant	(a, b) 6in (15cm) apart, single rows or staggered double row; (c) 15in (37.5cm) apart; (d) plant out in late May, 20in (50cm) apart
harvest	strictly the very young leaves. Old leaves are poisonous (oxalic acid). Dig the whole plant into ground (where brassica will go) against club-root. (maximum picking from each sowing should begin in 4–5 weeks and end at 7 weeks)
store	don't

Swedes   hardy;   *Turnips*   fairly hardy

soil	not freshly manured, deep dug, limed
site	not fussy, but not too dry in summer
sow	(a) seeds in spring for summer crops if liked; (b) June for August crop; (c) July–August for winter crop. ½in (12.5mm) deep

plant	small summer varieties: 6in (15cm) apart; winter types: 8–9in (20–22.5cm) apart
culture	well watered in summer or will bolt
harvest	(a) early types for eating as required from June–August; (b) autumn; (c) lift as required autumn to spring
store	(a) summer types won't keep; (b) clamp in sand or peat; (c) clamp some or leave in till wanted (swedes best)

Sweet corn   tender   Details: page 71

soil	rich, not freshly manured, moisture retaining
site	sunny, not windy
sow	in pots under glass in April
plant out	mid to late May, in block formation, 18in (45cm) between plants
culture	protect from late frosts in May. Stake if heavy crop. Water well. Pollinate if necessary
harvest	August to mid-September, as ready
store	frozen, dried, pickled

Tomatoes   very tender   Details: page 75

soil	rich, good compost etc, potash. Must be fresh bed every year in greenhouse
site	outside, maximum sun and shelter; also frame, large pots, growing bag, unheated greenhouse. (Heated greenhouse cultivation throughout year, not economic for amateurs)
sow	January–February in heat; under glass in March or buy in plants in May
plant	(a) outside in late May–June, 18in (45cm) apart in single row, or 15in (37.5cm) apart in staggered double row. Support on canes and/or wires; (b) in large pots, boxes or pots, one per 12in (30cm) pot, two per bag, supported by canes or wires; (c) in cold frame, two per sq yd of frame; (d) in greenhouse, ring culture, pot or direct in bed, 15in (37.5cm) apart, staggered row
culture	water well, spray against blight in July, take out side shoots, tie to supports as plant grows. (a) stop by pinching out top in July; (b) stop plant after four trusses are set; (c) stop plant at 3½–4ft (1–1.2m); (d) ring or pot, stop at six trusses, in bed allow to reach ridge before stopping. Shade greenhouse roof with nets in high summer. In autumn: (a, b) gather all fruit before first frosts; (c) lay down plant on straw inside frame and close light; (d) allow to finish growth in late autumn or collect fruit to ripen indoors, from pots or rings. Plants in beds should continue until Christmas

	in mild year if some insulation is added or slight heat introduced
harvest	from July. Fruit can be picked at first blush or left to redden on plant, according to weight per tomato bush
Store	bottle, chutney, pickle, purée. Keep fresh for limited period

Turnips

as swedes

Herbs

From the gardener's point of view herbs can be grouped into four types according to their growing habits: the first make relatively neat cushions or mats of low-growing plants; the second are the bushy plants, which at least start small; the third is the invasive type which sprawl across half the garden, and the fourth are the tall, mostly umbelliferous plants, grown for seeds or stems (Figure 31).

The first three groups need to be stationed somewhere near the kitchen, so the cook can rush out and pick a handful before the pot boils over. This is especially important in winter, when the trek down a muddy garden isn't inviting. Many of the herbs stay permanently on their sites, and would interfere with crop rotation if planted in the main vegetable plot. Therefore, it is best to keep them separate from other plantings, near the house, and at the edge of the bed where you can pick from the path.

Most of the first two groups of herbs are decorative and can be grown in the front garden if you are short of space. They make good edging plants, will grow on rockeries, and in pots or old sinks, which makes them useful for windowsills or balconies. They are generally not very demanding about their soil. Some will even go without watering for ages, provided the container isn't too small. They stand all kinds of ill-treatment—like being walked on (some are used for lawns) or given a rough haircut with scissors or clippers—and live in peace with babies and cats.

The bush plants, like rosemary and sage, and lavender, which is a household herb

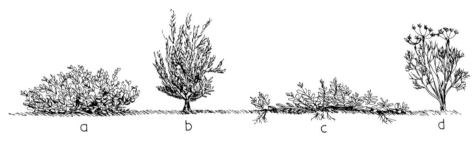

31 Herbs (a) cushion (b) bushy (c) sprawling (d) umbelliferous.

if not a culinary one, make useful windbreaks for small seedlings, and mobile ones if they are in pots.

The sprawlers, like the various types of mint, keep sending out shoots and putting down roots. Unrestricted, they will spread everywhere and strangle other plants beneath them. Therefore they must be grown in a space confined by brick or stone walls or in an old sink. This must be deep, as they need more moisture than can be maintained in a shallow sink.

The tall ones look handsome at a distance but untidy at close quarters, so they should be planted well to the back of the garden. Mostly they are allowed to ripen before use, so you will not need daily access. If the seeds scatter, you could have an invasion of huge monsters—4–5ft (1.2–1.5m) tall—and far more caraway, dill and coriander than you could use this century.

Most herbs can be started from seed in spring, and the commoner ones are readily available. The less common ones are advertised, but it is a lot cheaper to beg a cutting from someone with an established herb garden. There are always plenty of bits to spare. Some plants divide easily, giving a bit of rooted plant ready made. Others will be presented as a short length of stem. If you have the choice, take a piece that is about 4in (10cm) long, not too young, not old and woody or with flowers on. Strip back the lower leaves, and sink about half of it in wet, sandy soil. You can put rooting hormone on the cutting, but this is over-elaborate. Shove it in, keep it watered, and it will grow.

Once you have a herb, you usually have it for life. There are three growth patterns. Annuals produce, flower and die off all in one season. You can collect the seed carefully and sow it next spring, or let the seed fall on the ground and set itself. Only the odd tender plant doesn't react well to this. Biennials produce young leaves for using one year and then run to seed the next. This means a gap of one year unless you sow from bought seed for two springs, after which you have your own seed to work from. Perennials go on growing from year to year, though the plants tend to get tired and leggy after a time and should be divided, or restarted from cuttings or seed. They generally drop seedlings all round the mother plant which can be moved and grown on.

There are no rules about using herbs for culinary purposes—anything goes with anything you personally like it with. Experiment a bit and get some interesting combinations—but be light-handed at first. Home-grown herbs are much stronger than shop ones, and a little tends to go a long way. Annuals are mostly used first by picking some of the young leaves; later hang the whole plant upside down on a nail to dry off, then powder the leaves between thumb and finger and put the bits in a small closed pot. Perennials, and biennials planted in spring and again in summer, will be usable fresh all the year round, or pick a piece off and dry it as before. You can hurry up the drying in a cooling oven.

A lot of herbs or wild plants can be grown for medicinal use. They may need special treatment or harvesting according to which part of the plant is required. A good guide to these, with excellent illustrations, is *Herbs* by Dr Frantisek Stary and

Dr Vaclav Jirasek (Hamlyn). Some of the uses are incredible and rather terrifying, so on your own head be it. Gerard's *Herbal* is fascinating too.

Any of the seeds can be started out of doors in spring, with protection for basil or sage. The seeds are mostly so tiny that it is easier to mix a small quantity with sand before sowing in small pans or pots of mixed sand and soil, so that you know just where they are. Label the pots, to show which is what. When they are big enough to handle, plant out—quite wide apart for the cushiony type—in a well-firmed bed. Some of the plants have hard little seeds which are slow starters, so you tend to lose track of them in open ground.

Common culinary herbs

A = annual   B = Biennial   P = Perennial

Angelica   B   huge, striking umbellifer

propagate and plant	seeds sown *in situ*, very slow starters. Try keeping them in pot of sand through winter to break down hard coat and plant out in spring. 3ft (90cm) apart final position
harvest	young leaves (dull) stalks in second summer for candying

Balm   P   lemony, medium bush, invasive after first year

propagate	seeds in late spring, cutted, rooted bits in summer
plant	12in (30cm) apart
harvest	young leaves or dried

Basil   A   lowish cushion or bush version

propagate	seeds under shelter in late spring; frost-tender
plant	in May, 8–10in (20–25cm) apart
harvest	young leaves or whole plant dried for winter use; collect seeds for re-sowing and store till spring.

Bay   P   evergreen bush or small tree like laurel

propagate	cuttings of half ripe wood
plant	sheltered place or tub; rather frost-tender
harvest	young leaves and dried whole leaves most of year

Borage   A   medium low, attractive blue flowers

propagate   seeds in early spring, reseeds itself easily after first year
plant   12in (30cm) apart at first, later fills up sq yd
harvest   young leaves, old leaves dried quickly

Caraway   B   tall, untidy umbellifer

propagate   seeds *in situ* in summer
plant   well back, 24in (60cm) apart
harvest   seeds, next summer, before they drop

Chamomile   A   small cushion, bright yellow flowers

propagate   seeds in spring, reseeds itself
plant   8–9in (20–22.5cm) apart
harvest   flower heads for chamomile tea, shampoo additive

Chervil   B   floppy cushion

propagate   seeds in spring, reseeds itself
plant   12in (30cm) apart
harvest   leaves fresh most of year. Don't allow flowering except one for seed

Chives   P   narrow spikes in small cushion; onion family

propagate   seeds in late spring, division of clumps
plant   6in (15cm) apart
harvest   stems by snipping off about 2in (5cm) at a time from top— 'haircut'. Small onion bulbs from old plants

Coriander   A   medium height, messy appearance

propagate   seeds *in situ* in spring
plant   12in (30cm) apart, out of sight but in sun
harvest   seed heads, well dried and extracted from husk

Dill   A   tall, untidy umbellifer

propagate   seeds *in situ* in spring or summer
plant   10–12in (25–30cm) apart in sunny corner
harvest   seedheads, well dried, used whole in pickles

Fennel   P   tall, feathery foliage

propagate   seeds in April, divide plants in spring
plant   12in (30cm) apart
harvest   leaves, whole young sprays of leaves, dried seed heads

Florence fennel   (finocchio)   same, with turnip root

propagate   as for fennell, earth up root in summer
  and plant
harvest   as above, plus turnip root as vegetable

Garlic   P   medium spike, onion family

propagate   offsets (cloves) in spring, like shallots
plant   6in (15cm) apart, good in rich pocket of earth near fruit trees,
                       especially peach
harvest   whole bulbs when ripe, dry in sun and hang in net

Horse radish   P   about 3ft (90cm) tall, broad floppy leaves, very invasive

propagate   small thong (root section) about 4–6in (10–15cm) long
plant   18in (45cm) apart, good soil, in a corner
harvest   roots when mature, cut off still growing plant; re-generates at any
                       time from small roots left

Marigold, pot   A   ordinary garden plant, orange or yellow flowers and wide
                       leaves

propagate   seed in spring or summer, re-seeds easily
plant   6–9in (15–22.5cm) apart, flower garden
harvest   flower petals, young leaves

Marjoram, pot   P   small cushion

propagate   seed in spring or cuttings
plant   10in (25cm) apart
harvest   leaves, fresh or dried

Marjoram, sweet   A   low cushion; slightly tender

propagate   seeds in late spring or in shelter earlier
plant   12in (30cm) apart
harvest   leaves, fresh or dried, flower buds

Mint   P   low, sprawling, very invasive

propagate   root cuttings (stolons) in autumn in greenhouse, spring out-of-doors

plant   in container or walled-off bed, one plant will expand to sq yd if let; 3in (7.5cm) deep

harvest   leaves fresh or dried, or as mint sauce

Nasturtium   A   garden flower, orange, yellow, red trumpet flowers, sprawling

propagate   seeds in spring *in situ*

plant   about 12in (30cm) apart; will fill square or drape over walls, etc; space accordingly; sunny spot

harvest   young leaves; seeds fresh or pickled

Oregano (wild marjoram)   P   large cushion

propagate and plant   as for pot marjoram, but twice distance apart

harvest   as marjoram, but stronger

Parsley   B   crinkled foliage; medium height

propagate   seeds in spring (treat as annual); runs to seed second year; successional sowings in summer

plant   9in (22.5cm) apart in sunny place; good soil

harvest   sprays of leaves

Pennyroyal   P   very invasive and sprawling

propagate and plant   as mint

harvest   young leaves only, old ones very bitter and toxic

Rosemary   P   neat grey-green bushes, about 4ft (1.2m) high, feathery foliage, mauve flowers

propagate   cuttings (or seeds, but slow)

plant   solo bush or as hedge 20in (50cm) apart

harvest   handfuls of leaves or sprays dried and powdered

Sage   P   evergreen bush about 2ft (60cm) high

propagate   cuttings (or seeds, very slow); tender when young

plant   solo or 2ft (60cm) apart, sunny position

harvest   not in first summer, then leaves at any time, fresh or dried

Savory, summer   A   loose cushion, sprawling stems

propagate   seeds in spring
plant   12in (30cm) apart, warm damp place
harvest   summer, when flowering, gather and tie up to dry

Savory, winter   P   short bush, about 12in (30cm) high

propagate   seeds in summer, cuttings in spring; under cloche
plant   18in (45cm) apart, sunny place
harvest   from second summer on, young leaves, coarse after flowering
               each year

Tarragon   P   low, sprawling cushion

propagate   cuttings, rooted stems (seeds reluctant)
plant   sunny place, early summer (tender when young); will fill 2 × 2ft
               (60 × 60cm) eventually
harvest   leaves regularly fresh; collect before flowering for drying, or
               make vinegar

Thyme   P   low cushion, sprawling

propagate   seeds in spring; layering in spring; (cuttings in summer reluctant);
               division of clump in autumn
plant   12–15in (30–37.5cm) apart, well-drained soil
harvest   not in first year until well-grown, then whole side shoots at a time,
               fresh or dried, to keep it tidy

Thyme, lemon   P   sprawling, invasive

propagate   cuttings, division
plant   grows anywhere like weed, set in cracks in paving or by door
harvest   leaves any time, fresh or dried

Fruit

Summer is the time when fruit of all kinds is available in profusion—lovely taste, lovely smell . . . and a lovely price too, if you buy it at the greengrocer's. Wouldn't it be lovely to grow your own and always have top quality fruit? More or less anyone can grow soft fruit, grown on bushes or plants, but top fruit, from trees, is another matter.

Fruit trees

Bearing trees need all the nourishment of all the ground under their branches, which means that you can't grow anything on that whole area. A standard apple tree—which is the same size as any other standard fruit tree—will eventually cover a circle about 18ft (5.4m) across, so you must allow this final space for it. You can grow vegetables round it while it is very young, but never closer than 6ft (1.8m) to the trunk, and only top vegetables, not roots. When the tree is fully grown, all you will be able to grow beneath it is grass, and not very good grass at that.

There are specially bred trees which have been dwarfed to take up less space. A bush apple covers 10ft (3m) across, and a dwarf pyramid 9ft (2.7m) or even less. The bush, being smaller, does not bear as well as the standard tree. The dwarf pyramid either bears less, or bears well for a few years then suddenly dies. Neither goes on for thirty, forty and fifty years, like the big ones. They also grow much lower and the twigs get in your hair when you are picking the apples. It is best not to grass the area under a dwarf tree, because of the competition for food.

There is a newly developed mini-tree—a little bush with only a central stem, no branches. It takes up 4ft (1.2m) of space, and should fruit well on a limited scale while it lasts.

Older alternatives in a limited space include espaliers, fans and cordons, grown on walls or fences. A fan-trained tree is systematically pruned, from its youth, to have a fairly limited number of side shoots. These are tied firmly to a wooden trellis or strong wire and cane framework attached to the wall in a fan shape. Anyone with a lot of patience can buy a very young tree and do this himself. It

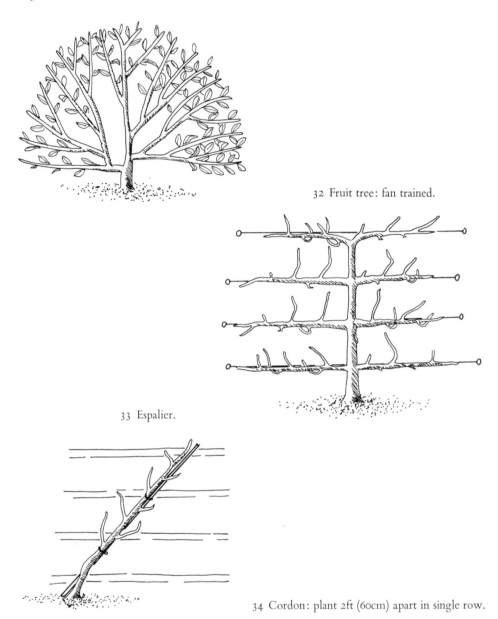

32 Fruit tree: fan trained.

33 Espalier.

34 Cordon: plant 2ft (60cm) apart in single row.

looks best if the fan is a decent size, and this needs a high, old-fashioned orchard wall or a house wall (Figure 32).

An espalier is even more rigidly pruned, leaving only a central stem and side branches at tidy intervals, trained at right angles (Figure 33). The branches are tied to wires 12in (30cm) apart and secured firmly to the wall. A cordon is even more severely pruned to a single main stem, and trained diagonally up the wall at an angle of 45° (Figure 34). These can be bought from a nursery ready trained, but both have to be kept that way, with annual attention to pruning. They bear well in their limited area. Because they have the shelter of walls, and can be covered quickly, they often do well in a year when trees in the open have lost their blossom through frost or winds. Peaches and apricots, which bloom insanely early for such delicate trees, do excellently as wall fruit. Soil near walls and fences is not very good, so the trees will need an extra ration of food at planting and regularly each year.

Apples

If you have room for a single apple tree, the question is 'Is it self-fertile?' It may need another variety to pollinate it. There is no point in choosing as your pair of apples a dessert apple which produces an early crop and a cooking apple which produces a late crop. The two types must bloom at the same time, so that bees can fly from one to another doing their good work. Some apples need *two* pollinators before they will produce. Unless you have space for two or three trees in your own garden, you must either do without apples or persuade a neighbour to plant the pollinator, so that you both have a good crop. Alternatively you can buy a 'family tree'. These trees are produced by grafting a number of compatible varieties on to one stock, so that the pollinator is there all the time. They cost more, naturally, but might be the answer for a small garden.

A national advertiser will have a wider choice of pollinating varieties available and possibly be cheaper than a nursery. If he offers a collection of six pollinators, these could be shared with neighbours to be sure of fertility. The local nursery, on the other hand, will have stock bred for your sort of soil and the plants will spend less time out of the ground and won't dry. This is important for success in establishing them. Container plants get over this difficulty, but can be damaged in transit, because they are awkward to handle.

Much the same considerations apply to pears and plums. One or two pears are rumoured to be self-fertile, maybe, but evidence suggests that they don't work very well yet. Several plums are self-fertile, including the popular Victoria, and so are damsons.

Most fruit trees don't bear until they are five, six or seven years old and are mostly sold as three-year-olds. Older than that, they are more difficult to get settled in and well rooted before they are ready to crop, and they may die in the effort. Bought younger, they are cheaper, but you have to wait an extra year or two. Dwarf trees get going sooner, but die off earlier. You won't get anything from them in a year or two, in any case.

Walnuts

Walnut trees, if you can find them at all, take eight or nine years to start bearing. Once going, they will keep it up for the next hundred years or so, producing very discreet flowers early in the season and surprising you in autumn by dropping their fruit cases—these are like spineless horse chestnuts and are almost invisible when growing among the leaves. If you inherit a walnut tree, let it do what it will—it is older than you are, for sure.

Cherries

Other fruit trees need a little more careful placing. Cherries will grow perfectly well in the open, but they are a magnet to birds. Even covering the branches with black filament webbing does not protect the fruit for more than a day or two. Word goes out, and clever Uncle Fred Bird comes to show the others how to get underneath.

Cherries do best on a wall, where you can cover them with thick nylon netting anchored top and bottom as protection. So also do peaches, apricots and nectarines, which in the open—except in the sunny south—are liable to damage by late frosts and winds. On a wall, they can be covered with curtains against the elements when necessary. This makes for competition for your sunny, south-facing wall. Morello cherries (cookers), however, will flourish on a north or east wall, preferably a tall or house wall.

Figs

Figs need special treatment. Only one, the Brown Turkey, is recommended for Britain, and this must be planted with a restricted root run, in a large container or brick-walled bed 3ft (90cm) square, or it will never fruit. The young figs appear in July, but these would never ripen, so they must be taken off. The tree will produce a second set, which are only tiny when autumn comes. Leave them on while the tree marks time through the winter and, provided the wind cannot blow them off, growth will start again in spring and you will have ripe fruit in summer. Obviously, the tree must be in a very sheltered spot to carry its fruit through the winter un-harmed, so here is another candidate for that south wall.

Planting

Whichever tree you choose, plant in autumn or spring, when the soil is warmish and dampish. Follow the directions for careful transplanting of a tree given on page 21. Prepare the earth well, removing all weeds and filling the bottom of the large hole with manure or compost. Stake the tree well and make sure the tie will allow for growth. Water until it is established, and whenever in the first year the weather is dry for long.

After-care

Most fruit trees need pruning to some extent. The general principles are to keep the middle open—which means removing crossing and centre pointing branches; take out any diseased or ancient non-fruiting wood, and trim short any branches going where you don't want them to.

You could guard against pests and diseases by spraying with some new chemical every few days, but the cost of this would make your crop very uneconomic. Better to stick to the simple things, such as banding the trunks with a grease bandage in autumn, to catch insects looking for a home. If woolly aphis appears on the twigs, squirt it with detergent-water or methylated spirit. If that doesn't shift it, well, is it so serious if you lose a few apples? They might have rotted in store anyway. Left to themselves, pests tend to cancel each other out. Don't be alarmed, by the way, if a tree full of little apples suddenly drops what seems like half of them in July. Despite the month, this is called the '*June* drop' and is nature's way of disposing of what she can't ripen.

Soft fruit

Soft fruit, grown on bushes or plants, is much easier for the small-garden owner with limited space. Even so, bushes of gooseberries and red or black currants need a square metre—what the old gardener called 'a square yard and a bit for luck'—or even more for access. These bushes cost around 75p each, and are mostly sold in threes or fives, rather than ones.

Plant in spring or autumn, no deeper than the soil mark on the stem in a prepared hole with a tidy dollop of manure about 12in (30cm) deep, topped with compost and good weed-free soil. Spread the roots out well in the hole and make sure there are no gaps in the earth. Tread well in—it will be there for the next twenty or thirty years.

If the bushes arrive unpruned, cut back any long shoots to the third or fourth bud on each. Remove broken or twisted shoots and leave an open middle to the bush. There should be no fruit at all the first year; take off anything that shows, or the plant will be weakened. The next year there will be a small crop, and after that a lot for the foreseeable future. Don't prune unless you must, and then confine yourself to old, diseased or straggly branches. Black currants can be semi-pruned every harvest time by cutting off a whole bunch of fruit plus a little stem, when picking the berries.

You can increase stock at any time by layering. Anchor a long, low branch to the ground with wire and cover with soil where it touches. Gooseberries will throw down roots very quickly; black currant stems may need cutting half through where they enter the ground to encourage them. Healthy cuttings of wood 9in (22.5cm) long may also be stuck in sandy soil, and will probably root. The resulting bushes should be moved to their own planting station where they will fruit in their second year.

Raspberries

Raspberries can be grown as bushes, but being taller and floppier than gooseberries and currants, they are generally grown on frameworks. These are quite simple:

just two posts, set firmly in the ground every 6ft (1.8m), projecting about 5ft (1.5m) above the surface. String four or five wires tightly between the posts at intervals.

Raspberry canes can be planted in October or April. They sell in fives, tens or twenty-fives, from about 10p to 25p each. 'Glen Cova' is the earliest common variety and 'Malling Admiral' the latest 'ordinary' kind. To extend the season, you can buy autumn-fruiting raspberries, which are always labelled as such.

Plant the raspberry canes to the depth of the nursery's soil mark, 15–18in (37.5–45cm) apart, and tie them to the wires. They will probably have three stems cut to about 2ft (60cm)—if not, trim them to this length. Sideshoots will develop, but no fruit the first year. In November, cut off the old brown canes and trim the six best side shoots to different heights so there will be fruit at every level. Tie these to the wires, so that they are trained to grow straight instead of sticking out in all directions. The next year, they will fruit, and for many years after. Each year just cut out the old canes and tie in the new (Figure 35).

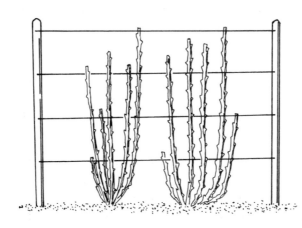

35 Raspberry canes: trim to different heights to spread crop evenly and tie to wires.

Autumn-fruiting raspberries planted one October will produce a little fruit the following autumn and plenty afterwards. Normally, cut them down in spring to produce new growths during the summer which will fruit that year.

All raspberries send up dozens of suckers from the base. These can be detached, plus their own bit of root, and planted in a new line, but not within 5ft (1.5m) of the first row or they will shadow each other.

Blackberries

These sometimes arrive in the garden of their own accord, as a result of berries dropped by birds. However, the cultivated forms, like 'Himalayan Giant', are much better croppers. Plant them on a fence or a post-and-wire framework, but give each one 6ft (1.8m) of space—more if possible. For your own convenience, tie the shoots in a rough fan if you can—they are vicious beasts, which will savage their owners as well as marauding small boys, so use an old walking stick, leather gloves and an iron determination. Trim off any dead wood and any stem which is wildly out of line, but don't touch healthy old wood, since there will be another crop from it. The prunings are excellent as guards for seedlings against the birds.

Loganberries

Loganberries and some of the fancy crosses, like Boysenberry, related to black-berries and raspberries, need fence or wire support and 6ft (1.8m) of space. Cut out all the old wood of loganberries after fruiting and start again; follow the manufacturer's instructions for the hybrids. The fruits are mostly sourer and less vigorous than raspberries or cultivated blackberries, so they can serve as thief deterrents.

Strawberries

These are the easiest fruit to place in a small garden, since each plant can manage on a sq ft—or less if you never want to increase the stock. Some varieties fruit in June—'Cambridge Rival', for instance—and others carry on until early August. The old 'Royal Sovereign' is what most people think of when they visualise a strawberry and interesting new varieties have been bred for size of berry. Once the summer crops are over, autumn fruiters, like 'Hampshire Maid', carry on till the frost comes. All are widely sold and advertised, and some claim to be virus-free stocks, which would be vital if you were thinking of growing them as a cash crop. A typical price is ten plants for £1.40, but there are considerable local variations.

Clean the site of perennial weeds and put in a good dose of manure at one spade's depth. Cover with compost and good soil, then build up a shallow ridge or mound, on which the straggly roots of the plant are spread out (Figure 36). Firm down the soil over the roots and water well round them. Summer-fruiting strawberries should go in in August or early September; autumn fruiters can wait until October–November. These will all fruit the following year. If you wait till spring for planting, there will be no crop that year, except in very favourable climates.

Fill in with soil

36 Strawberry plants: setting out.

The crop can be advanced by covering the plants with a cloche in February. Water the young plants, but reduce the amount sharply once the fruits have formed, or the plant will run to leaf. Tuck straw or dried grass under the stems to protect the fruit while it is ripening. A polythene collar can be used instead, but this encourages slugs and holds water round the stems, which rots the fruit.

After fruiting, the plants send out little runners which produce tiny plants at the end. Anchor these stems down with a stone or wire and they will root, to produce new plants. These can be set in the space left between the rows, if you planted the strawberries 12in (30cm) apart. If you planted closer, pin the runners down into pots of earth on the path or adjacent soil, which must be kept watered. Restrict the number of runners to one or two per plant or it will be weakened.

The original strawberry lasts about three years, after which the crop decreases greatly. So, each year, take the rooted runners and set them out in a separate bed of their own. They will fruit the next year, which will double or treble your crop, and eventually take over from their parents.

You will have a permanent succession of strawberries, as long as disease does not strike. The worst offender—grey mould (botrytis)—can be sprayed with chemicals at the flowering stage, never later or the fruit would be poisoned. However, if trouble strikes when you have two or three different strawberry patches in the garden, it would be better and cheaper to quickly root out the affected few before the rest are hit. The other healthy plants will remain to crop then, with no risk of poisoning.

Strawberries will also grow happily in flower pots, barrels, frames, and green-houses. They cope quite well in window-boxes, provided they are given good earth and plenty of water. Some will grow up trellises; although this looks pretty, the crop will be a bit miserable, since they are putting a lot of effort into clinging on.

Alpine strawberries

Available under various names, usually concealed as 'continuous fruiting', these have smaller berries with a slightly raspberry tang—some people actually prefer them to strawberries. The variety 'Baron Solemacher', which can be grown from seed, makes an outstandingly attractive edging plant for the ordinary garden and can be set 4–6in (10–15cm) apart as it does not produce runners. 'Tumbleberries' are rather untidy, but do reasonably well on a rockery.

Protection against predators

All soft fruit is attractive to predators—insect, feathered and human. Take any necessary precautions before the fruits appear. Slugs can be disposed of by carefully placed pellets. Ants are more difficult, since what gets rid of them tends to get rid of people too. Two-legged thieves are by far the worst, though, and these can be discouraged by putting the fruit under nets or in cages.

Strawberries, being low plants, are easy to net over. A narrow strip of net over each row makes it easier to pick the fruit than a large chunk of netting over all the plants.

Fruit bushes can be netted individually, or caged—either in a metal framework covered with nylon net, or much more expensive wire or plastic mesh. A typical 9 × 8ft (2.7 × 2.4m) cage for a few bushes costs about £19, while a much larger one, 24 × 12ft (7.2 × 3.6m) can be bought for less than double, which may make it worth the initial outlay. A good temporary cage can be made by setting up the frame of a frame tent over the bushes and draping netting on it.

The less sophisticated birds are discouraged by fluttering strips of coloured rag, or plastic wheels which whirl in the breeze, or by the rattle of twisted metal spirals cut from old beer cans. But there is no real substitute for the lad who runs up and down shouting—if you have children, they will probably do this anyway.

When in Drought

Without water, even the strongest plant will die or fail to produce a crop. What can we personally do to compensate for nature's shortcomings in time of drought?

First, we can hang on to every scrap of rainwater, instead of letting it flow away uselessly down the drains. There is a limit to the storage space available in the garden, of course, but in summer the use of water keeps up with any temporary extra supplies. Rain falling on the house roof can be collected in water-butts—diverted in summer via the down pipes from the gutters. Rainwater is much better for plants than hard, chlorinated tap water, and it is sheer wastefulness to use the purified water supply unnecessarily.

Once-used water—from baths, basins and sinks or washing machines—can be collected, direct from the waste pipes or by siphonage, for watering the garden. Any soap or detergent content will not hurt the ground—in fact, a lot of it is nourishing, but see page 197.

Rain or waste water can be stored in tanks, old baths, or packing cases lined with plastic. You could make a garden pool, lined with cement or plastic, and fill that. A swimming pool can be pressed into service in a crisis—the soil will not be harmed by the chlorination of its original water, though it should be diluted with rain or waste before being applied to plants direct.

Naturally, any open tanks or pools should be fenced off if there are children about. Thick wire mesh or slatted wood, well secured, will prevent toddlers getting drowned. The water will get coated with algae, if left standing, which won't hurt plants. In mid-summer, it may attract mosquitoes wishing to breed; as soon as you notice the antics of the spring-tailed larvae, put a few drops of paraffin on top of the water, and they will curl up and die. This won't harm plants either.

The more humus there is in the soil, the better it will cope with extremes of rainfall. Thin soil lets rain run straight through to the sub-soil. Heavy clay gums up and holds pools of water on the surface. Good, rich soil is evenly wetted and holds moisture for a long time a few inches down, where the plant roots can get at it. The more compost and similar humus-producing material we can get into the soil, the less of a problem it will be.

When a long drought comes, the soil dries from the top, so small seedlings and shallow-rooting plants die first. Any plant with a lot of leaves will give off moisture to the air fast and, if it can't replace this, it will be in trouble. This loss of water can normally be replaced by long sessions with the hose, drenching the earth and spraying over the leaves. But, in time of prolonged drought, this is not allowed. As all the water has to be carted around the garden in cans, you will want every drop of it to work hard.

It is easier to water effectively round the roots of a plant if it has been set in a shallow trench or pit; this is the best method for most of the summer-growing plants. Those which have a soft stem may need a little rampart just close to it, with a circular trench outside that, to ward off rot. If drought threatens while you are planting, start the plants off with a handful of wet peat in the planting hole. It will retain this moisture and future waterings, just where the roots need them. Newspaper or tea-leaves in the bottom of the planting trench will serve the same purpose, rotting down slowly as the amount of moisture in the soil increases. Old sacks will do—or even old socks, provided they are woollen, for nylon and other synthetics won't rot and may interfere with plant growth.

Water at night, after the sun has gone down, especially if you are spraying leaves. In the daytime drops of water left on leaves act as burning glasses for the sun, and the leaves would be scorched to death.

Your trenches could be lined with plastic, to keep in all the water you supply. However, unless you buried the plastic very deeply—which would mean a lot of watering to get the area damp—the roots would soon hit the plastic and be unable to proceed to the deeper layers of soil where the nourishment lies. Also, if it rained, the plastic trench would flood and wash out or rot the plants.

You can line a wooden box with plastic, but be sure to make a lot of drainage holes in the base. An inch of peat in the bottom of the box does the same job less riskily.

Always water plentifully at one time. It is heavy work carting two-gallon cans of water around, and the temptation is to spread it over as large an area as possible per can. Too little water only wets the surface of the soil above the plant roots. Either it evaporates in the heat of the sun before they get to know about it, or they start struggling upwards towards it. The nearer the roots are to the surface, the more likely they are to be dried up by the sun, or attacked by surface pests looking for something juicy to eat.

Once the soil is really wet, you can mulch, by covering it with peat, grass mowings, newspaper—anything which will rot reasonably quickly. Don't let it wad together and block the air from the plants. Even a dust mulch is better than nothing. Hoe the top surface of the soil loose to keep the sun off the lower layers.

Shade plants, particularly young seedlings, from the fiercest sun, with pots of shrubs, wooden screens, paper, doubled-up netting—even strategically placed washing, which can drip over the garden too.

And, if you have faith, pray for rain.

Pocket-handkerchief Gardening

The modern housing estate tends to devote the minimum possible space to private gardens. In some cases there is an unfenced 'landscaped' area in front of the house and only a tiny yard at the back. The same may apply to houses built on part of a plot belonging to an older property. Town houses may have hardly any garden space at all, and often this is paved or cemented over. Flat-dwellers may have only a balcony, and people in bedsitters not even that. What can they do if they want to grow a few vegetables?

Back-to-front layout

Anyone with a front garden available can plant vegetables—just go ahead and lay it out precisely as you would a back garden. This may cause comment, since Britons are a conservative lot, and the lazy, non-gardening neighbours will be the most censorious.

A front vegetable garden can be laid out in an attractive way by using the more decorative plants and setting them out in patterns. Runner beans make a handsome fence, with red-orange flowers and light green fruit. The rich wine-purple of red cabbage and beetroot; the contrasting greens of lettuce, parsley and the cushion-forming herbs like marjoram and thyme; the feathery foliage of carrots, narrow mid-green spears of onions; luxurious ropes of ripening tomatoes and elegant bushes of rosemary can be arranged to look like a very expensive piece of land-scape design (Figure 37).

Avoid the messy plants, like potatoes, parsnips, swedes and savoys, and whip off any dying leaves from your chosen plants as they mature. The cucurbits—marrows, cucumbers, pumpkins—sprawl, but there is a certain panache about a single pumpkin, confined in a circular bed half-hedged with rosemary bushes or red cabbage. Cucumbers look fine planted in a raised bed with the fruit trained down the side. Judicious inter-planting with showy, bright blue or yellow flowers relieves the greenness of the vegetables when young.

An unfenced front garden is a problem, because it can be attacked by marauding

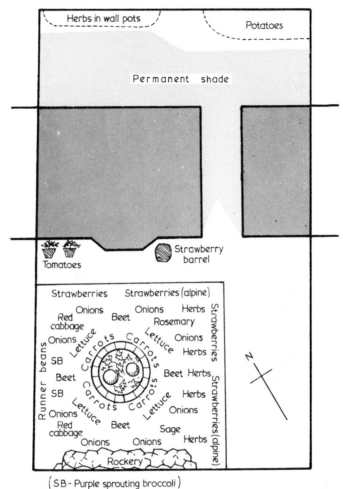

Herbs in wall pots

Potatoes

Permanent shade

Tomatoes

Strawberry barrel

Strawberries   Strawberries (alpine)

Onions   Onions   Herbs
Red cabbage   Beet   Rosemary
Onions   Lettuce   Onions
SB   Carrots   Herbs
Beet   Beet Herbs
SB   Carrots   Herbs
Onions   Lettuce   Onions
Red cabbage   Beet   Sage
Onions   Onions   Herbs

Runner beans

Strawberries   Strawberries (alpine)

N

Rockery

(S B - Purple sprouting broccoli)

37 Using the front garden for vegetables. Make a circular bed with red or coloured brick edging in centre for pumpkins, cucumbers, etc in summer, lettuce or spring onions in winter. Plant out purple sprouting broccoli in two rear beds in autumn for striking winter-spring colour effect.

dogs and neighbourhood children. Make sure the title deeds allow fencing off before you pay for your house. Prickly mahonia bushes, roses or a series of tubs of plants do something to discourage invasion. Front-garden produce is vulnerable to theft, but a nosy neighbour may be a godsend in preventing this.

Patios and yards

The patio-only householder can make good use of pots, boxes, old sinks, tubs and wire baskets. It may even be possible to lift paving stones or break up a cracked bit of concrete in order to make a planting area. The bed can be filled with compost and good soil, after the sub-soil has been broken up and extracted. Top soil can be bought, or obtained from building sites or where driveways are being laid.

For any planting bed or container which is relatively shallow choose stump-rooted carrots and round beet, onions, lettuce, radishes, herbs, tomatoes and cucurbits. Plant close together; feed and water them plentifully.

If you have a dark little courtyard, paint the walls white, to bounce back every bit of available light. Things can be grown all the way up the wall—trained on wires; in boxes of earth on long legs, or in pots and baskets hung from strong fixed nails. Wet earth weighs a lot, so err on the massive side for these supports.

Balconies

Anyone with a balcony can grow vegetables and herbs in pots and boxes—but make sure the structure is sound or it could come crashing down, which won't make you popular with passers-by or the police. As for window-boxes, a full-sized one is only possible when you have a sash window behind it. With a casement window, you are stuck with a half-width box and some interesting gymnastics.

Any indoor window-sill, french door or glazed porch will provide the necessary light space for you to grow something. Just add water and ventilation. If you have no such space, there are always bean sprouts, which can be grown fast in a warm dark place.

A most useful innovation for the would-be grower who has no space or soil is the growing-bag. This plastic container holds good potting mixture, and there is no need to buy pots or boxes. Bought ready-prepared for about £1 or more, a growing-bag will take two tomato plants, say, or a number of smaller type crops. It will be good for only one growing season, but the used medium makes a base for starting off new compost, mixed with fresh soil. Don't grow the same plant in it, though, as this would be a sure invitation to disease.

Hydroponic growing

Another popular method of cultivation, using no soil at all, is hydroponics. Originally this was the growing of plants in water only, dosed with chemical micro-nutrients, but propping up the plants proved difficult. Plants grown by this means are now set in an inert base material—like sand, pea gravel, vermiculite, etc—regularly watered and fed with selected nutrients to make up for those naturally found in the soil. On the large scale, hydroponic growing has made the desert bloom; on a small scale, it can do the same for your back yard.

However, it does mean a lot of work, keeping up the scientifically calculated watering and doses, and there is also the cost of the chemicals. If you want to try it, read *The Beginner's Guide to Hydroponics* by James Sholto Douglas, the expert on the subject; and Phostrogen Ltd market a kit with all you need. We have tried the system, but regard it as an interesting experiment only. The same amount of work, applied to conventional cultivation, brings better results even on the small scale.

What About an Allotment?

The first thing is to find out if there are any allotments in your district, whether one is available and how much is the rent.

Local authorities have a legal obligation to provide allotments for their rate-payers, but this is more often honoured in the breach than the observance. Ask at the town hall, district council offices or wherever you pay your rates. If they claim there is no space for allotments, remind them of their obligation in law and organise a pressure group.

Usually an allotment is of 5 or 10 rods, which is disposed as 30ft × 45 or 90ft (9 × 13.7 or 27.4m) and a path around it. The rent varies, but it can be as cheap as £2 a season, a truly remarkable bargain. Check that you have security of tenure for eighteen months at least, or it will be no use to plant overwintering crops like brassicas and beans. Find out whether water is laid on to the site, and if there are any odd regulations.

You will certainly not be allowed to erect a greenhouse, and in some places not even cloches or frames. You must not sell any of the produce, since the use of allotment land for commercial purposes is illegal. Some allotments forbid machinery; while others frown on children and animals—which could be awkward, since baby or dog sitters might cost as much as the produce you gain.

If the allotments are far from your home, think about the time involved and cost out the journey. If you have to drive five miles each way, are you going to be able to pop out at night and cover this or stop that? If there is no water laid on, can you carry enough with you to satisfy hungry plants in a hot summer? In a one-car family, will the person with access to the allotment by day have the use of a car full-time? You can't go by bus if your wellies stink of dung or if you are carrying a bag of peat.

Take a look at the site of the allotments on offer. Are they fenced off? Is there any form of supervision in your absence? An unguarded site overlooked by other gardeners will probably be fairly safe, but one in full view of a block of flats, where no one works an allotment, will probably be vandalised regularly. You don't want to work for months and have your crop smashed or stolen.

Is there a shed for tools, to save a lot of carrying to and fro and avoid nasty scratches on the car's simulated hide? Is it lockable? Are there any borrowable watering cans and wheelbarrows or a hirable cultivator?

On the whole, the key to the matter is how close the allotment is to your home. The nearer it is, the less it will cost you to get there, in money and time, and you will be more likely to keep up with the work. The more you are there at unpredictable times, the less likely you are to suffer losses from pinchers and vandals. If there is a choice, go for 5 rods this side of town, not 10 rods 4 miles away. Unfortunately, an awful lot of people have been getting the allotment bug, which means waiting lists for years to come in many places.

Borrowed land

Some elderly folk own large gardens where they would dearly like to be producing vegetables, but are just not capable of the work any more. They might be willing to let you work their land in return for a share of the fresh produce, which takes a lot out of a pension. Try approaching the local Darby and Joan Club or the council welfare department, or write to the local paper, which might start a local movement.

There would, naturally, be some control by the garden's owners over how much of it was dug and what structures were erected there. Against this, they would be on the site to keep an eye on things, from the security angle and for early warning of pest attack. Light work—like covering plants against frosts and limited watering—could be shared, to mutual advantage, while the arrangement lasted.

The reverse situation can arise, where a couple who are out at work for long hours and really can't cope with their garden during the week might be glad to let an able-bodied pensioner plant up part of it and share the produce. Obviously, there must be an agreement from the first about the area to be cultivated. We once had neighbours who employed a paid gardener and arrived home from holiday to find an unwanted rose-bed filling their lawn. They were too anxious not to lose him to remonstrate.

Schools, colleges and firms quartered in country houses often have spare land of which they make no use. It is always worth asking—they might say yes.

In Your Absence

A really dedicated, not to say manic, gardener would take a holiday only in dead of winter, but not many people are going to be that self-sacrificing. But going away at more or less any time in the summer poses problems, mostly concerned with watering and gathering of ripe crops.

In the normal British summer, outdoor crops will probably get enough rainfall to manage on. But a sudden drought may well occur, and even the semi-dedicated gardener will want to do what he can to preserve the crops he has worked for.

Just before you leave, soak the planted area very thoroughly—2 gallons of water for each square yard is about right. To prevent the moisture being evaporated by the sun, cover the wet earth with a mulch of any absorbent material—peat, lawn mowings, tea leaves—or top 'it with stones or straw.

Tall plants, like runner beans and tomatoes, lose a lot of moisture through their leaves, so apart from watering and mulching see that they are shaded by a nylon net with bits of foliage stuck in it, a white net curtain, an old sheet hung on wires a couple of feet away—anything which will impede the sun's direct rays. Less light will slow down the growth a little, but this is no bad thing while you are away.

Stake everything firmly and check that tomatoes are tied as high as they can be. Stop rampant growers like marrow and grapes so that their long tendrils do not roam all over the garden. Net fruit against birds, and set slug traps or sprinkle slug pellets.

Plants in pots can be thoroughly watered and then sunk to their rims in the ground. Cover with peat, lawn mowings or ashes to keep in the moisture. Raise them very carefully when you return, as they may root into the earth.

Pots and boxes from the greenhouse can be stood outside in a sheltered place or in a frame. Plants in pots which must stay in the greenhouse can be placed inside a second pot or bucket of peat or sand, which will hold in the moisture. To sink them in a bucket of water would be too much, causing their soil to go soggy or float away, and the roots to rot.

You can place several plant pots round a large bucket or tank of water. Trail a strip of rag or, better, candle-wick, from the water to each pot and tuck its end well down in the soil. The wick should transfer water to the plants as they need it,

38 Capillary watering. Secure candle wicks to stones at bottom of reservoir and tuck other end well down into soil of pot.

by capillary attraction (Figure 38). An equally effective method is to sit pots on a tray of gravel filled with water to half its depth. If you can trail a bit of wick from the base holes of the pot to the water reservoir, so much the better.

Plants in beds in the greenhouse can be watered and mulched, but they are subject to much higher temperatures than outdoor plants and thus lose their moisture much faster. Shade the greenhouse roof with whitewash or blinds and arrange a capillary watering system if possible. Leave all doors and ventilators open—also frame lights.

A fairly simple automatic spray-watering system can be set up for the greenhouse. Outside, you need a reservoir of water, large enough to last for the holiday,

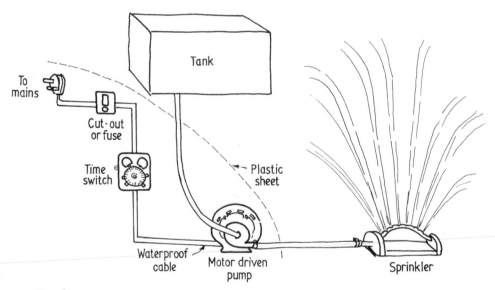

39 Greenhouse automatic watering system using rotating spray head. All electrical parts must be covered against water and isolated from the mains.

Inside, you need a waterproof pump, controlled by a time switch set to go off twice a day, in morning and afternoon. Attach a hose to an oscillating lawn sprinkler—the type which waters in an arc rather than a horizontal circle (Figure 39).

It is as well to try out any of these devices in advance to make sure they work. Ensure that the automatic sprinkler system is thoroughly safe in operation, with all the electrical connections and the pump shielded from water penetration by secure plastic barriers. Even so, it is wise to put a fail-safe cut-out between the time switch and the electricity source in the house.

If you have a reliable and cooperative neighbour, some of these precautions can be omitted, but try to leave as little to be done as possible, so that goodwill doesn't wear thin. You can offer an incentive by encouraging the waterer to help himself to ripe crops. This will be an act of mercy in the case of beans and peas, which must be regularly picked or they stop producing new pods. If the neighbour isn't much of a gardener, take him or her on a tour first and indicate which plants are which, especially if there are any particular instructions concerning them.

If your neighbours are incapable or unwilling, and you can't make a reciprocal arrangement with a gardening friend, you may have to consider paid help. Payment in kind is best if it can be arranged—someone expecting to benefit from the produce is likely to be more careful of it. The choice may be between a pensioner, keen to earn a bit extra or have a supply of produce during the year, and an unemployed school-leaver or a student at a loose end in the holidays. It may seem sense to take on a youngster, who can heft cans of water around and spot odd jobs that need doing better than a somewhat frail old gentleman with weak eyesight. But many teenagers have not been brought up to have a conscience about doing properly what they are paid for. The call of the record-player may prove too strong to allow long watering sessions.

There is a security problem to consider too. If at all possible, instal a tap on the outer wall of your house, so that the waterer does not have to be given the key and a free run of the premises. Even a teenager you know well can't be trusted in those circumstances. Given access to a whole house, he or she will inevitably let word get around the crowd. This could result in a break-in, the loss of your possessions or the contents of the drinks cabinet. If you must give the waterer access to the kitchen, lock or bolt the door leading to the rest of the house.

If you know well in advance when you will be away, plan your crop sowing accordingly. Leave out the successional sowing which would ripen then. Plant—in trenches or circular dips lined with peat—a main crop earlier or later, so that it is not too small or too far advanced to manage by itself for a week or three. Early to middle July isn't a bad time, if you have the choice. The further you get into August, the more things are busting out all over and will need dealing with daily.

Harvest Home — Natural Storage

When autumn comes, the average idle person feels depressed by the chill in the air, the certainty of winter to come and the equal certainty of bills to follow, and has only a wasted year to look back on. The virtuous gardener, on the other hand, now reaps the reward of his labours throughout the summer and has tangible evidence of his virtue. He collects and piles up his gathered crops, and knows they will stand him in good stead for months to come.

To stand the cold and storms of winter, all the produce must be stored carefully in a well-chosen place, by the best method for that crop, and in the best possible condition. As you gather your crops, look them over carefully for any slight sign of damage or insect attack. Any affected article will have to be used up as soon as possible or processed before storing.

Storing vegetables

The bulkier, hardier crops can sometimes be left in the ground until required. When the cold weather comes, they cease to grow to any noticeable extent, are held in a kind of natural refrigerator in the dark, and can be lifted when they are wanted for use. This applies to root crops, like carrots, turnips, parsnips, beet; brassicas tough enough for winter, like brussels sprouts, broccoli, kale, winter cabbage; and stem crops, like celery, chicory, etc, which are earthed over for blanching (pages 82 to 83).

This is fine for the brassicas, which have their edible bits above ground. It is not so good for root crops since, when the weather is frosty, they are held fast in the ground and cannot be dug without great demands on time and temper. They are also attacked by the ground-borne pests, which welcome your thought in providing food stores for them. As time goes on, root crops become hard and woody and eventually start shooting again, producing new leaves at the expense of the root.

Clamps

On the whole, it is best to raise at least half your root crop and store it in clamps.

Dig up the individual plants cautiously, taking care not to break the tip or spear the side with your fork. Reject anything with broken skins and then twist off the tops for composting, using a screw action to prevent tearing any of the root itself. This is especially important with beetroot, which should be left with a couple of inches of stem, otherwise they bleed to death. Leave the crop out for a day or two to dry—if the ground is already damp, spread them on wire or nylon netting to get both sides dry. Some of the dirt will fall away as it dries, but don't be tempted to wash off the rest to make the vegetables look nice—this will make them go wizened and shrivel up, if they haven't rotted first.

The crudest form of storage is the simple clamp. Straw or dried grass is spread on the ground or in the yard and the vegetables are piled on it in a pyramid or ridge, steadily decreasing in size. The pyramid is covered with more straw and then topped and sided with a thick layer of earth, smacked hard and smooth with the back of a spade. Stick a few upright straws in the earth to let a little air get to the crop. The finished clamp should be like a low thatched house (Figure 40).

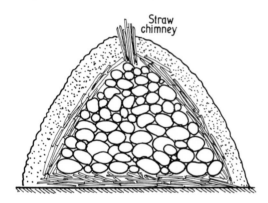

Straw
chimney

40 Clamp: simple heap type, covered with straw and earth.

The thick covering keeps the frost off the crop and the rammed earth 'roof' lets most of the rain run down the side. The snags are mainly two. First, if there is even one secretly diseased or damaged vegetable in the clamp, the whole lot may catch the ailment and go bad. Potatoes and carrots which have turned rotten smell really disgusting. In Lincolnshire a clamp is called a 'grave', hence such doom-laden remarks as, 'When I opened the grave, 'twas naught but black slime to be seen.' Secondly, it is very hard to take a few potatoes or carrots out without letting wet in, and a re-made clamp is never quite as weatherproof as it was at first. You can allow for this by making the clamp in sections divided by internal straw walls, but this is rather fiddly.

An improved method of clamping is to isolate each vegetable as far as possible. Either divide each layer of an ordinary clamp with straw, and extract one layer at a time, re-earthing the rest, or store the whole crop in a box, barrel or other container. The vegetables are stacked individually, with sand, peat or vermiculite between each one. Carrots of the stumpy sort stack upright, and triangular carrots

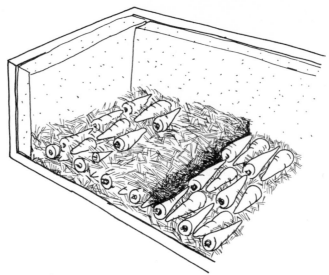

41 Clamp: box or barrel type, with all vegetables fully separated by straw, peat or sand.

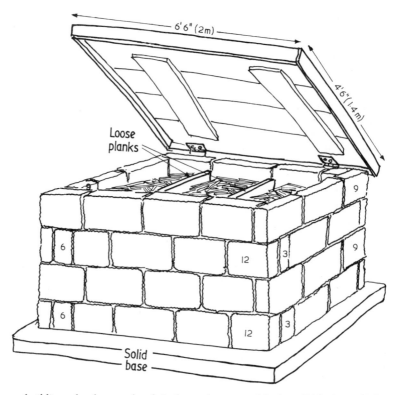

42 Clamp: building a bunker, made of 3in (75mm) concrete blocks. All blocks are full size except as indicated. 3 = 3in (75mm); 6 = 6in (150mm); 9 = 9in (225mm); 12 = 12in (300mm). Cover and separate every vegetable as in Fig. 41 and divide types with loose planks.

or parsnips flat, with every other one reversed (Figure 41). The container can be lined with straw or polystyrene for frost protection and the top should be well covered in the same material. It is easy to move the cover and fish out as many vegetables as are required without disturbing the rest, and as long as the stored vegetables are dry and dark, they will keep.

The containers can be ordinary boxes, barrels, a bottomless frame of four bits of wood resting on the yard, or they can be purpose-built. An old.coal bunker, or a similarly shaped container built of blocks, stationed just outside the kitchen door, will be frost-free, handy and rain-proof (Figure 42). It is very simple to build, and good practice for anyone contemplating constructional work around the house. The inside can be divided with loose bits of plank as required. This is a lot easier than storing your boxes in a shed full of other junk.

Blanchers

The whole class of plants which are blanched before use can be left in trenches in the garden, but the same problems apply as to roots left in the ground. Frost makes it difficult to lift them, and they are attacked by pests and frost. They can be moved into boxes and covered in the same way as roots or transported with their own earth and slates to a site in yard or shed and left to finish their blanching (see pages 82 to 83).

Heeling in

Other plants—like Jerusalem artichokes, roots, leeks—can be moved nearer the house and inserted into a slit trench in a convenient part of the garden. Some of the same problems will apply, but a site near the house is likely to be more sheltered than in the open garden, so they shouldn't freeze in the ground. Parsnips, incidentally, are supposed to taste better when they have felt their first frost; this is a matter of opinion.

String them up

Onions are traditionally kept hanging in strings from the ceiling. Always dry off the plants in warm sun before bringing them in. If it is chill and rainy, sit them on a length of wire netting with a roof propped over it. Collect them with plenty of stem for stringing (Figure 43). Hang the string in a cool but frost-free place and pull as required. Kept in the kitchen, they look impressive, but they will sprout and rot. Garlic can be strung or tied in bunches when well dry.

Hang them up

The tough-skinned cucurbits—pumpkin and marrows—will keep for some months

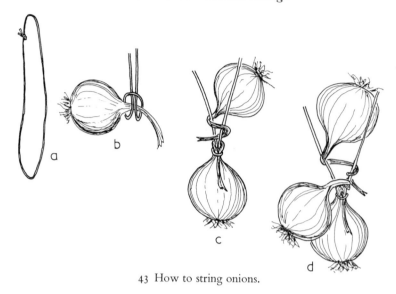

43 How to string onions.

if they are stored in a cool, frost-free place, but they must be able to get to the air on all sides. Sling them in a strong net from a sturdy beam, and check for pressure marks from time to time. Don't hang a pumpkin by its curved stem, since this dries up and drops the fruit like a small bomb. Ridge cucumbers keep a while, but are best pickled. Melons have a limited store life. Onions without stems and shallots can also be hung in nets, though shallots are mostly pickled.

Storing fruit

Only hard top fruits, like apples and to a lesser degree pears, will store well without processing. Only the very best of the crop should be selected for this purpose.

Pick the fruit from the tree by hand—don't shake the branch to accelerate the process, or the whole lot will be bruised. The fruit is ripe and ready to come when a gentle twist of the stem will detach it. If it fights back, leave it for a few days. Set the fruit down carefully in a bowl or bucket—don't throw it in or, again, it will bruise.

Inspect every fruit closely after it is picked, and sort into heaps; perfect; very slightly bruised or specked; rather bruised or specked, and half-way gone. These are respectively for dry storage; process and store; use right away, and wine. Anything worse goes straight on to the compost heap.

Each perfect fruit should be individually wrapped in paper and stacked on a slatted tray, preferably in a single layer, but two if you are short of space. The wooden trays with little projections at the corners, made for tomatoes, are ideal: they can double as apple trays and potato chitting trays at different seasons (Figure 44). Stack them in an airy place with not much light—under stairs or in an attic will do.

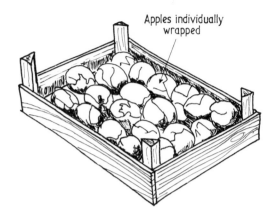

Apples individually wrapped

44 Apple trays: wrap fruit in newspaper or tissues, not plastic, and inspect regularly.

Apples will usually keep till spring, and individual wrapping means that even if one goes bad it won't get at the others, provided you check over the trays occasionally and shift any rotten ones before they ooze out of their paper. When apples are stored unwrapped, the skin wizens and the taste changes. They are then very mellow, which some people prefer.

Pears don't store as well as apples, and you will be lucky to keep any past Christmas. Conference and russet pears, which have a tougher skin, keep the best. Soft-skinned types, like Williams, have no lasting power at all, so you might as well make a complete pig of yourself and preserve the rest. Rotting in the juicy type of pear can be retarded for a while by wrapping them in greaseproof paper or aluminium foil, but check them every day. The moment they feel soft, they must be eaten or the next day they will go sleepy—like rotten cotton wool. Then they are only fit for compost.

Any apples which are less than perfect must be eaten or processed as soon as possible, to arrest their slide into the next category down. The majority of the pear crop and all the stone and soft fruits need processing. Many of them will freeze and retain most of their fresh characteristics. Most will bottle, jam or purée, and some are regularly used in pickles or chutney. Nothing of the whole harvest which can be caught in time need be wasted.

Harvest Home—Food Processing

Apart from storing produce more or less as it comes from the plant, there is a whole repertoire of traditional tricks for keeping food through the winter in a reasonably palatable and nutritious form.

Drying

Bacteria and moulds need moisture to grow, so if you can deprive them of it, your food stays safe from attack. Unfortunately, some foods are made so brittle or leathery by the drying that they are hardly worth keeping—biltong, for instance, is a sun-dried meat that is no doubt better than starvation, but not much.

Apples

The kinds of apple that do not store well in trays can be dried to apple rings. Peel and core the fruit (save the scraps for making pectin stock, page 161); cut them into slices about $\frac{1}{4}$in (6mm) thick, and spread them out on baking trays or a piece of board. You can dry them either in a cooling oven, after baking, or in a solar-heated dryer (see page 238). In either case, try not to let the temperature go over about 180°F (80°C) or the rings will be leathery when dry and mushy when reconstituted. It should take about four days to get enough moisture out—you can check on progress if you weigh a few of the rings first and use these particular ones to follow the process. When they have reached a quarter of their fresh-sliced weight they are dry enough.

Apple rings made this way are useful for pies, apple sauce, curries, etc, and are really quite nutritious. They retain a little of their vitamins B1 and C, although most of the C disappears during subsequent recooking.

Mushrooms

These and other edible fungi can be dried in the same way as apples. They make a useful source of protein for winter soups and stews, but lose a lot of flavour. Many people prefer salted (page 156) or pickled (page 163) mushrooms, chanterelles, etc.

Onions

Cut onions into slices and dry them like apples. As they contain a lot of natural moisture you will need to wait until they have shrunk to one-eighth of their original weight, otherwise they could rot in storage. Don't dry them in a closed oven or solar dryer with other foods! The food value of dried onions is not very great, but they are useful for flavouring. Sometimes strung onions that are going slightly soft can be salvaged by slicing and drying them.

Plums

These can be dried to prunes for storage. Pack the fruit neatly in a shallow wooden box or deep baking tray, with the stalks uppermost. Put aside any with insect bites or gummy spots for immediate eating or cooking. Be careful not to bruise the others; cover them with a sheet of kitchen paper or aluminium foil and put them into the solar dryer, or pop them in the oven after baking. As they shrink, pack them closer together; if you have more than one tray full at first, transfer from one to another as the fruit shrink, so that you keep one tray completely occupied. The prunes are ready when they have shrunk to just over a quarter of their original weight. Keep them in tins with tight lids, or well-stoppered jars in a dark place. Prunes are mostly sources of sugar (about 40 per cent), but also contain useful amounts of iron, vitamin A and nicotinamide (niacin, one of the B2 vitamins). Tradition praises or condemns them as a laxative, but they make very little difference to a well-balanced diet, as their action is almost entirely due to the fibre they contain.

Sweet corn

The cobs can be dried in the sun until the grains peel off with a fairly blunt knife. Store these in a dry place until you need them, then boil for about 20 minutes in the minimum amount of water. Corn stored in this way is a stop-gap food—the grains never regain the plumpness or taste of fresh corn, and are inferior to deep-frozen corn.

You can make the grains a little more exciting by wetting fresh-stripped corn with milk, rolling the grains in sugar, and drying these in a cool oven. This makes 'corn flakes' with the same texture as sugared popcorn, and was a traditional American snack food for children. It has no particular food value except calories, but is better for children than sweets.

Tomatoes

Tomatoes can be concentrated in the form of purée, a traditional ingredient in Italian cooking. Dry the tomatoes, in an oven or solar dryer, on a piece of smooth board, and scrape the pulp off every day, spreading it afresh until it is quite thick. The acid in tomatoes helps to preserve this pulp, although it is not nearly as de-hydrated as most dried foods. The purée contains some vitamin C and traces of B1 and other useful nutrients, but its main value is as a livener for dull winter menus.

Green tomatoes can be treated the same way, but the purée is rather acrid to some tastes. It is probably better to save surplus green tomatoes for chutneys and sauces, where they will add an edge to ingredients with a blander taste.

Peas and beans

Allow these to ripen thoroughly and then dry them for use in later cooking. Shell them and spread them out for some time in an airy place until all moisture has evaporated. Then store them in covered jars or pots, to keep them clean and safe from mice.

Herbs

These can be picked as sprays or handfuls of leaves and hung up in an airy place to dry naturally in a week or so, or the process can be accelerated by putting them on trays in a cooling oven after baking. The leaves go dry and brittle, and can be powdered or fragmented between thumb and finger, over a plate. Store them in airtight jars. Label the drying herbs as you go, since several tend to look alike when powdered.

Salting

Salting is really another method of drying, except that salt is used instead of heat to withdraw the water. Some traditional foods—bacon, for example—depend on the salt for their taste. Others need to have it boiled out before they become palatable.

Beans

A crock or bucket can be used for salting beans. Most people prefer earthenware, but a plastic bucket with a lid is just as good—if you can get over the psychological block of using such a thing for a folksy recipe.

Pick runner or French beans on a dry day, and put aside any bitten or bruised ones for immediate cooking. Dust the bottom of the crock with salt (cooking salt is cheaper, but table salt will do just as well); add a layer of beans—one bean deep— then more salt, and so on until the beans have run out or the crock is full. Put a lid on it and store it in a dry place.

To cook the beans, take out as many as you need (with *dry* hands); wash off the salt with cold water; dunk them in boiling water for about five minutes; then drain, and finally cook them in fresh boiling water. This should get rid of enough salt to make them eatable. Beans stored in this way do not lose any protein value, but most of their vitamins B1 and C are lost either in storage or in the successive washings and boilings.

Curing

Bacon and ham

Many people prefer home-cured bacon and ham, even if they have to buy the pork from outside. The necessities are salt to preserve the meat, and sugar of some kind—molasses, even honey in some recipes—to make it soft and moist. Bacon can be made with salt alone, but it has the consistency of old shoe-soles. Saltpetre—potassium nitrate—is added in most curing recipes, because it gives the bacon or ham a good colour. Bacon cured with just salt and sugar is quite tasty, but greenish-grey instead of pink. The pink colour of commercial cured meat is due to substances called 'nitrosamines' which are produced by the saltpetre. Some researchers believe that these can cause cancer. If you therefore decide to leave out the saltpetre, replace it by an equal weight of salt.

For a 10lb (4.5kg) ham or flitch, rub the meat well with ordinary salt and leave it to sit in the curing tub for twenty-four hours. Wipe away any blood or moisture that has exuded after this time, and then cover it with the curing brine. The basic recipe for this is:

2lb (.9kg) salt
1lb (454g) sugar
$\frac{1}{4}$oz (7g) saltpetre
1gal (4.5l) water

Bring the mixture to the boil and pour it, hot, over the meat in the tub, making sure that there is enough to cover it completely. Put a piece of board with a stone on it to hold the meat under the surface of the curing brine—don't use an iron weight, it will rust and discolour the brine.

There are dozens of minor variations on this: you can use brown sugar (the same weight), or treacle or honey (twice the weight), instead of ordinary sugar; old beer instead of some of the water (as in Derbyshire ham); and sea salt instead of common salt—if you don't mind bromides in your ham. Whatever cure you use, leave the meat in for at least two weeks, preferably three days per lb, turning it every day to make sure it is thoroughly impregnated by the brine. Look out for bacterial attack, which is revealed by sliminess or 'stringiness' of the brine—it actually hangs from your fingers like thin jelly. If this starts, pour away the brine, wash the meat under the tap until all the slime has gone, and make up some fresh brine with a little more salt in it than usual. The ham or bacon should be all right if replaced in fresh brine promptly.

When the meat is cured, wash it and hang it up in a cool dark place for about a week—and make sure that flies cannot get at it. You can eat it green (unsmoked), but if you prefer the smoked flavour, as most people do, smoking is quite easy to arrange. You need twigs or chips of hardwood—oak is traditional in Britain, hickory in America, but any hardwood seems to work. Don't use softwood, or your meat will taste of turpentine. Get an old, but clean, galvanised dustbin, the sort with corrugations in the lid (see Figure 45), and knock a few holes in the bottom to let the smoke in. Stand it in a secluded part of the garden, with enough bricks or stones under it to keep it about 12in (30cm) off the ground. Invert the lid, and hang your cured meat from the handle, so that it is clear of the sides and bottom of the bin.

45 Cutaway diagram of galvanised dustbin converted to smoker.

Nearby, start a small fire with your hardwood scraps. Don't use a paraffin firelighter, or the smell will get into the meat; if necessary, ignite the wood with a blowlamp. When it is smouldering well, but not actually burning, shovel it under the bin, so that the smoke goes up through the holes and out under the lid. Keep the fire fed with occasional bits of wood, for about three days if possible. The temperature should not go above about 120°F (50°C) or the meat will start to cook, and then does not keep well. When ready, wrap the meat in greaseproof paper, or preferably cooking foil to exclude light, which makes cured meat turn rancid.

Any type of meat can be cured in this way. Leg of pork makes ham; gammon or back makes lean bacon; belly of pork makes streaky bacon. Lean beef can be salted for traditional salt beef, or salted and smoked for pastrami. Even joints of mutton can be cured—'macon' isn't very exciting, but it keeps well.

Fish

You can use similar brine for curing fish, but omit the saltpetre, as this makes very little difference to its colour. Fillet and gut *fresh* fish, spreading out the two halves of herrings and similar small fish, or cutting up larger ones into chunks of about 1lb (454g). Put them in the brine for twenty-four hours—using it cold, not boiling. Then get two heavy pieces of clean plank; lay the fish out on one and sprinkle coarse salt thickly over them, then press them down with the other plank. Put the fish to dry in the open air for three days—keeping cats away—then brush off loose salt and either wrap the fish in cooking foil for storage, or smoke them. A simple wooden or basketwork rack, or a wire cake tray, will serve for your smoker. About twenty-four hours of smoking is usually enough. You will find that the fish have far more flavour than most commercial 'smoked' fish—these are often only brined and then painted with a solution of 'smoke flavour' and brown dye.

Preserving with sugar

Sugar is another way of baffling bacteria and moulds; when the sugar concentration is over 70 per cent they cannot grow. This is one of the oldest chemical treatments for preserving food, for even before cane sugar was readily available people preserved meat and other foods in jars of honey.

Black and red currants

These can be stored simply by surrounding them with sugar. Put aside any broken or squashy fruit for immediate cooking or wine-making; drop a few cloves into the bottom of a jar, then alternate layers of currants and sugar—use equal weights of each—until the jar is full. Tie a paper cover over it and the currants should keep for at least six months.

Candied fruit

This will keep almost indefinitely; the idea is to impregnate the produce with a sugar syrup so strong that it crystallises. Hard produce, such as orange or lemon peel, chestnuts, walnuts and angelica (see page 124) should be pre-cooked in plain water until they just begin to soften. Then boil them with the sugar syrup as described below. Early May is a good time to cut the angelica, as it is then firm but not too tough. Peel chestnuts and shelled walnuts first by dropping them into boiling water, then cold water. Soft fruit (pears, plums, greengages, peaches, cherries) need only be cored or stoned and added directly to the syrup. You can treat tomatoes the same way; select them red but not squashy, and be prepared for a shock when you taste the finished result. A few very delicate things, like crystallised violets and candied rose petals, should be made by completing the sugar boiling first, then adding the flowers at the last possible moment before it crystallises.

In every case, start with a syrup in the proportions 1lb (454g) sugar to 1pt (.5litre) water. Add the fruit, nuts, etc—pre-cooked if necessary—and bring to the boil for about twenty minutes. Then leave for at least twelve hours for the sugar to impregnate the produce. Then add another 4oz (113g) sugar for every 1lb (454g) you originally used and bring to the boil again. This time carry on with the process until the syrup temperature reaches 240–250°F (115–120°C). It is at this point that flower petals are added for making these confections. If you have no sugar-boiling thermometer, boil to 'soft-ball'—when a spoonful of the syrup dropped into a saucer of cold water can be rolled up into a soft ball like toffee; brittle strings, or a hard ball like a marble, show that the process has gone too far.

Drain off the syrup, put the fruit, etc, on to a baking tray, and finish drying it in a cool oven. When cold, store the produce in a stoppered jar, or wrap chestnuts (marrons glacés) individually in kitchen foil.

Jam

A useful way of preserving the flavour, at least, of summer fruits, this is basically a jelly of fruit and pectin—a natural thickener that occurs in many fruits (but not all, see below)—and enough sugar to preserve the mixture, usually about 70 per cent of the total. There are countless recipes for jam-making, but all of them—if they are going to work—reduce to a very few simple principles:

1   Use approximately equal weights of fruit and sugar
2   Adjust the water used to boil the fruit so that you have approximately 1pt (.5 litre) cooked fruit for ever 1lb (454g) sugar. By always using the same wooden spoon and saucepan for your jam-making, you can save a lot of time—measure out 1, 1½, 2, 2½ pints and so on of water into the saucepan, and make a notch in the spoon when it is held upright. In that way you will easily know the volume of liquid.
3   Pectin and acid help to make jam set, so fruits with plenty of both (apples, Morello cherries, black, white and red currants, quinces, oranges and lemons) never need help in setting. Medium-pectin fruit (apricots, blackberries, greengages, loganberries, peaches and plums) may need to be mixed with one of the high-pectin kind or dosed with extra pectin or acid. Low-pectin fruits (sweet cherries, pears and strawberries) and marrow or swede—often used to add bulk to jam—always need assistance to set.
4   You can make up for lack of pectin or acid by adding any of the following: 2 BS tablespoons of lemon juice or ⅓ BS teaspoon of citric or tartaric acids per 4lb (1.8kg) fruit; 2oz (56g) powdered commercial pectin to 4lb (1.8kg) fruit; ¼pt (142ml) pectin stock (see below) to 4lb (1.8kg) fruit. Don't overdo these measures, or add any

of these things to jam made from high-pectin fruit, or you will have to cut your jam up with the breadknife.

5 If you have a sugar thermometer, boil until the temperature of the jam is about 220°F (104°C). Otherwise test for setting point by spooning a little of the jam on to a cold plate to see whether it solidifies.

6 Warm the jars before pouring in the jam, otherwise they will crack. Seal them well, but first put a disc of greaseproof paper on top of the jam so that condensed moisture inside the lid does not dilute the surface—if the sugar concentration is reduced below about 70 per cent, mould can grow. As long as you scrape it off before eating the jam, it does no harm but it can spoil the flavour a long way down the jar.

Pectin stock

This is a good way of making use of surplus apple peel, cores, and so on. Simmer 1lb (454g) of apple scraps in ½pt (284ml) water until the apples are pulpy; strain the mixture through a jelly bag; put the juice back in the pan and bring to the boil, and then pour it into pre-heated jars. If you want to use it immediately, just cover the jars until you are ready. You can keep the pectin if you use Kilner jars and seal properly (see page 167).

Honey

If you have large supplies of honey, you can use it in most of these preserving recipes—though it will not set for candying. As honey is about 75-per-cent sugar, use 1⅓ times as much compared with cane sugar.

Sugar and health

If you are thinking of writing to tell us that excess sugar is bad for you—*we know*. Jam is no substitute for protein, or minerals, or vitamins. However, in moderation, jams (or crystallised violets, for that matter), are pleasant and harmless decorations for a balanced diet. You can use brown sugar for any of the recipes, though the taste is a bit overpowering, but it really makes no difference to the food value.

Vinegar and lactic acid

Acids are far more effective than sugar in stopping mould and bacterial attack. Ordinary vinegar, which is 5–6 per cent acetic acid, will preserve most food. Lactic acid is a similar material produced in many traditional preserving processes, and often the two are used together.

Vinegar, as most home wine-makers know, is the final product when wine, cider, or beer goes sour, and you can in fact make your own vinegar quite easily by disregarding all the precautions given in the brewing section (pages 175–177). For wine vinegar, select a bottle of wine that is already a little sharp to the taste, and let

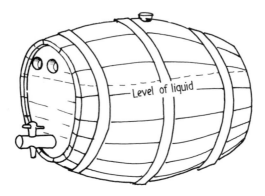

46 Vinegar making: barrel method.

it go sour by deliberately exposing it to the air in a jug. Put some muslin or similar material over the top to let air in but keep insects out. Now get a small cask or barrel—preferably wooden, but plastic would do—and make holes in the ends so that air can circulate above the level of the liquid (Figure 46). Pour your sour wine in, put the barrel on its side, and fill up to just below the level of the holes with more wine. Plug the holes lightly with muslin so that air can circulate, but insects cannot. Keep it in a warm place, and you should find that a thick mat of bacteria— called 'mother of vinegar'—will form on the surface of the liquid. You should be able to run off wine vinegar after about six weeks and, if you are careful to retain most of the mother of vinegar in the barrel, it will make further quantities every time you fill the barrel with wine.

This is a slow and rather tricky process; if you can get hold of beech shavings, there is a quicker and more reliable method. Use a cask with a detachable lid, and three-quarters fill it with the shavings—beech is best; most other woods give the vinegar an odd taste. Put the lid back on and arrange the set-up shown in Figure 47, where wine from a barrel or jar can trickle in at the top of the cask, over the shavings and out through the tap at the bottom. Sour a little wine as before; pour it into the cask so that it soaks well into the shavings; leave it for a couple of days for the acetic acid bacteria to start multiplying, and then allow a thin trickle of wine to pass through. Try not to get the shavings wine-logged, or air will not be able to penetrate to complete the process. If the product from the first run does not seem as sour as wine vinegar should be, pour that lot through again, and slow down the rate a little by controlling the tap on the wine barrel. It does no harm if you put the vinegar through several times. When you have made a batch or two, the mother of vinegar will have become established and the process can be speeded up. This method works for cider vinegar also.

With this home-made equipment you can produce malt vinegar. Make up a brew, as described on page 179 for beer but without hops; let it ferment to the stage of bottling, then use either of the methods above. Hops not only give a bitter flavour to the vinegar, but may in fact slow down the process by their preservative effect.

Vinegars made like this can be used for flavouring. If you boil them with herbs,

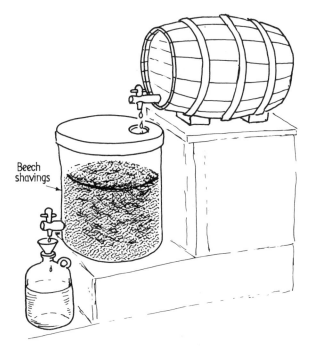

Beech shavings

47 Vinegar making: wood-shaving method; make sure the shavings are not flooded.

such as tarragon, onions or shallots, spices, and so on, you can make a whole range of exotic vinegars that are ideal for marinating food or simply to serve at table. The amount you use is obviously a matter of taste, but if in doubt try 1oz of spice or herbs to 1pt vinegar (50g per litre), and go up or down from there.

They can also be used, with or without flavourings added, to preserve red or white cabbage (rub the slices of cabbage with salt, leave them for about two days under a cloth, and pack them in jars with hot vinegar); mushrooms and other fungi (boil them for about twenty minutes and then pack them, not too tightly, in jars and cover with hot vinegar); boiled beetroot, either in the form of baby beets or in slices; nasturtium seed pods, which make a very pleasant substitute for capers; small sweet-corn cobs (you often find some left on the stalk at the end of the season— they cannot grow any more, but are quite a delicacy if pickled); apples cut into chunks, and cherries.

Other vegetables and fruit can be packed in vinegar if you only want to keep them for a short time, but they may turn soggy if left for more than a month or two. To get over this, you need to brine them before putting them in vinegar. This salt treatment is not just to extract water or improve the flavour, but helps to encourage lactic acid bacteria to develop in the produce, so that it is pickled 'from the inside'.

To preserve beans (French or runner, use only the young ones), cauliflower, cucumber (especially the small outdoor type, for gherkins), marrow, and onions or shallots, make up a brine with 10-per-cent salt (1lb per gallon, or 100g per litre) sufficient to immerse all the produce you have. Cooking salt or coarse preserving salt is better than table salt for this. Use only wooden or plastic containers—not metal (and particularly not copper, which may dissolve in the lactic acid and actually make the vegetables rather poisonous); stir with a wooden or plastic spoon, and have an effective insect-proof cover.

Prepare your vegetables—cut beans and cauliflower into conveniently sized pieces; peel onions, and so on—weigh them, and put them in the brine. Now weigh out more salt corresponding to one-tenth of the weight of produce, and add this as well, stirring it in. Cover the vessel and leave it in a cool dark place, stirring every day. To brine the vegetables properly, at least two weeks will be needed, and more for some: with marrow and gherkins you can tell how well the process is going, because the lactic acid production turns the flesh from white or cream to a translucent green.

When the vegetables are thoroughly brined, wash them in several changes of warm water to remove excess salt, and leave them to soak overnight in water to extract some from the inside. Then pack them in jars and cover them with hot spiced vinegar. Your own tastes will tell you what spices to use; the traditional ones are chillis, garlic, pimento, black peppercorns, cloves and allspice.

Dill pickles are made with gherkins brined in 10-per-cent salt solution, as above, but with about 4oz of sugar added to each gallon (25g per litre), and the dill, allspice, coriander, bay leaves and so on added to the brine, so that the flavour penetrates right from the beginning. You need to watch this preparation very carefully, as it can easily develop mould if you do not stir regularly.

Sauerkraut

This is made with firm white cabbage pickled entirely in naturally formed lactic acid. The white cabbage must be really firm, and you will need a vessel with a well-fitting *heavy* lid that rests inside it (Figure 48). The lid is there to hold the cabbage

48 Sauerkraut vessel: use an earthenware dish as a lid.

under the surface of the pickling liquid; some commercial manufacturers actually use chunks of solid concrete with handles set in for this purpose. A large round stoneware dish would do very well, as long as it can move up and down in the crock or bin. Never use metal containers or utensils.

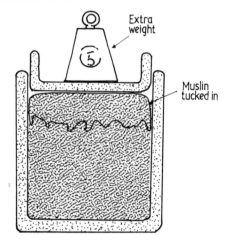

49 Sauerkraut making: cover with muslin and weight lid.

Slice your cabbage thinly with a sharp knife; weigh it, and then weigh out salt at the rate of 4oz for every 10lb of cabbage (25g per kilo)—cooking or coarse salt is best. Pack the cabbage tightly into your crock, with salt dusted in between the layers; cover it with a piece of cheesecloth tucked down the sides (see Figure 49), and put your weighty lid on, pressing the cabbage down well. Try to keep the temperature of storage between 60° and 80°F (15–25°C). After a day or two, the salt will have extracted enough juice for it to be visible just under the lid; make sure that all the cabbage is held under the surface, or it can go mouldy. After about four weeks, your sauerkraut is ready. You can keep it in the crock, if you remember to put the lid on and push the cabbage down every time you remove some, or you can pack it into Kilner jars and sterilise it (as described on page 167), when it will keep almost indefinitely.

Cheese

Another food preserved by lactic acid, cheese is well worth making if you have your own supplies of milk, or can buy it in bulk direct from the producer or the dairy. It is not economic to make cheese from milk delivered to the door, because of the dairy overheads, but you might conceivably make a profit if you could master the art of making, say, Stilton or Camembert to professional standards.

The starting-point for all the various types of cheese is the same. Milk consists of a mixture of casein, lactose (milk sugar), fat, and a few other ingredients, in water. You need to separate the casein (curds) from the rest (whey). This happens naturally as milk goes sour, when lactic acid bacteria work on the lactose and the acid precipitates the casein. Other acids, such as fruit juice or vinegar, will do the same. Natural digestive enzymes, like rennet or pepsin, also have this effect: you can buy rennet, which is also used for making junkets, and pepsin is sometimes sold as a meat tenderiser.

Let the curds settle; pour off as much of the whey as you can, then strain the curds in muslin or a fine-mesh wire strainer. Curds made in this way and lightly salted become cottage cheese; if you press them in the cheesecloth to get out more whey, then salt them, you have farm cheese. These cheeses will keep for several days in a cool place, but should not be left too long.

To make hard cheese that will keep well, you need to press out a lot more whey, and this means some kind of mechanical help. You can make a very primitive press from and old saucepan, using stones as weights to get the pressure (Figure 50). If you can turn a wooden screw on a lathe, or get hold of some heavy-duty threaded rod from some machine, you can contrive a really effective screw-press. An old-type mangle might give you the screws—we use iron screws from an inherited embroidery frame.

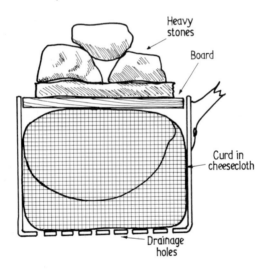

Heavy stones

Board

Curd in cheesecloth

Drainage holes

50 Simple cheese press made from saucepan.

Take about 5gal (22.5l) of milk—it is not really worth using less for hard cheese; if you have a small quantity to use up, make cottage cheese—and let about 1gal (4.5l) stand in a warm place until it is just on the turn: not smelly, but ready to separate. Warm the rest of the milk to blood heat (98°F, 37°C), add your ripened gallon, then rennet (follow the manufacturer's instructions for quantities), and hold the temperature until the curds begin to separate throughout the milk. If you cannot get rennet, use lemon juice or vinegar, at about 1 BS tablespoonful to the gallon (4.5l), though the cheese may not mature quite as well. An extract of the leaves of nettles, or lady's bedstraw (*Galium verum*), is supposed to act like rennet, but we have never tried this. Any slightly acid plant should work, if it is not poisonous and does not interfere with the lactic acid bacteria.

Strain off the whey from the curds; add salt—try about ¾oz (20g) to the quantities above, but adjust more or less to taste when you have the system working regularly; chop the curd well to mix in the salt and allow whey to escape, and wrap it in two layers of cheesecloth. Put it in your press and squeeze it until no more whey appears—you can spread this process over a few days, pressing a little more each day. Then put your cheese, in its inner cloth, in a cool dark place to mature for about two months minimum. If you notice signs of mould on the surface, peel off the cloth and rub the cheese with salt. You should get about 1lb of cheese, resembling Cheddar, for each gallon of milk (1kg from every 10l).

Yoghurt

This is milk partially fermented with *Lactobacillus bulgaricus,* a particular variety of lactic acid bacteria. You can make it most easily by buying a sample of 'live' yoghurt—not pasteurised and not fruit-flavoured—and stirring about 1BS tablespoonful of this into 2pts (about 1l) of ordinary milk warmed to blood heat. Keep it at this temperature for about eight hours—in a warm cupboard or a wide-mouthed vacuum flask. Once you have successfully made one batch of yoghurt, some of this can be used to start off the next, and so on. You will find after a time that an off-flavour begins to develop, due to 'wild' bacteria getting in. By keeping everything clean and covered, and washing all your utensils in very hot water or dilute household bleach, this can be staved off for a while; if it does happen, get rid of your culture and buy another pot of yoghurt.

This is an easy and cheap method of making yoghurt. Don't, however, believe all the fairy tales about its health-giving properties—it has just about the same food value as the original milk.

Bottling and canning

One of the simplest ways to preserve food it to shut it in jars, sterilise it by heat and then seal the containers. Home bottling—Americans call it 'canning'—necessitates a supply of Kilner or similar heat-proof jars with lids that can be screwed down; rubber rings to make the seal under the lid, and a saucepan deep enough to immerse the jars up to their shoulders in water.

All types of fruit can be preserved in this way. For berries and currants, simply clean the fruit and pack it straight into the jars, trying not to bruise it. Apricots, plums, greengages and cherries can be packed as they come, or stoned. Peaches, unless they are very small, are best halved and stoned. Apples and pears should be cored and halved or quartered, according to size.

Make up a syrup with 1lb of sugar in 2pts of water (400g to 1l), and pour warm, not boiling, over the fruit to immerse it. Dip the rubber sealing rings in boiling water to sterilise them and fit them to the lids. Screw the lids down—then *unscrew* a quarter-turn to let steam out during the sterilising so that your jars don't burst.

Put two or three pieces of wood or a coiled-rope mat at the bottom of the saucepan to keep the jars from contact with the hot metal—these will do just as well as the special racks and trivets sold for this purpose. Stand the jars in place; stuff some bits of folded paper down beside them to stop them rattling against the side of the saucepan, and cover them to the shoulders with warm water. Now bring the water to the boil, turn down the heat, and simmer for about twenty minutes at around 190°F (88°C). This temperature need not be exact—just make sure the jars stay near boiling point without actually being battered about by the bubbling water.

When this is done, turn off the heat altogether and, with a cloth or oven glove, screw down the lids tightly. It is important that you do this before the jars have cooled appreciably, otherwise they will suck air and fresh bacteria in from outside. Stand them on a wooden surface, or on an old towel spread out, and let them cool. Next day, unscrew the rings and hold up each jar by the edges of the lid. If the lid comes away, the sealing is inadequate; you should either eat the contents straight away or repeat the sterilising process—with a new rubber ring, as this is probably the cause of the leak. If all is well, pack away your jars until needed.

Acid vegetables, like tomatoes, can be treated in the same way. You can cut down on the sugar, if you like, but add a little vinegar to the water to aid preservation. However, this method should not be used for other vegetables or meat, because the temperature is not nearly high enough to kill all the bacteria and there is a risk of botulism—a particularly nasty form of food-poisoning.

You can also sterilise your jars in a pressure-cooker (or autoclave), if it is deep enough to take them plus a wooden or rope spacer at the bottom. Put about 2in (5cm) of water in the cooker; place the jars in position, remembering to unscrew the lids that crucial quarter-turn; put the 5lb per sq in (0.024kg/sq cm) weight on the valve and, as soon as the cooker is up to pressure, lower the heat, maintaining the pressure for two minutes for soft fruits, like berries and currants, and four minutes for larger fruit, rhubarb and tomatoes. You can pack pectin stock (see page 161) for jam-making: give it 5 minutes, as it contains hardly any sugar to preserve it.

Turn off the heat and leave the cooker to cool for ten minutes. Take the valve off cautiously, open up and, as soon as you can, screw down the lids of the jars. Test them the next day as above.

When bottling vegetables, clean them thoroughly, pack them in jars and cover them with 2-per-cent brine (1oz of salt in 2½pts water or 20g per litre). Sterilise them for ten minutes in the pressure cooker using the 15lb/sq in (0.070kg/sq cm) weight—this will give you a temperature of 250°F (121°C); at least 240°F (115°C) is needed to sterilise vegetables properly. Make sure that your cooker is not leaking, even slightly, or the pressure, and therefore the temperature, will be lower.

Freezing

Preserving food in ice has been practised for a very long time. Freezing slows down the growth of bacteria, though it never quite stops it; but it is certainly one of the best methods of retaining the taste and nutritional value of food. Running a modern deep-freeze successfully is quite easy, if you follow a few general guidelines:

1   Don't put in too much food at a time. Food at room temperature is 'hot' compared with that of the freezer, and the machine can only cool it at a certain rate. Your freezer should have a rating—quoted in the instructions or specification—that tells you what weight of food you can freeze in twenty-four hours. If you put in more, or try to freeze hot food, stocks already in the freezer may be warmed up and spoiled.

2   Freeze everything as quickly as you can. Slow cooling makes large crystals of ice, and the food becomes broken up and soggy when thawed. You may also lose vitamins during a slow freeze. All appliances have a quick-freeze compartment near the cooling coils, and many have a booster switch to enable you to get more power when you put food in.

3   Don't let food stay in the freezer indefinitely. A year or eighteen months is as long as you can reasonably expect anything to keep, and many foods go off sooner than this (see table below). Try to code or date every packet of your own produce, so that you always know what to use first. You can buy labels that will stick on plastic without peeling off in the cold. We simply cut out small pieces of coloured paper and seal them inside the bag, so that they cannot get lost.

4   Pack food in air- and moisture-tight material. This stops one food tainting another —fish and ice-cream, for example; and it helps prevent drying out and 'freezer burn', which is the effect of combined low temperatures and oxygen getting at the produce. Plastic freezer boxes are quite cheap, and polythene bags bought by the hundred from specialist companies are so inexpensive it is not worth using them a second time in the freezer. Shut the bags with clips or a heat-sealer—you can buy a small hand-operated one for about £10 or a practically automatic one for about £40.

5   Pack food in meal-size portions, then you will not have the bother of having to break up a pack and re-freeze part of it.

6   Do not let the freezer temperature rise above 0°F (—18°C); ideally it should run at —6°F (—21°C). If there is a power failure or other emergency, resist the temptation to open the freezer, kept tight shut and undisturbed, with luck it will stay cold for at least three days, unless you have recently put in fresh supplies.

7   All your home-grown vegetables, except herbs, need to be blanched (treated with boiling water or steam) before they are packed—unless, of course, you cook them completely before freezing, as with beetroot. This hot-water treatment destroys enzymes in the plants which can spoil the flavour, texture and food value in quite a short time. To blanch: cut or otherwise prepare your vegetables, and drop them into *ready-boiling* water for the set period (see table below). Drain off the water rapidly through a colander; wash the produce with cold water, then leave it to drain thoroughly. Pack it when cold. If you have a steamer, get the water boiling rapidly before you put the vegetables to steam, and again cool rapidly under the tap as soon as the blanching period is complete.

8   You can save yourself a lot of trouble by freezing your vegetables on flat trays covered with polythene; then, when they are quite hard, pack them into polythene bags. This stops them from freezing together into a large lump, and you can take out part of a bag without having to repack or re-freeze the rest.

9   Fruit is best frozen either in dry sugar (allow half the weight of the fruit, and sprinkle it so that each fruit is surrounded completely); or in syrup—40-per-cent sugar in water (8oz to a pint or 400g to a litre). Recommended methods are given below.

Deep-freezing your own produce

Fruit	Method	Storage life (months)
Apples	Peel, core, slice into slightly salted water, drain, dry sugar pack	12
Apples	Peel, core, slice direct into 40 per cent syrup	15
Apricots	Skin, stone, dry sugar pack	12
Blackberries	Dry sugar pack	12
Cherries	Stone if required, 40 per cent syrup	15
Currants (black, red, white)	Dry sugar pack	15
Gooseberries	Dry sugar pack	15
Greengages	Halve, stone, 40-per-cent syrup	15
Loganberries	Dry sugar pack	15
Peaches	Skin, halve, stone, 40 per cent syrup	12
Pears	Not really suitable for freezing	
Plums	Halve, stone, 40 per cent syrup	12
Raspberries	Dry sugar pack	15
Rhubarb	Boil, 40 per cent syrup	18
Strawberries	Dry sugar pack	12

Vegetables

Asparagus	Blanch 3 min water, 5 min steam	12
Aubergines	Slice, blanch 3 min water, 5 min steam	8
Beans, broad	Pod, blanch $2\frac{1}{2}$ min water, $4\frac{1}{2}$ min steam	8
Beans, runner	Cut, blanch 2 min water, 3 min steam	12
Beans, runner	Slice, blanch 1 min water, 2 min steam	12
Bean sprouts	Seal loosely in polythene	3 weeks
Beetroot	Boil completely; slice large beets	18
Broccoli	Separate florets, blanch 4 min water, 6 min steam	15
Brussels sprouts	Trim, blanch 3 min water, $4\frac{1}{2}$ min steam, freeze on flat before packing	15
Cabbage	Trim, slice, blanch $1\frac{1}{2}$ min water, 3 min steam	12
Carrots	Trim, slice large carrots, blanch 3 min water, 5 min steam	15
Cauliflower	Trim, separate florets, blanch 4 min water, 6 min steam	15
Mushrooms	Use buttons only, blanch 2 min water, 4 min steam	8

Parsnips	Trim, slice large parsnips, blanch water 2 min, steam 4 min	18
Peas	Pod, blanch 1 min water, 1½ min steam, freeze on flat	12
Peppers	Use green only, slice and remove heads and seeds (do not blanch)	6
Potatoes	Peel, chip, blanch 1 min water, 1½ min steam, freeze on flat	6
Spinach	Wash, separate, blanch 2 min water, 4 min steam	8
Swedes	Peel, dice, blanch 2 min water, 4 min steam	12
Sweet corn	Trim cobs, blanch 5 min water, 8 min steam	12
Sweet corn	Boil, strip grains, freeze on flat	12
Turnips	Peel, dice or slice, blanch 2 min water, 4 min steam	2

Preserved food and good health

Of the main diet factors, there is usually no difficulty in storing carbohydrates and fats, the calorie foods. Grain, honey, sugared preserves, butter, cheese and nuts all retain their energy value for long periods, and the usual trouble is that we tend to stuff ourselves with high-calorie food in the winter, to the detriment of our health and waistline.

Proteins are also easy to store: meat can be frozen, dried beans and peas keep for months, bacon, cheese and eggs can all be kept for a reasonable time in a cool place. The main shortages arise, as they have for centuries, in providing the essential vitamins during the winter months. A variety of vegetables is, on the whole, the best safeguard against vitamin deficiency. Preserved—and particularly frozen— ones can fill the gap when fresh vegetables are harder to come by. This is the real argument for the trouble of preserving produce and the cost of running a freezer— one week's loss of time through illness or lethargy due to diet deficiency can easily cost you more than running a couple of freezers throughout the year.

Vitamin A, essential for the health of the eyes and other organs, is destroyed by drying—and, for that matter, by any high-temperature treatment like roasting— but it is usually easy to get enough from carrots, green vegetables (brassicas go on through the winter), and butter or margarine (and full-cream cheeses). Freezing does not affect the vitamin, neither does pickling in salt or vinegar.

Vitamin B1 (thiamin) is rather more delicate, and is lost to a large extent during high-temperature cooking, such as baking and bottling. It is also soluble in water, so if you cook your food in a lot of water and then throw this away, you throw away the vitamin as well. Blanching of vegetables before freezing reduces the B1— though, if you have a lot of produce to freeze, you can save some loss by using the same water over and over again; this also saves fuel, if you don't have to heat up every batch from cold. Fortunately bread and potatoes, as well as fresh vegetables, contain thiamin, so you are unlikely to contract beri-beri, the deficiency disease, in Britain even in the winter.

Riboflavin occurs in bread, cheese and other milk products, and most vegetables, including pulses, like peas and lentils; green vegetables, and mushrooms (a good source). It is hardly affected by processing, except that it can be dissolved out in water; so dried, bottled, pickled or frozen foods retain their riboflavin. Light destroys it, however, so don't leave your bottled foods in the open or your milk on the doorstep.

Nicotinamide (niacin) is one of the most stable vitamins, and stands up well to drying, boiling, pickling and freezing. The most serious losses are invariably due to boiling food in too much water, so use conservative cooking methods. Meat, grains and most vegetables contain fair amounts of this vitamin. Beer contains nicotinamide *and* riboflavin, which may give some people a novel excuse for drinking.

Vitamin C (ascorbic acid), on the other hand, is the most difficult vitamin to get throughout the winter, and many people actually show signs of a shortage. Scurvy, the major deficiency disease, is fortunately rare, but minor symptoms are common: bad skin, broken blood vessels, minor wounds that will not heal up, and soreness or bleeding of the gums. The trouble is that vitamin C is destroyed by heat, light and exposure to air, so not only most methods of preserving, but even cutting up fresh food for cooking, cause losses. Freezing does the least damage, and you can ensure your winter vitamin C by storing frozen (not bottled) fruit; frozen vegetables, especially green-leafed ones, and some roots—swedes and turnips are quite a reasonable source. Potatoes are the main source of vitamin C in Britain, and provide most of the vitamin in the summer, but old potatoes from clamps have lost a lot of the vitamin before you get them.

Vitamin D (calciferol) is necessary for bone formation, so a shortage causes rickets. It is normally formed naturally in the skin by exposure to sunlight, so inevitably it tends to disappear in winter—and may be slightly lacking all the time if you live and work in a very dark area, or wear very concealing clothes. Fortunately the main food sources—butter, margarine, eggs, cheese and so on—are all easy to store throughout the winter. Once the vitamin is in a food, it is hardly affected at all by processing.

Vitamin B12 (cobalamin) is the only other vitamin that is likely to be deficient in even the most processed diet; ironically enough, shortages are normally confined to enthusiastic food reformers. Lack of B12 leads to pernicious anaemia—unfortunately, while the vitamin is fairly widely distributed in animal products such as meat, liver, eggs and cheese, it is almost entirely absent in most vegetable foods, so Vegans suffer more than the thoughtless mob of meat-eaters. Now for the good news: it is hardly affected by any kind of processing.

Home-grown Hooch

Wine and beer

From the true economic point of view—which is to say the proper utilisation of raw materials—brewing liquor from fruits and grains is not efficient. True, the alcohol has some energy value, but rather less than you could obtain from the sugar or starch it is made from. Many wines and beers contain valuable vitamins and minerals, but again only things that you could absorb more efficiently by eating the raw materials.

However, in the crazy money-system in which we have to live, making your own wine or beer is vastly cheaper than buying it—and, in psychological terms, most people would prefer to have a bottle of 1954 Château Margaux than a handful of 1954 sultanas, despite the fact that they are both basically grapes.

If you work with the normal fruits and grains, and follow the simple principles set out below, you should be able to turn out wholesome drinks at a fraction of the commercial cost.

Raw materials

All brewing operations depend on yeast breaking down sugars to alcohol. The sugar may be glucose or fructose naturally present in fruit or vegetable juice; lactose in milk (as in the eastern European drink *koumiss*, made from mares' milk); glucose made by breaking down starches in potatoes, grain, etc; extracts from sugary plants, such as molasses, used for rum; or refined sugar or honey added deliberately to the brew to increase the alcohol content.

There are several plants in the tropics that produce very sweet juices: the sugar cane itself, of course, and the toddy palm, used to make palm wine or arrack, but only one European plant—the grapevine—*regularly* makes enough sugar for a decent wine of full strength. Cherries, apples, and so on, make weaker wines, which sometimes do not keep. Most other products need help from added sugar, or the conversion of starch to sugar by malting (see page 178).

However, it is worth looking at the available resources of starch and sugar in a number of fruits and vegetables:

	Sugar per cent	Starch per cent
Apples (eating)	11	0.3
Apples (cooking)	9	0.4
Apricots	˙7	—
Bananas (peeled)	16	3
Blackberries	6	—
Cherries (eating)	12	—
Currants (black)	6	—
Currants (red)	4	—
Currants (white)	6	—
Damsons	10	—
Gooseberries	9	—
Grapes (black)	13	—
Grapes (white)	16	—
Greengages	11	—
Loganberries	3	—
Medlars	9	—
Peaches	8	—
Pears (eating)	11	—
Pears (cooking)	9	—
Pineapple	12	—
Plums (eating, Victorias)	9	—
Plums (cooking)	6	—
Raisins (dried)	64	—
Raspberries	6	—
Beetroot (boiled)	6	—
Carrots (raw)	5	—
Parsnips (raw)	9	2.5
Potatoes (old)	0.5	20.3
Swedes (raw)	4	0.1
Turnips (raw)	4	—
Barley	—	70
Maize	1	68
Oats	—	60
Rice (polished)	—	79
Rye	—	72
Wheat	—	71
Golden syrup	79	—
Honey	76	—
Molasses (blackstrap)	67	—

So, for example, if you were making a gallon of parsnip wine, and had 4lb of parsnips, this would give you $(9 + 2\frac{1}{2})$ per cent of mixed sugar and starch—as it all ends up the same way, it is quite sound to add them together. This amounts to about $7\frac{1}{2}$oz of fermentable material. You could add 1lb of raisins, which will give you a further $10\frac{1}{2}$oz. If you want $2\frac{1}{3}$lb of sugar/starch per gallon, a normal figure, you must therefore add a further 1lb 6oz of sugar per gallon. [In metric terms: if you want 5l of wine, and have 2kg of parsnips, this provides 230g fermentable material. A further 226g of raisins will give 320g more. If you need a total of 1,250g of sugar/starch, you must add 700g of sugar to your 5l batch].

Yeast

This is a living organism, and the requirements of its life-style account for much of the complication and mystery in fermenting. You will usually find that it behaves if you note the following points:

1   Yeast dies if it gets too hot, and gets sluggish when it is cold. Try to keep your brews in the 60–80°F (15–25°C) range. In any case, when the temperature gets over 80°F, alcohol starts to evaporate at a serious rate, and bacterial attack is encouraged. A warm cupboard can easily be fitted up for fermenting, with a small lamp or heater worked by a thermostat if you want to get really organised.

2   Yeast needs organic material to grow on, just like a plant. Most fruits and vegetables provide this, but if you have rather a 'thin' brew with a lot of plain sugar, add ammonium phosphate as a 'fertiliser'. You can buy this as yeast nutrient.

3   Yeast needs air to multiply, so there is a first stage in fermenting where you leave the wine in an accessible tub or bin so that you can stir it and work air in. Once you have enough yeast, you can let it work in the absence of air (anaerobically, the second stage) in bottles or barrels (see below).

4   Yeast is eventually killed off by the alcohol it produces. Some yeasts, such as ordinary bakers' yeast, may be killed by alcohol at 8 per cent or even lower, but special wine yeasts have been developed that struggle on until the alcohol level is around 15 per cent. Your own yeast will gradually adapt itself by natural selection to take higher concentrations of alcohol. The 15-per-cent level is about the top for any yeast, and as this will be produced from roughly 30-per-cent sugar or starch (3lb to the gallon, 300g per litre), any sugar over this concentration will never be fermented and will stay in the wine as sweetener. If you come across a home-made wine that is sickly sweet, it is often because the maker did not realise this limitation, and just bunged in sugar in the hopes of making stronger wine.

Other organisms

There are other organisms just as interested as yeast in your sugar solution and they will try any tricks to get into it. Unfortunately, the most common ones are the acetic acid bacteria that turn wine to vinegar (see page 161). Fruit flies—tiny things that will be depressingly familiar to any wine-maker—carry large numbers of these bacteria and can thus infect the wine. You should therefore cover all vessels carefully; wash everything that has had fruit or juice in it, and treat all bottles, funnels, corks and so on with a solution of sodium metabisulphite (1oz per pint of water; 50g per litre). You can also put this solution in a fermentation lock (see below) to make sure that bacteria do not sneak in through this.

Metabisulphite is also used to kill bacteria naturally present on the fruit; it is fairly harmless to yeast. This is a tricky job on the small scale, and some people prefer to sterilise the fruit by bringing it almost to the boil, then cooling before fermenting. You can buy measured amounts of metabisulphite in the form of Campden tablets from wine-makers' suppliers; follow the manufacturers' instructions.

Carbon dioxide

When yeast works on sugar solutions, it converts about half the weight of sugar into alcohol, and the rest into carbon dioxide gas. You can see and hear the bubbles when fermentation is going well, and in fact a gallon of wine of average strength produces about 12 cu ft of the gas during making (5l of wine give 380l of gas). Obviously, if you bottle up wine in a closed container before this process has finished, a build-up of pressure will blow out the cork or perhaps burst the bottle. Yet you need to keep air and bacteria out of the wine, so you must have protection of some kind.

51 Fermentation lock for wine making.

The most efficient way to do this is to fit a fermentation lock (Figure 51) to the top of the container. This has a little pool of liquid—preferably bisulphite solution—which allows gas to bubble out from the wine but stops anything getting in. If you don't want to go to this trouble, close your bottles with corks *very lightly* pushed in, or tie paper or parchment over the top, until you are quite sure that fermentation has stopped.

The exception to this is making bottled beer, with some gas in it. Here you let the fermentation go to completion, taking care that the alcohol content is not above 8 per cent, then put the beer into bottles with a spoonful of sugar in each bottle. This gives the yeast something to work on, and a small amount of gas is produced. Sparkling wines are made the same way.

Clearing wine

Apart from alcohol and the flavouring compounds from your fruit or vegetables, your wine will contain residues of fruit, dead and living yeast cells, and other debris. The large bits you can strain off before you put the wine into bottles or barrels; the rest has to settle naturally—you can filter wine, but it is a long and usually unsatisfactory job on the small scale. When the debris has settled, carefully pour or siphon the clear wine into another container. This is known as racking.

Tannin, which is present in most fruits—in the skins of grapes, for example, and very obviously in damsons and sloes—helps to speed up the settling process. Some fruits contain very little tannin; there is none at all in vegetables or flowers, so recipes for, say, parsnip or elderflower wine may specify cold tea as one of the ingredients. You can try this yourself if your wines do not clear properly.

Acid is necessary for the most efficient fermentation. Most fresh fruit contains enough, but dried fruit, vegetables, and honey need some added. Lemon juice can be used, or you can buy powdered citric or tartaric acid from a chemist or winemakers' supplier. Go easy with it, unless you like alcoholic vinegar.

Basic wine recipe

Taking into account all these requirements, it is possible to make up a general method for wine which should give a drinkable product, and you can then go on to adapt it to your own tastes and raw materials.

Take 3lb (1.4kg) of fruit or vegetables of the sugary kind, and 2pts (1l) of water. Crush or pulp the fruit in the water, and boil the vegetables till soft. Heat the fruit to about 180°F (80°C). Put your pulp in a bucket or tub (plastic or wooden, never metal) with a cover to keep out fruit flies. Calculate how much sugar your raw material contains (see page 175). Weigh out enough sugar to make this up to 2lb (1kg) total, dissolve this in 6pts (3.4l) of warm water, and add it to the stock in the bucket.

Add about 1oz (30g) of yeast and 1oz (30g) of ammonium phosphate (and either the juice of 2 lemons or 4g of tartaric acid, if you are working with vegetables). Cover the vessel, and let the mixture ferment at about 60°F (15°C) for 8–10 days. Then strain off the solids, squeeze out any liquid trapped in the mass, clean out the fermentation vessel, and put the liquid back in it. For a medium to dry wine, add a further 1lb (454g) of sugar; for a sweet wine use 1½lb (.75kg). Leave the mixture to ferment again for about 4 days, then strain it into a gallon jar fitted with a fermentation lock; put it in a warm place (around 60–65°F, 15–17°C) and leave it until all signs of bubbling have ceased. Pour it carefully, or siphon, into another bottle to collect the clear(ish) wine and leave the sediment. You may have to 'rack off' like this several times. Leave the wine for at least 4 months, longer if possible, before drinking any.

You can scale up these quantities as much as you like—you may have fruit and sugar to spare. Many batches seem to work better on the large scale and, of course, you lose less, proportionately, in straining, racking off and similar separations. A 20gal plastic water butt with a lid makes a good vat.

Malt

You can ferment starchy things with yeast, but it is rather slow, because it has to break down the starch to sugar before it can make alcohol. A centuries-old way of speeding up this process is to let grain sprout, which naturally produces sugar by enzyme activity. Barley does this particularly easily, and the process is called 'malting'.

You can malt barley on the small scale by an adaptation of the method for making mung bean sprouts (page 98). Get a large food can or similar container of about ½gal (2.25l) capacity, and punch a few holes in the lid to drain off water without letting the barley grains through. Half-fill it with clean dry barley, soak the grain in warm water for twelve hours, then drain off the surplus water and leave the barley to sprout at about 70–75°F (21–23°C). Moisten it with warm water from time to time, but do not let it get submerged for long. When the sprouts are about half the length of the grains (after around four days), the malt is ready for drying.

The intensity of the drying makes a lot of difference to the taste and colour of the malt and the liquor you produce from it. If you bake it very lightly so that its colour does not change appreciably, the malt will contain a lot of sugar, but will not develop the characteristic 'malty' taste. If you put your sprouted barley in the oven on a baking tray, or in your solar dryer, and dry it until it is only just browning, you can produce such a light malt. This can be used for pale beers of the lager or American style, or even for wine, as an extra source of sugar. Purists may shudder at the thought of mixing grain and fruit, but in fact a light malt gives no 'beery' taste to the brew. This is one way to get over the problem of sugar supplies for wine, if you do not want to use commercial sources. You can also add malt to other starchy materials, like potatoes or wheat, to speed up their breakdown to sugar.

If you roast the malt until it is golden brown—in an oven (your solar heater will not get hot enough)—you get the normal malty taste and a beer that is amber. Further roasting makes 'black malt' and dark beers like porter or stout, with a taste of burnt sugar from the caramelised malt.

Hops

Traditionally used to flavour beer, hops have no effect on the alcohol, whatever the advertisements imply. Apart from the bitterness, they help to preserve the beer. You can grow your own hops (see page 94), or buy them ready-dried from wine-makers' suppliers. While the quantity used is a matter of taste, for a start try 2oz of dried hops per gallon of beer (65g per 5l).

Basic beer recipe

Beer is usually less alcoholic than wine, except barley wines that can be up to 15-per-cent alcohol. If you are going to drink the stuff by the pint, far better to work at 6–8 per cent—even this is stronger than some commercial brews.

Take 5lb of malt, roasted to the colour you fancy; beat it with a mallet to crack the grains, and soak it in 1gal of water (2.5kg malt to 5l), warming the water to 140°F (60°C) and maintaining this temperature for several hours. The idea is to let the enzymes in the malt work on the starch and convert it to sugar; if you use cold water the process is very slow, but if you steep at more than about 140°F (60°C) you run the risk of destroying the enzymes by heat. After about 12 hours, or whatever you can manage in the way of steeping, strain off the liquor ('wort'), squeezing out as much as possible from the malt residues, and boil the wort with 2oz of dried hops (65g for 5l). You can just dunk the hops in and strain them off again, but it saves time and trouble to put the hops in a cotton or muslin bag and tie or sew it up; then you can simply lift it out when the boiling (about 20 minutes is enough) is over. If you want stronger beer, start off with more malt, or add sugar—up to 1½lb per gallon (.75kg per 5l)—at the wort stage, but the quantities given will make quite a strong brew without additions.

Let the wort cool to about 98°F (37°C), add yeast, and ferment as for the wine recipe, except that you will not have to add extra sugar half way through. This beer should be ready for drinking in about a week or two. If you want a bottled beer of the gassy sort, wait until the fermentation has completely stopped, then take some clean beer bottles with good screw stoppers, put a BS teaspoonful of brown sugar into the bottom of each one, fill them with your beer, and screw them down. Don't be tempted to put in more sugar to make the beer stronger—you will just burst the bottles. If you want it stronger, start the whole fermentation process with more malt or sugar.

Cider

Cider is difficult to make in the traditional style—by fermenting pure apple juice—because not many varieties of apple produce enough juice or enough sugar. Most people are more naturally interested in cider as a way of using up surplus apples as they come. The best solution is to use the basic wine recipe (see page 177), with 3lb of apples per gallon (1.5kg per 5l) and added sugar to make up the total. With cider, as with beer, don't overdo the strength if you intend to drink pints—a total of 1½lb of sugar per gallon (.75kg per 5l) is plenty, taking the apple sugar and added sugar together.

We find it best to boil most varieties of apple—partly because apples are usually earmarked for cider when they are scarcely fit for eating or cooking, and the boiling at least helps to sterilise them; and partly because it releases the juice from the hard, crisp type of eating apple. The only disadvantage is that this also releases pectin, which can make the cider slow to settle.

Such cider looks, and tastes, quite drinkable after about two months, but if you aim for crystal clarity you can buy a commercial enzyme, *pectinase*, that breaks down the last cloudy specks of pectin. This can be used in other fruit wines, for the same purpose.

Mead

If you have only tasted commercial mead, which is usually imported grape juice flavoured with a little honey, you can have no idea of the distinction of real mead, made entirely with honey. It is a luxury well worth indulging if you can get hold of honey in bulk.

Honey usually contains about 75-per-cent sugar (see page 174), to obtain maximum alcoholic strength make up 4lb of honey to a gallon (2kg to 5l) with water. Very tolerable mead can be made with lower strength, and 2lb per gallon (1kg per 5l) is more appropriate for quaffing from goblets. For best results add the juice of 2 lemons or 4g of tartaric or citric acid for each gallon (5l). Some people add cold tea, for tannin, but nothing much needs to be cleared from mead so this is an unnecessary addition and may spoil the delicate flavour of the honey. Try to keep your mead—it really improves with time.

Storage Costs

Most of the costs of food storage, where they are quantifiable at all, are very low compared with the value of the produce. By collecting every bottle and jar you can lay your hands on—especially glass ones with well-fitting lids or caps—you can keep your dried food, jams, pickles and wine properly packed for almost no outlay. For larger amounts, empty sweet jars may be obtained from a confectioner, although some of these are now thin PVC and not much use for long-term storage. Wooden barrels are sometimes available second-hand from importers of fruit juice and similar commodities—you will find them advertised in the *Exchange and Mart* and gardening magazines; use these for wine or cut them in half to make sauerkraut tubs or salting vats. Wash them out carefully with several changes of hot water— you can usually tell by the smell whether you have got rid of all the sour juice— and, when used for wine or sauerkraut, rinse them with sodium metabisulphite solution (page 176) as a final precaution.

Stoneware crocks and jars tend to be collectors' items now, and very overpriced. You can occasionally pick them up in out-of-the-way junk shops, and they are well worth having.

The freezer

This is not only a substantial capital item, but has running costs. Unless your garden is very small or you are very unlucky with your crops, about 20 cu ft (570l) of freezer capacity will be needed for the average family living on its own produce. As this is larger than any domestic freezer, you have to decide whether to buy two or get a semi-commercial freezer. You may be lucky and find a second-hand commercial model, but because of discounts, special offers and general availability, it is usually cheaper to get two domestic models than buy a new commercial one.

Two chest freezers, each of 12–14 cu ft (340–400l) capacity, will hold upwards of 700lb (320kg) of assorted food; they will cost you, new, about £300 if you shop around. You can get second-hand and reconditioned models, and these are usually a good buy, because freezers are among the more reliable of domestic electrical appliances. If you buy a new one, it should give you about twenty years' active service, so the annual amortisation is about £15. The running costs will be roughly 1.8 kilowatt-hours (units) per cubic foot per week, or a total of 2,500 units per year —say, £56.

Don't add unnecessary costs by entering into an annual servicing agreement. It is surprising—except perhaps to the cynic—how often a freezer which has been running perfectly well seems to need attention and extensive repairs after being 'serviced'. Many of the things which can go wrong with a freezer can be put right without a refrigeration engineer's experience. If you keep your freezer in a cool, dry area you should not really anticipate much trouble—damp surroundings can cause corrosion, which means expensive repairs.

Insurance of the contents may be worth your while if you store a lot of expensive cuts of meat, but most insurance policies specifically exclude losses due to deliberate power cuts.

Against your costs, set the gains. You can store around 700lb (320kg) of food for the winter months and other times of shortage, and even if most of it is in the form of garden vegetables, it can easily be worth £250–300 at market prices during those periods, so you are making an easy profit even after deducting the cost of producing the food. Add to this the more intangible benefits of having a constant supply of food with the minimum loss of vitamins and other food value, and the argument for the freezer is even more convincing.

Surplus Produce

Having worked hard at your garden in a reasonable year, planting a few extra thises and thats to allow for crop failure, there will probably come a time when you have far more produce than you will need in the next year. Even when you have squirrelled away what you can and given some to a deserving cause or to the man who showed you how to prune, there may still be a surplus.

Selling from a stall

You could just take a table down to the gate, and set up a stall and clear the lot in a couple of hours—but your first customer would probably be a policeman asking if you had a street trader's licence, and the second a snooper from the local council wanting to know if you have permission to change your house into a shop.

The best sales from wayside stalls are made on main or busy roads. If people can pull off the road into your own driveway, this is all right, provided you have the licences; but you must not encourage them to stop or wait on double yellow lines or a clearway, or cause an obstruction anywhere. You can set up a stall in a layby, but only temporarily—and with the permission of the local authority, for ordinary roads, or the county council, for trunk roads. If you sell from a car moving about, or go from door to door, you will need a pedlar's licence—costing about £1 for variable periods—and will get some old-fashioned looks at the police station when you ask for one.

If there is a regular market in the town, you could try to rent a stall on a casual basis. Approach the market superintendant well in advance; make sure there is a stall available and that your goods will be accepted. Naturally, the regular traders who work the markets all the time have priority; if there are four of them already selling fruit and vegetables in a small market, it is unlikely you will be allowed to set up shop as well.

The rent for a stall usually works out quite reasonably, if you have plenty to sell. A typical northern market may charge £1.50 a day; in the south it is more likely to be £2.50 to £3, and some places charge extra for a temporary market traders' licence, which might double the cost. You are provided with a stall, board and canvas cover, but you have to provide your own scales, which should have certified weights. If any customer complains of having been short-weighted, the inspector of weights and measures may check and can prosecute you. Your kitchen scales might be accurate, but check them first or allow a bit extra in every bag—though this will lower your profit. You will need a plastic cover for delicate fruit, in case it pours, and a macintosh for yourself—same reason.

For selling, you will want paper bags, which might be created out of twisted cornets of newspaper; boxes for display and carrying the goods to and fro; price tickets; a secure satchel for money and a float of small change to start you off; and, if you mind about your hands getting filthy from handling coins, a pair of gloves.

Find out what rules apply to vehicles delivering to the market in the morning and where you can park safely during the day, without incurring a fine which would dent your profits. If there is no easy access to the stall, enquire about use of trolleys or bring a pram.

Wash all the produce and trim off stems. Pack it securely to withstand the journey and humping to the stall. Small fruit is best pre-weighed and sold in containers, especially if it won't take much handling. Cost this bit of the operation very carefully. Unless you have adequate packaging material to re-cycle, the boxes could cost more than the fruit.

Don't try to work a stall alone for a whole day. It is astonishingly hard on the feet, if you aren't used to it, and even the most iron-bladdered will need to go to the loo some time. Two pairs of eyes are better than one when light-fingered children are about—besides, you will need moral support as an amateur in a competitive profession.

The market folk are tough, but cheerful and friendly—as long as you are. Pulling rank or playing helpless will get you nowhere. But don't expect to be let into the fellowship that has been forged over years of working different markets in all weathers. And don't try to undercut the other traders' prices. They have a living to make and they won't appreciate this a bit; it is too bad if playing children crash into your stall and upset all the fruit, or a van splashes a puddle over it and you—accidentally, of course. Try to avoid being placed next to a regular trader selling exactly the same produce. Probably the market superintendent will avoid this, but you could ask if there is a choice of site.

Unless you have enough produce of your own to fill a stall, the operation won't be economic. Even though the stock comes 'free', there are still the overheads to consider: rent, packaging, transport, equipment and any extra costs, like baby-sitters or loss of wages.

The Women's Institute may have a stall in the market which would sell your produce. They pay the rent, provide the scales and possibly the bags; you might or might not have to do full-time selling. The WI takes a cut of the profits. If they have had a stall there for any length of time, the natural suspicion of the market traders will have changed to resigned acceptance, from which you will benefit.

If you do run a stall or join WI's, check first before bulking out the produce with home-made cakes, cheese or wine. Some markets just don't allow prepared foods; others do, but you will have to comply with all kinds of food and hygiene regulations. You must provide washing facilities, have a loo nearby, and cover all prepared food with plastic against flies. You can't sell home-made wine without a licence, for example, and a good many other commodities are affected by some bit of legislation or another. The environmental health department of the local authority can tell you about this.

In some areas, Sunday markets are run on disused airfields or similar out-of-the-way places. These are generally illegal, because of the antiquated Sunday trading laws, but much more free and easy, once the initial fee has been paid. You must be prepared to pack and run for it if the police decide to put a stop to it—but mostly they have too much sense to bother about it. They do have to act if a local trader complains, though, and when they do you lose your stall and profit.

Selling to a shop

You could try selling through local shops. The greengrocer will have regular contracts with commercial growers, but if you offer him produce which is very early, or out of the ordinary or specially fine, he might buy it from you so as to be able to display it as 'local grown'. A general shop of the more enterprising sort might accept your produce, even if it does not normally sell fresh vegetables. Tomatoes or strawberries early in the season will sell anywhere; old carrots or cabbage, on the other hand, are doubtful starters. Take a sample of your wares, well presented in a box, to a shop to see if the owner is interested. He will expect strawberries or raspberries to be in punnets, to save them being damaged by handling; these cost money and will reduce your profit. The price he offers you will bear very little resemblance to the price he will charge his customers; and the more perishable your goods, the less you are in a position to haggle.

Growing for sale

An unplanned surplus is most likely to occur at the end of the season, when it has no scarcity value—unless you grow nectarines or Chinese cabbage. If you are really keen to sell, perhaps you should set out from the start to grow something marketable. Sound out your markets first: make sure that your ideas are acceptable and fix a tentative date. To keep that deadline, you may have to protect your crops with glass; the purchase of this will dent your profits the first year, but be re-usable afterwards.

The crops most likely to sell on a small scale and a casual basis are earlies, exotics and certain 'old-fashioned' varieties. You will certainly need glass and a favourable growing area, if your earlies are to live up to their name. You may be able, without impoverishing yourself, to undercut a distant commercial grower sufficiently for the local shopkeeper to consider it worth his while to take your produce—since transport costs add a lot to central-market prices.

Exotics and old-fashioneds are probably easier to grow competitively. Most commercial growers go for the big markets and don't bother with items for which there is not a large guaranteed sale all over the country. Asparagus has a limited season, and therefore a limited public. You may be able to supply enough from a good-sized bed to meet local demand. Chicory, endive, leeks, herbs, globe artichokes, or the Chinese and Japanese varieties of plant might all sell well.

Commercial growers have practically stopped producing some types of fruit, like raspberries and greengages, because they don't travel well into and out of central markets. Delivered locally, they are quite unharmed. Some of the popular varieties of apples, plums, tomatoes, lettuces, etc are no longer grown commercially because they don't yield huge crops or uniform sizes. In a high-class area, there will be a sale for these 'old-fashioneds' among people who value good flavour.

Cacti, another cash crop which can be produced on a small scale, grow easily from seed and even more easily from offsets. A few bought-in plants will reproduce themselves for ever. You will need winter shelter, a lot of tiny pots and labels, potting soil and pea gravel—plus a good book, such as *The Pocket Encyclopaedia of Cacti in Colour* by Edgar and Brian Lamb, to help you identify the plants.

If your crops can be classed as 'organically grown'—which they can be once your compost is under way—you might be able to sell them to a 'whole food' restaurant. These enterprises are generally run by amateurs, who are quite happy to deal with other amateurs. Unfortunately, they often lose enthusiasm or go bust, so you may find yourself minus a market at an awkward time. You could get together with some friends and start your own bistro—with home-grown food a speciality.

Setting up in business brings problems in its wake: VAT, income tax, accounts, licences. The odd casual sale is neither here nor there, but when done regularly, especially if you make a success of it, someone is bound to bring it to the attention of the authorities. If you are asked to declare your profits, then do just that—deducting the cost of seeds, pots, packaging, peat, soil, nutrients and labour from what you have received from sales.

Exchange or barter

If you do not fancy getting involved in the commercial side of gardening, try advertising your surplus produce in the local paper or on a newsagent's noticeboard, and pass the word round among your friends and people at work. You may be able to arrange the exchange or barter of surpluses between a group of neighbours. Do this in advance of planting, and agree who will grow a possible surplus of which crop; otherwise everybody will have lettuces, or apples, and consumer resistance develops. Decide on a fair basis for exchange—by weight or by value of produce—and keep a solemn record of debits and credits. If one person is for ever popping round for the odd pound of tomatoes, you must be sure how much in produce she owes, otherwise things can get nasty and local feuds build up.

Plant Foods

Chemicals v. organics

The popular picture of a self-sufficient agricultural community or unit is one in which nothing ever needs to be brought in or taken out. By a mysterious, intricate, but laudably natural series of processes, everything is recycled; all the wastes find use as raw materials for the next generation of plants or animals, and life is as self-contained as the inside of a bottle-garden. The theory is that, as long as you return the dung and composted vegetable wastes to the soil, your eco-system will flourish for ever. Sadly, although the picture is often painted very attractively—and certainly dung and compost are immensely valuable—the great plan does not work out very well in practice. There are too many losses.

Soil is so complex that, for every process that tends to increase natural fertility, there is a contrary one that works against it. Rain washes out soluble nutrient salts from the earth, and carries them, via the rivers, to fertilise seaweed. Phosphates react with lime or acids also present in the soil and become so insoluble that the plant roots cannot assimilate them. Denitrifying bacteria break down the nitrates that have been laboriously built up by the nitrifying bacteria.

Once you start to take crops away from the growing area these losses become even greater—for example, every ton of wheat harvested removes from the soil about 65lb (30kg) of nitrogen, 55lb (25kg) of potash, and 30lb (14kg) of phosphates; and other plants have similar appetites. Of course, you can replace some of these materials by composting the waste from the vegetables, but all the other losses have to be made up from sources outside your own land, whether you rely on dung carted from horses and cattle fed and grazed elsewhere; phosphates dug out of the ground, or ammonium salts from chemical factories.

However, although we must accept that strict self-sufficiency is not possible, there is no need to go to the other extreme. Gardeners, smallholders and farmers buy and spread far too much fertiliser, most of which goes to waste. Encouraged by the advertisements of the large fertiliser companies, they seem to think that, if two bags of 'Phosphoblogg' doubles the crop yield, four bags will quadruple it. Plants do not work that way. Fertiliser, whether organic or artificial, should be used like salt in cooking: not too little, but certainly not too much.

The aim for the businesslike grower should be to find out the optimum quantities of each nutrient for the particular crop and soil, and then to shop around for the cheapest and most effective way of obtaining any extra nutrients that may be needed. The following notes may help you when it comes to choosing a fertilizer.

Nitrogen sources

Nitrogen compounds play a key role in the nucleus of every plant cell, so a certain amount of nitrogen is essential for every crop. However, leaves and stems need more than the rest of the plant, so it follows that produce grown specifically for the leaves—such as lettuce, cabbages, brussels sprouts, globe artichokes and, of course, grass—needs more nitrogen, than those plants grown for edible stalks, such as celery, asparagus and rhubarb. Plants grown for their fruit, seeds or pods, and roots do not need as much nitrogen, and indeed may give poor results if over-fed with nitrogenous fertilisers. Root crops like carrots and beet, for example, tend to produce luxuriant foliage and tiny twisted roots if their soil is too rich in nitrogen.

Plants live in an atmosphere that is roughly four-fifths nitrogen gas, but unfortunately they cannot absorb the gas itself. They can only take up the necessary nutrient in the form of soluble nitrates or ammonium salts in the soil. Some nitrates—annually about 11lb per acre (12kg per hectare)—are formed by lightning flashes; the nitrogen and oxygen in the air are united by the electrical arc, and a very dilute solution of nitric acid comes down in the rain during thunderstorms.

Nitrifying bacteria that live in the soil, and more particularly in the root-nodules of peas, beans, and other pulses, can absorb nitrogen gas from the air and turn it into usable plant food—hence the importance of beans in most systems of crop rotation (see page 61). Their roots, left in the ground, serve as a reservoir of nitrogenous material for the next crop. Unfortunately the work of the nitrifying bacteria tends to be undermined by a busy little tribe of denitrifying bacteria that can convert nitrates back into nitrogen gas. This is why the nitrifying bacteria dispersed generally through the soil do not in fact have much effect on the nitrogen content; it is only when they are concentrated in colonies, as on bean roots, that they manage to keep ahead in the nitrate race.

The other main natural source of nitrogen is any plant or animal that has died on the land. Various groups of bacteria break down the complex nitrogen compounds in proteins, cell nuclei and so on, and eventually release these as simple nitrates that can be assimilated by plant roots.

Where plants need more nitrogen than is provided by these natural processes, there is a wide choice of supplementary sources, which are listed below in order of nitrogen value.

Nitrogenous fertilisers

	per cent Nitrogen	Other Nutrients	Comments
Urea	42–46	none	quick acting, produces slightly acid conditions
Urea-formaldehyde	36–40	none	slower acting, produces slightly acid conditions
Ammonium nitrate (nitram)	34.5	none	quick acting, produces slightly acid conditions
Ammonium sulphate (sulphate of ammonia)	21	none	quick acting, produces very acid conditions
Calcium cyanamide	21	calcium	quick acting, produces alkaline conditions
Sodium nitrate (Chile saltpetre)	16	none	quick acting, produces slightly alkaline conditions
Nitro-chalk	15.5	calcium	quick acting, produces alkaline conditions
Calcium nitrate	15	calcium	quick acting, produces alkaline conditions
Hoof and horn meal	13	phosphates (small amount)	slow acting
Dried blood	10	phosphates (very small amount)	fairly slow acting
Fish meal	9	phosphates	slow acting
Pigeon manure	6	phosphates, potassium, calcium	slow acting
Ammoniated superphosphate	3–6	phosphates	quick acting, almost neutral
Tea leaves	4	phosphates, potassium	slow acting
Meat and bone meal	4	phosphates, potassium, calcium	slow acting
Bone meal (steamed)	3	phosphates, calcium	slow acting
Seaweed meal	2	phosphates, potassium	slow acting
Dried sewage sludge	2	phosphates, potassium	slow acting
Fresh horse manure	1–2	phosphates, potassium	slow acting
Poultry deep litter	$1\frac{1}{2}$	phosphates, potassium	slow acting

	per cent Nitrogen	Other Nutrients	Comments
Mushroom bed compost	I	phosphates, potassium, calcium	slow acting
Fresh poultry manure	$\frac{1}{2}$	phosphates, potassium	slow acting
Fresh pig manure	$\frac{1}{2}$	phosphates, potassium	slow acting
Fresh cow manure	$\frac{1}{2}$	phosphates, potassium	slow acting
Garden compost (average)	$\frac{1}{2}$	phosphates, potassium	slow acting

These are the cold facts about nitrogenous fertilisers; the large chemical manu-facturers have predictably devoted a great deal of publicity to the high percentage of nitrogen in their products, and the low figures of the 'natural' materials. How-ever, before you rush out and buy hundredweights of urea or ammonium nitrate, consider carefully where and when you might need additional nitrogen, if at all, and how much.

Taking, for example, vegetables such as cabbage, brussels sprouts and kale, grown exclusively for leaf production, these obviously need more nitrogen than most other plants. Yet if you lift a 4lb (1.8kg) cabbage, you are only removing from the soil about ⅓oz (9g) of nitrogen; allowing for losses from denitrifying bacteria and nutrients leached away by the rain, the total nitrogen loss per plant is about ⅔oz (18g). If you grow the cabbages at the intervals recommended on page 106 this amounts to about 1⅓oz (37g) of nitrogen per square yard (44g per square metre).

You could obviously provide this necessary replacement with 4oz (113g) of ammonium nitrate or 8oz (226g) of nitro-chalk, but 8lb (3.6kg) of ordinary compost —a bucketful—will make up the loss just as well, and costs practically nothing. Some agricultural writers sneer at compost because of its very low analytical figures for nitrogen, phosphates, potash, and so on, but this totally ignores the fact that, even in a small garden, you can easily accumulate a ton or so of excellent com-post just by processing vegetable waste, weeds, grass cuttings and fallen leaves. A ton of compost may only contain as much nutrient material as a hundredweight of branded fertiliser, but it costs a lot less.

In addition, compost provides humus, an essential ingredient for good soil which is more difficult to put a price to. Humus is the generic name for the mass of fibres left after the softer parts of vegetable materials have rotted away; the fibres them-selves disappear in time, but this process takes much longer, and meanwhile they fulfil several vital roles in the health of the soil.

First, the presence of this network of fibres helps to retain a controlled amount of moisture, just like a sponge, and holds together particles of soil in an elastic 'crumb' structure, so that the surface does not dry out very easily, and in any case does not break down to dust in dry or windy weather. One of the most damaging effects of the long-term and exclusive use of artificial fertilisers, as in much modern farming, is that this network of fibres, present in the virgin soil, finally decomposes and cannot be replaced, because no vegetable waste is returned to the ground. The result is erosion of the topsoil, either by water, which washes away the loose powdery soil, or by the wind, as in a dust-bowl. The topsoil is literally blown away, leaving only the hard infertile subsoil. Once this has been allowed to happen, the land is ruined. Cash crops are out of the question, and only years of careful planting and ploughing in the green manure crops (see page 26) can revive it—and, of course, this costs money.

Apart from purely mechanical improvement of the soil, the fibres in humus also play a part in the natural processes of nitrogen provision. The bacteria that produce nitrates from more complex nitrogen compounds need oxygen to thrive, and humus fibres assist them by making air channels through the soil, and holding these open even when the earth is pressed flat. The deeper the penetration of humus, the more nitrate you will get in your soil, and working in humus will improve the fertility as well as the texture of heavy or clay soils. Straw and similar vegetable matter with hollow stems can help in the same way; and, of course, the tunnels made by earthworms are extremely useful for admitting air—the only trouble is that the worms will come only if there is already some nutrient in the soil.

Lastly, humus acts as a long-term food supply for the many kinds of bacteria that live in the soil and are essential for its health. Worms again help in this process, by dragging bits of leaves and dead vegetation deep into the ground, where they act as a nucleus for colonies of bacteria.

Fibrous manures—such as hoof and horn meal, seaweed, animal dung mixed with straw, and similar materials—are therefore always to be preferred to simple inorganic salts, if you obtain them at an economic price. However, 'organic' manures have no magic powers; they are simply sources of useful chemicals. Plants absorb nitrates, not the elixir of life—and plants do not care whether their nitrates come from ICI or the dung of sacred cows.

If your plot needs nitrogen in a hurry, do not be too proud to buy artificial manures. They may well spell the difference between success and failure in the early years, before you have had a chance to build up a stock of good compost. Just try to work towards a system that provides not only nutrients, but humus.

Of the commercial nitrogenous fertilisers, the cheapest, in terms of cost per unit weight of nitrogen, is usually ammonium sulphate. Its major disadvantage in most situations is its extreme acidity—as you will notice if you handle the powder without gloves and happen to have a cut or graze on your hands—which tends to upset the balance of the soil. You cannot correct this acidity by adding lime or other alkaline materials, because they merely cause the loss of all the nitrogen in a smelly and expensive cloud of ammonia gas (see page 194 for more details on the compatibilities of various fertiliser materials).

However, it can be used in moderation on chalky soils, and the acid finds two

specific uses in the garden: in the form of 'lawn sand', ammonium sulphate mixtures kill moss and other weeds on grassland (as the mixture is washed into the soil,
of course, the nitrogen is then available to give a boost to the grass leaf production),
and ammonium sulphate is also useful as an activator for compost. A little sprinkled
over the heap seems to speed up the breakdown of fibrous materials. Do not use
very much in this way, as most of the nitrogen is lost during the process, and does
not contribute to the ultimate food value of the compost.

Urea and ammonium nitrate are almost as cheap in terms of weight of nitrogen
per unit cost, and far less acid-producing. Neither of these fertilisers should be
mixed with lime or other alkalis, as this will cause loss of nitrogen in the form of
ammonia, but they seem to tolerate chalky soil quite well, and may help to balance
the pH a little more towards neutrality. Urea-formaldehyde, a development from
the plastics industry, has nearly the same nitrogen content as urea, but breaks down
far more slowly; at the moment it is mainly sold in rather expensive small packs for
the gimmick-conscious gardener.

For soils and crops that need a neutral or slightly alkaline environment, better
sources of nitrogen for quick growth are nitro-chalk, calcium cyanamide, calcium
nitrate and sodium nitrate. The first three, as their names suggest, actually introduce
calcium as well as nitrogen, and reinforce the action of any lime that you may have
used previously. Sodium nitrate acts as a mild neutralising agent for soils that are
getting a trifle acid, but should not be used instead of lime on very acid soils, as this
causes loss of nitrogen and makes the treatment very costly. Any of these four
fertilisers can be mixed with lime for application, or added to freshly limed soil,
without any danger of nitrogen loss.

Sodium nitrate is traditionally used as a dressing for asparagus beds just before
the tips begin to show. The nitrate helps to boost rapid stem production, while—as
asparagus is essentially a salt-marsh plant—it tolerates a high sodium level in the
soil better than the weeds which could compete for the nitrogen. Some growers
also use a salt dressing (agricultural sodium chloride) to intensify the sodium level.

Phosphorus sources

Phosphates play a part in almost every chemical reaction in the plant cell, and are
therefore essential for growth. They are particularly important in root formation,
and root crops should always be provided with ample phosphate nutrients. Fruit
and seeds also benefit from phosphates.

The phosphorus cycle in the soil is far less complicated than that of nitrogen,
because there is no reservoir of phosphorus corresponding to the nitrogen in the air.
Plants remove phosphates, sometimes in large quantities—a 100lb (45kg) crop of
potatoes, for example, means a loss of phosphate equivalent to about 8oz (226g) of
calcium superphosphate, and these phosphates have to be replaced. Ideally this
should be done by returning to the soil all the vegetable and animal materials that
originated from it, but there must inevitably be losses. In addition, phosphates have

an unpleasant habit of reacting with other soil ingredients to form insoluble and practically useless compounds, so there are losses from this process as well.

Phosphate minerals are fairly widely distributed, but mainly in the form of calcium phosphate—phosphorite, apatite—which is almost insoluble in water and therefore not assimilated by plants. If phosphate rock of this kind is ground up finely and buried in the soil for a long time, the natural acids will release phosphate in soluble form, but this is a very slow process that may take years. The most common 'organic' forms of phosphorus—bones and bird droppings (guano)—also contain calcium phosphate, so they are no better than the rock.

In 1842 John Bennet Lawes of Rothamsted discovered that if phosphate rock was heated with sulphuric acid, quite a lot of the phosphate appeared in a soluble form, and the resulting calcium superphosphate was in fact the first artificial manure ever to be used in agriculture. It is still one of the most important sources of phosphates.

When you are using phosphate materials, whether bought from a chemical company or in the form of compost, it is important to know what proportion of the phosphate is soluble and how much is still insoluble calcium phosphate.

Phosphate fertilisers

	per cent P_2O_5 (phosphoric oxide)		Other	Comments
	Soluble	Insoluble	Nutrients	
Ammonium phosphate	48	—	nitrogen	usually used in solution; quick acting
Phosphate rock	—	30–36	none	very slow acting
Steamed bone meal	—	28–29	nitrogen	fairly slow acting
Bone meal (unsteamed)	—	24–26	nitrogen	slow acting
Ammoniated superphosphate	18–20	8	nitrogen	quick acting
Calcium superphosphate	18	8	none	quick acting
Basic slag	—	15–18	none	slow acting
Meat and bone meal	1–2	16	nitrogen	fairly slow acting
Fish meal	8	—	nitrogen	quick acting
Dried sewage sludge	3	—	nitrogen (very little)	quick acting
Pigeon manure		2	nitrogen, potassium, calcium	slow acting
Fresh horse manure	0.5	—	nitrogen, potassium	quick acting
Fresh pig manure	0.5	—	nitrogen, potassium	quick acting
Garden compost	0.5 •	—	nitrogen, potassium	quick acting
Fresh cow manure	0.2	—	nitrogen, potassium	quick acting

When selecting a phosphate fertiliser, exactly the same arguments apply as for nitrogen. Once you have lifted, say, your 100lb (45kg) of potatoes, you need to replace the phosphate they have incorporated in themselves. You can do this with 8oz (226g) of superphosphate, but you will get just as much phosphorus by adding 18lb (8kg) of compost or horse manure, and improve the condition of your soil at the same time. If, however, you haven't enough compost and cannot get farmyard manure, by all means use superphosphate or one of the other 'artificials' rather than let your soil stay impoverished.

One minor complication of all phosphate application is that soluble phosphate tends to get locked up in various insoluble forms. In limy soil, for example, super-phosphate and organic phosphates are gradually converted to calcium phosphate. The process usually takes about six months, which means that if you are going in for intensive growing, with the soil in use all the year round, you should boost your phosphate levels twice a year, and in any case add fresh phosphate at the beginning of each spring.

In acid soils, another process locks away soluble phosphate: under these conditions aluminium and iron react with the phosphate to make insoluble salts. This should not worry you if you keep your land adequately limed, but when you are starting to cultivate a new garden or plot you may need extra phosphates until the soil is brought to the right pH balance.

A good plan for most soils is to add a slow-acting phosphate fertiliser, such as steamed bone meal, at about 2oz per square yard (70g per square metre) to act as a 'background' source, and use faster-acting soluble phosphates, either organic or artificial, to suit the particular needs of the crop. The bone meal will keep up a limited supply of phosphate for up to three years. If you can get meat and bone meal at a reasonable price, this is even better, as it contains some soluble phosphate. However, apart from local bargains, meat and bone meal tends to be more expensive than simple bone meal, even weight for weight, and as it contains a lower proportion of phosphate this makes it uneconomic.

Soluble phosphate materials should never be added to lime or calcium salts— nitrate, cyanamide, etc—or put on freshly limed soil, or the phosphate will be rendered insoluble.

Potassium sources

Potassium—the third of the elements that play a vital part in cell processes—is particularly important for the production of fruit (including tomatoes and melons, cucumbers, marrows, and similar cucurbits); seed and seed pods (peas and beans); tubers (potatoes and artichokes) and leaf bulbs (leeks, onions, garlic, shallots). It is thus important for almost all vegetables except the purely leafy ones.

Potassium is widely distributed, though it tends to disappear from the soil, partly because many of its compounds are very soluble in water and therefore easily washed out by rain into the rivers, but mainly because many plants store up large quantities of the mineral in their edible portions. Our 100lb (45kg) potato crop, for instance, carries off the equivalent of 1¼lb (566g) of potassium sulphate.

On some soils, particularly the clay type, there is often a lot of potassium tied up in the form of insoluble complex compounds. These can be decomposed by liming, which thus releases the mineral for plants—and, as lime is far cheaper than any of the commercial potassium salts, this is good economics if you work on a clay soil.

As wood and coal (the fossil remains of prehistoric forests) contain a good deal of potassium, ash from fires is a useful source. The main active ingredient in ash is potassium carbonate (the original 'pot-ash') which is rather alkaline, so it should not be allowed to come into direct contact with plants, nor mixed with materials like ammonium sulphate which cannot tolerate alkali. Coal ash is quite safe to use in the garden or smallholding, but it is probably better to let it 'mature' in the compost heap for a month or two before it is applied to the soil.

Some gardeners burn other vegetable waste under the impression that the potassium is somehow only obtainable through ash; this is, of course, a mistake. The potassium is there all the time, and burning the waste merely destroys other valuable materials, such as nitrogenous fertiliser and humus.

When further supplies of potassium are required, there are a few useful chemical fertilisers available—as analysed below in comparison with some organic fertilisers.

Potassium fertilisers

	per cent potassium (as K_2O)	Other nutrients	Comments
Potassium chloride (muriate of potash)	60–62	none	
Potassium sulphate	50–53	none	
Wood ashes	20–35	phosphate (small amount)	alkaline
Pigeon manure	2	nitrogen, phosphate	
Fresh horse manure	0.6	nitrogen, phosphate	
Garden compost	0.5	nitrogen, phosphate	
Fresh pig manure	0.2	nitrogen, phosphate	
Fresh cow manure	0.1	nitrogen, phosphate	

Other essential elements

Several other elements contribute to the health of plants and the maintenance of a fertile soil. Deficiencies of these could be detected by chemical analysis, but the behaviour of plants grown on the particular soil is a far more sensitive indicator of shortages—or, occasionally, excesses.

Nitrogen deficiency: Leaves and stems yellowish instead of bright green, slow and dwarfed growth, drying up of leaves early in the season. In many plants this starts as a browning of the lower leaves and spreads upwards, long before leaves should start to wither. Cure by applying appropriate nitrogen source.

Phosphate deficiency: Purple shades in leaves and stems, slow growth, thin stalks. Low yield of fruit and seed. Spindly roots in root-crops. Correct by applying phosphates.

Potassium deficiency: Mottling and curling of leaves, starting at the bottom of the plant. Scorching or browning of the tips and edges of leaves. Premature fall of leaves. Poor root development, often resulting in plants falling down in the wind. Correct by applying appropriate source of potassium.

Calcium deficiency: Young leaves in the terminal bud become hooked, and die back prematurely. Leaves have a wrinkled look. Roots short and excessively branched. Correct by applying lime, or by using a calcium-based fertiliser such as nitro-chalk, spent mushroom compost, or similar materials. In cases where the soil is already rather alkaline, and would not therefore benefit from lime or chalk, another useful source of calcium is gypsum or anhydrite (calcium sulphate) which is neutral. Such a condition is rare in untouched soil, but sometimes occurs on an old plot if it has been overdosed with wood ashes. Very sticky clay soils can often be improved by digging in gypsum or anhydrite at about 8oz to the square yard (250g per square metre).

Magnesium deficiency: General loss of colour, starting at the base of the plant and spreading upwards—the veins of the leaves often stay green. Brown patches on the leaves of potatoes, between the veins, but not starting at the edges—which is more often a sign of blight. A similar patching of the leaves of apple and cherry trees, and reddish borders to the leaves of gooseberries. Magnesium is vital for the production of chlorophyll, which controls the whole growth process of plants, and, apart from the colour changes, the plants are usually stunted and have misshapen leaves, curling up at the edges. Magnesium deficiency is not common naturally except on chalky soils, where the chalk locks up magnesium in the form of insoluble dolomite, but the same thing can happen if you are over-enthusiastic with lime. Correct by adding Epsom salts (magnesium sulphate) at about 1oz per square yard (35g per square metre); this may be necessary as an annual treatment for chalky soils. In the long term, farmyard manure or dried sewage sludge can be used to build up a reserve of magnesium.

Sulphur deficiency: Young leaves are very light green, with the veins even paler. In some plants (potatoes, for example) the pallor appears as light spots or mottling on the leaves. Fruits appear prematurely and remain small and immature instead of ripening. Sulphur deficiency is fairly rare in the British Isles, largely because of the rain of dilute sulphuric acid that results from air pollution. This starts in the big cities, but drifts everywhere, so that even the most rural situation is not denied its share of sulphur. In cases where the element is short, however, the simplest strategy is to add a small amount of gypsum to the soil, or use one of the sulphate-based artificial fertilisers: potassium sulphate, ammonium sulphate, or superphosphate, which contains gypsum, according to the other needs of your plants. A very small amount will suffice, as sulphur is only required in trace quantities by plants. Of the above fertilisers, 1oz to 4sq yd (10g per square metre) should be ample.

Boron deficiency: Boron is one of the 'micro-nutrients' required in minute amounts by some plants; deficiency signs include brown cracks at the base of celery stalks; brown rot in cauliflowers; rotting in the hearts of swedes, beet and other root crops; and yellow tops on some leafy plants. The textbook way to add boron to a deficient soil—usually chalky (boron gets locked up as insoluble calcium borate)—is to water it with a solution of borax at the rate of 1oz of borax in 1gal of water per 2sq yd (20g in 4l of water per square metre). For many people, however, the most convenient source of boron is the waste water from washing with powdered synthetic detergents; these all contain sodium perborate bleach, which leaves a useful residue of boron after the washing is done. It may be necessary to carry out the borax or detergent-water treatment annually on chalky soils. Be careful not to overdo the application; many plants are sensitive to overdoses of boron. Don't use borax or detergenty water on soft fruit, like raspberries, strawberries and black-currants, or near tree fruit, such as apples, pears, plums and cherries. Peas, radishes, tomatoes and potatoes are fairly tolerant to boron—but it is better to apply it at the beginning of the growing season, not over the plants themselves—while lettuce, cabbage and other brassica, onions, beans, beetroot and asparagus seem quite tolerant to the dressing.

Keep this in mind when using household waste-water in times of water shortage (see page 139). Wastes from washing *powders* should only be used on plants that are tolerant to boron; washing-up *liquids* are quite safe to use, as they contain no perborate.

Iron deficiency: When nitrogen and magnesium needs are adequately met, yellow tips to leaf shoots, particularly on fruit trees such as plums and cherries, are probably caused by iron deficiency. A couple of ounces of ferrous sulphate (sulphate of iron) crystals dissolved in water and applied to the foot of the tree may actually do some good for the same season, if you have spotted the pale shoots quickly enough. In the long term, bury a handful of rusty nails among the roots of the tree. Soils that are chalky or very rich in manganese may suffer from a permanent shortage of iron, in which case you may have to treat your fruit trees with ferrous sulphate every year or two.

It is unfortunate that many of these deficiencies can be spotted only by partial or complete failure of the crop, but at least this enables the grower to be ready for next season. Some deficiencies show up in the early growth—nitrogen, magnesium and iron shortages can all be spotted quite early if you are paying the right amount of attention to your young plants—and in these cases it is often quite possible to save the crop by emergency action.

In the long term, the best strategy against deficiencies is to build up plenty of compost, which will conserve the trace elements, and—when taking in fertiliser from outside—use the organic materials, like farmyard manure or sewage sludge; rather than chemical fertilisers. Some of these, especially the nitrogenous ones like urea and ammonium nitrate, are now so pure, chemically, that they lack the traces of iron, magnesium, sulphur and so on that used to occur in the older, cruder materials.

Compost – The Conservation of Resources

All crops remove vital raw materials from the soil and these have to be replaced to ensure fertility for further produce. While the cost of buying these raw materials as commercial fertiliser chemicals is not excessive—even the greedy potato only consumes about 30p worth of chemical fertiliser per 100lb (45kg) yield, assuming you buy only the essential chemicals and not overpriced branded fertilisers—it obviously makes sound economic sense to recycle as much of the surplus raw materials as possible. This not only saves money but improves the texture of the soil and the future yield from it.

Composting methods

The aims of any composting system are that it should: produce plenty of humus; not lose excessive amounts of soluble minerals; kill weed seeds, so that these cannot germinate when the compost is spread; kill insect pests and their eggs or larvae, so that they are not perpetuated from one season to another.

In addition, most people would vote for a method that does not involve back-breaking amounts of work, produce smells or attract insects. Fortunately all these requirements can be met by a number of composting systems.

Despite all the fuss made by the proponents of rival methods, there are really only three essentials for good composting: bacteria, air and warmth. Any method which provides all three will be effective.

Bacteria

The actual work of breaking down vegetable material from the lumps in which it usually appears to the even texture of fibrous humus is performed by bacteria, so you must encourage them as much as possible. You can increase the numbers of active bacteria right away by mixing dried sewage sludge, farmyard manure, or any similar animal wastes, with the vegetation; put a layer of weeds, etc, then a little dried sludge, then more weeds, and so on. Seifert, in his 'bio-dynamic process' for making compost, recommends making a pit or channel at the top of the heap of vegetation, and pouring liquid farmyard manure into this. The layer system seems to work just as well and is a lot less messy. If you can manage it in some fairly hygienic way, and without scandalising the neighbours, urine has quite a useful speeding-up effect on compost—the Chinese used to call it Chairman Mao's secret ingredient in the fight for improved agriculture.

Do not despair if you have no ready source of manure or sludge. The bacteria that cling to particles of earth on weeds, etc, will multiply quite rapidly given the right conditions. A very little nitrogenous fertiliser, even artificial material like ammonium sulphate, will give them enough nitrogen to keep them active, and after that they should be able to survive on the vegetable waste itself.

There are branded 'compost accelerators' on the market, usually blends of sewage sludge and lime, or similar mixtures, but we find them very expensive and not much better than ordinary composting. A sprinkle of lime on each layer will help to prevent the compost getting too acid, but do not add much or it will inhibit the bacteria.

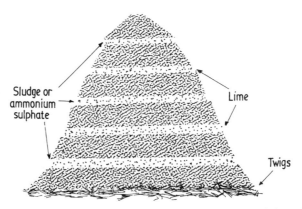

Sludge or ammonium sulphate

Lime

Twigs

52 Compost heap layers. Do not mix lime and ammonium sulphate directly.

Air

To ensure that the right kinds of bacteria develop, air is essential. The aerobic bacteria are the goodies, taking in oxygen and breaking down vegetation without producing any unpleasant by-products—a well-made compost heap has hardly any odour, apart from a slight and rather pleasant mushroomy smell—and they produce compost with a fine springy texture like shredded peat, very useful for lightening heavy soil. If the heap is too dense or wet, and the supply of air is cut off, aerobic bacteria cannot thrive, and their disreputable relations the anaerobic bacteria take over. These produce evil-smelling gases, particularly from meat and other animal products, and tend to give the compost a slimy texture which is quite unsuitable for soil conditioning.

Make sure that there are air channels of some kind right through your heap. If a container is used, have it made of slatted or perforated material—not with solid sides—and mix in plenty of straw and similar plant fragments with any wastes that tend to be sticky or close textured—fine lawn cuttings, for instance. Cow manure, if it comes from the modern type of intensive farm, often contains very little straw, and tends to go sour and malodorous if composted in this form. Mixing it with straw will soon give a fine, highly nutritious compost with good texture and hardly any smell.

If you cannot get straw easily, other 'hollow' plants will do almost as well. Long grass from road verges is often left to lie after cutting, and is less likely to have been treated with herbicides than grass from, say, the municipal park. Chopped-up cow parsley can be laid as 'pipes' to the middle of the heap. Even corrugated cardboard torn up into small pieces is better than nothing.

A layer of twigs, hedge cuttings, or similar stiff material at the bottom of each heap will let the air in, but do not make the layer too thick or spiky, otherwise earthworms will be discouraged from creeping up into the heap. Worms form the best aeration system of all; they carry on mixing and churning up the compost, leaving air channels behind them, until the natural rise in temperature gets too much for them. If you have a number of heaps at various stages, the worms may even be persuaded to migrate from one heap to the next as the process goes on.

Aeration is obviously assisted by turning the heaps over from time to time; this not only lets the air in, but makes sure that all parts of the heap have a turn in the warm interior. At Dorking, in Surrey, where the enlightened local authority composts all its domestic waste instead of burning or burying it, very rapid results are obtained by pushing the heaps round a field with a bulldozer from time to time.

Warmth

Bacteria work about twice as fast at 86°F (30°C) as at 68°F (20°C). As the process of composting goes on, the temperature will begin to rise spontaneously, as fermentations get going, and it is this increasing warmth that is necessary to kill weed seeds and insects. The temperature of a successful heap should reach some-where between 120° and 160°F (50° and 70°C), which is hot enough to kill nearly all seeds and insect eggs or larvae. Some insects are remarkably hardy; flies' eggs can withstand temperatures of 113°F (45°C). A really well-made heap can get a lot hotter than this—we had one recently that caught fire, and we had to run water over it all night to keep it under control. So look out for overheating, and pour a few buckets of water over any heap that is getting too enthusiastic. Farmers used to poke an iron rod into the middle of a haystack and feel the temperature when it was withdrawn, as a check on overheating—this is quite a good way to test your compost heap.

Making a compost heap

The simplest method is just to pile up all the vegetable waste, with a little manure or sludge, if available, scattered at intervals of about 6in (15cm), and lime dusted over the layers at similar intervals. Make sure that there is plenty of fibrous material like straw, peat, or long grass to aerate the softer and closer vegetation. If you put meat scraps from the kitchen on the heap, cover them immediately with earth to discourage flies. Keep the pile damp but not soaking wet. With luck you will have reasonable compost in the middle of such a heap after six to nine months, but the outsides should be cut away and used as the basis for the next heap, as they will not have become warm enough to be thoroughly composted.

A minor improvement that costs very little is to cover each heap, when completed, with a sheet of black agricultural polythene held down by pegs or heavy stones. Water the heap really thoroughly before you cover it, as it may be inconvenient to moisten it afterwards. The plastic will not only keep moisture in, and flies away, but will also absorb heat from the sun—black polythene collects more than the translucent sort—and thus keep the compost warmer. Again, you will probably have to cut away the sides and top for further composting.

If you make your heap against a wooden fence, protect it with a thick sheet of polythene, otherwise it may rot with the compost.

Compost containers

If you want good compost in a relatively short time, build a compost box (Figure 53) in some shaded part of the plot. A 3ft (1m) cube box will hold enough compost to prevent the mass cooling down quickly, without stopping aeration— the problem with very large boxes. You will need one compost box for every 10 sq rods under cultivation or grass—say, 300 sq yd or 250 sq m—more if you add other wastes to your home-grown compost. While you are at it, you might as well build two boxes—one for collecting current waste while the other is maturing.

The boxes can be made from any old timber; they should not be close-boarded, so battered second-hand floor boards would do. Alternatively you can set up strong corner posts and make the sides of wire netting, in which case you must provide insulation to keep the working heap warm. The whole secret of constructing a good compost box is to maintain this balance between aeration and overcooling. Make the front of your wooden box as a sliding panel—a discarded sheet of steel shelving would be ideal.

Paint any wood with creosote and leave this to soak in for at least a fortnight before you start putting in vegetable matter. A further coating of bitumen waterproofing is sometimes recommended to stop the creosote getting into the compost, but this does not seem to make much difference. Metal parts should be given a good coat of aluminium metal primer paint.

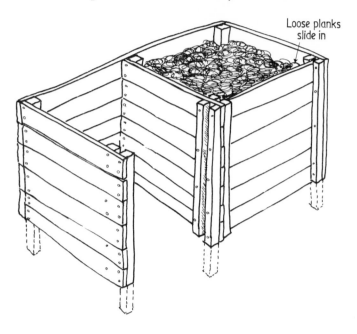

53 Compost boxes. Fill as in Fig. 52.

Pile the vegetation directly on to the ground, so that worms can get in, and keep the lid on, especially in wet weather, so that the heap does not get too wet or cold. In autumn and winter you may have to provide some extra insulation—a length of fibreglass roof insulation can be tied round the box with string to form a sort of overcoat; this material is so porous that it will not interfere with aeration. Alternatively you could get panels of polystyrene foam insulation about $\frac{1}{2}$in (12.5mm) thick, and tie these against the outside, If you paint them black or dark green—using water-based acrylic gloss paint—they will collect more heat on sunny days. If you use polystyrene, make extra sure that your heap does not get to smouldering temperatures, or your insulation may go up in a cloud of black smoke!

You can, of course, buy ready-made compost containers, the commonest being folding wire baskets—which, again, will need insulating in winter—and the barrel shaped bins with staves that can be slid out for access. These will make perfectly good compost and look tidy in a very small garden or patio. Even the largest of the 'barrel' containers takes only about 20 cu ft (.56 cu m)—not enough for the compost from a 10-rod plot. If you had $\frac{1}{4}$ acre (1,000 sq m) under cultivation, you would need about six of these commercial bins, at a cost of around £150; whereas for a fraction of this, using second-hand timber, you could build a highly-efficient compost 'production line' of several boxes for successive heaps.

Composting materials

You can put almost every kind of vegetable matter into a well-built compost heap and turn it into useful plant food. Weeds of all kinds—apart from one or two exceptions (see below)—should go in as you pull them up or hoe them; grass cuttings are valuable for quick rotting, and you can get rid of all the waste bits of produce. Even poisonous material like rhubarb leaves can be used—composting destroys the dangerous oxalic acid.

Leaves of most kinds rot down so fast that it is probably better to keep them in a separate heap (see page 13), but the tougher varieties, such as horse chestnut, can go into the general compost heap. Manure from animals and birds will increase the nitrogen and speed up the action, and even the bedding of pets, such as guinea pigs or rabbits, can be used. Kitchen scraps can be composted, but meat, sausages past their prime and similar material should be covered with earth or buried deep in the heap, so as not to attract flies or cats.

Tougher materials—such as hedge cuttings, cabbage and brussels sprouts stalks, the roots of docks and thistles, and cow parsley—will compost in time, but will disappear more quickly if they are sliced or chopped beforehand. In fact, bruising or shredding helps along all types of compost (see page 19). The finer you shred the produce, the quicker the composting, so long as you do not make the mass too soggy and thus exclude air. Fine lawn cuttings, for instance, may need to be mixed with something coarser, like straw or long grass, as they tend to rot down to an impervious mat; this does not allow air to penetrate and its centre begins to smell and turn black—evidence that anaerobic bacteria are at work.

Old newspapers and magazines, well shredded, can be added to the heap—they do not add anything to the nutrient value, just increase the bulk of humus. (There must be a lesson for editors somewhere in this.) The contents of the vacuum cleaner can go the same way, and any rags, as long as they are animal or vegetable fibres —wool, cotton or linen.

Don't add to compost:

Evergreen leaves, like privet, yew, pine needles or ivy. They poison the bacteria and slow down the composting action.
Fresh perennial weeds—particularly buttercups, couch grass, convolvulus and bindweed. Dry them thoroughly in the sun to kill their roots or runners; then you can add them to the heap.
Any plants that have been dressed with selective weed-killers or other herbicides— except the simple ones recommended in pages 218. This can arise if you collect weeds or grass cuttings from neighbours who are not compost-minded. Some of the selective weed-killers used for grass are very persistent and could kill plants treated with the compost.
In general, think of the compost heap as the natural resting place for all your

wastes. Keep a large covered bin outside the kitchen door in which vegetable trimmings, tea leaves, coffee grounds, apple cores and leftovers can be collected before being taken down to the heap. If you have a workshop, put all the sawdust, shavings and similar wood or paper scraps in a bin, and distribute these on the compost heap in a while—shavings are very good for aeration. When you gather produce, carry a knife with you to trim away outside leaves and uneatable roots or tops and put them straight on to the heap. Such simple time-and-motion study will make your kitchen and plot tidier, and your compost heap grow, without apparent effort.

Ban the Bonfire!

One of the surest signs of uneconomic and inefficient gardening is the smoke signal rising from a bonfire. The nuisance is bad enough—clouds of acrid smoke blackening washing, turning leaves brown before their time—and, at close quarters, a risk of lung cancer just as great as that from cigarette smoking. Even more serious is the wastage. Every pile of leaves, grass or weeds sacrificed to the Firedrake means a corresponding reduction in the fertility of the soil. You can replace some of the chemical nutrients with artificial fertilisers, but the humus never—and even the chemicals cost money. In quite a small suburban garden, the nutrients contained in the annual crop of grass, leaves, weeds and vegetable waste may well be equivalent to £25 worth of bought fertiliser—so each weekly bonfire costs 50p. There are, admittedly, a few plant diseases so serious that affected produce must be burned, but these are so rare in normal gardening that they would scarcely justify one bonfire per year.

Pests and Diseases:
Are you Licensed to Kill?

The witch-hunters of the seventeenth century saw themselves as beleaguered in a world permeated by evil, where the agents of the devil could assume a thousand different and confusing shapes, fly through the air, creep under the earth, sidle into houses through cracks in locked doors and shutters, and cause mysterious and fatal pestilences.

You have only to look through the advertisements in *Farmers' Weekly* and gardening magazines to get exactly the same feeling. The modern agents of the devil have names like Gummosis, Botrytis, Anbury, Tortrix—or, more simply, scab, rust, and smut—and the only protection against them is a constant repetition of the magic words Dimefox, Zineb, Endrin, Tecnazene, Thiram and Malathion—the last actually sounds like some kind of curse.

Farmers and intensive growers of one crop may be forgiven for their responses to this haunted feeling. They know that one outbreak of rust or eyespot can spell the difference between profit and loss in cereals, and that some diseases like potato wart can wipe out a whole crop, or even a complete potato-growing area, so they have little option but to pray and spray. However, many farmers even now admit that the cost of these chemicals, on top of seed, fertiliser, and labour, can itself wipe out the profit on the produce, and one feels that only a belief in magic, rather than economics or science, could persuade fruit growers, as some do, to spray up to twenty times a season.

The smaller grower with a reasonably mixed range of crops is very unlikely to have a catastrophically bad attack of any of these pests or diseases, and in any case the loss of one crop does not mean economic disaster. So before you go out into your plot and blast everything in sight with a spray, think carefully about the economics of the process, and then think just as carefully about the long-term effects.

For instance, among the insecticides, there is no doubt that the chlorinated hydrocarbons—DDT, aldrin, dieldrin, BHC alias Gammexane alias Lindane, and so on—have done an almost miraculous job in making habitable parts of the world that were once completely overrun by dangerous insects: tsetse fly, malaria-carrying mosquitoes, lice that carry typhus, etc. On the other hand, in the more delicately balanced world of the average farm or garden, they tend to have much the same effect as a sawn-off shotgun in a crowded room. They wipe out not only insects that are pests, but also bees, ladybirds, earthworms and other beneficial insects, and even reduce the numbers of insectivorous birds, hedgehogs and moles, because these absorb the poison with their prey.

The systemic insecticides are a little better from this point of view, as they are absorbed by the plants and only kill those insects unsporting enough to bite into the produce—unlike bees, for instance, that only take nectar. Unfortunately, human beings also bite into the vegetables and fruit eventually; despite all the assurances that systemic insecticides are completely safe for warm-blooded animals, it is well to take note that there are warnings not to eat anything that has been sprayed for at least three weeks afterwards.

Some of the systemics—the organo-phosphorus group—are related chemically to the so-called 'nerve gases', of which a few milligrams of vapour or a drop absorbed through the skin can be fatal. One ounce of the insecticide TEPP, for example, could kill 500 people; agricultural workers using it are obliged to adopt gloves, overalls, leggings, helmets and respirators. Again, despite assurances that the insecticide is quite safe after a period, putting such a deadly substance on food at all seems an unacceptable risk compared with any possible advantages it might possess. Many of the more modern insecticides are less dangerous than this, but TEPP is about as poisonous as prussic acid, so this is not as reassuring as it sounds and their long-term effects have still to be discovered.

The indiscriminate use of insecticides is also counter-productive because it interferes with the natural balance of predators and prey. Apart from birds, moles, hedgehogs and other useful pest eaters, a whole range of insects live on aphids, mites and similar pests. Spraying often kills these beneficial insects while sparing the destructive ones. Red spider mite, for example, used to be confined almost entirely to greenhouses and similar closed situations, but it is now spreading to orchards, fruit plantations and other outdoor sites, because its natural enemies have been decimated by spraying.

One further argument against the use of some insecticides is their long-term effect on the flavour of food. Many of the chlorinated hydrocarbons, particularly BHC, have unpleasant 'moth-ball' tastes that can taint fruit and root crops, anything up to three years after application. This makes proper rotation of crops almost impossible once the insecticides have been used.

Fungicides are not usually as poisonous as insecticides, but there are long-term hazards connected with the organo-mercury compounds used by some seed suppliers as an anti-mildew measure. Mercury is a cumulative poison, so small amounts taken in with food can build up to a dangerous level. The Japanese found this out in tragic circumstances when nearly 100 people died at Minamata Bay after eating fish that had been living on sea plants contaminated with mercury—the food chain concentrated the metal at each stage.

Having said all this, what is the grower actually to do when blackfly are nibbling the tops of the broad beans, eelworms making subway systems in the carrots, and the apple trees seem to have been struck by Poe's 'red death'?

The thing *not* to do is to dash out and buy an expensive back-pack spray apparatus and some even more expensive branded insecticide, and blast everything in sight. This is not only costly but usually completely ineffective, and the long-term effects of the sprays may be worse than the disease.

First make sure that your troubles are really due to outside agencies. Many deficiency diseases, caused by minor shortages in the soil, can look very much like the work of insects or fungi. Yellowing leaves and falling fruit in apples and pears, for example, are more likely to be caused by dryness in the subsoil than anything above ground. Strange tints in leaves—brown edges, yellow stripes, etc—need not be blight. They are far more often symptoms of a deficiency of nitrogen, potassium, or calcium (see page 195). Critical shortages of boron can cause brown and hollow centres in swedes and beetroot, with all the appearance of sabotage by millipedes or eelworms. Even such a common event as frost can seem wildly dramatic if it happens at an unusual time of year. We vividly remember coming back after a weekend visit to find our plot ravaged as if by a rain of weedkiller: potatoes and tomatoes were black and dying, and even hardy shrubs like laurels had scorched brown leaves. It turned out to be an unseasonable frost, right at the end of May.

Next, if the trouble is definitely due to insects, fungi or bacteria, try to identify the exact cause. Some, like greenfly and blackfly, are obvious, but underground pests and fungus diseases may take a little more time. There are many excellent books which will help here; try to find one with illustrations of the type of damage, such as A. G. L. Hellyer's *Garden Pests and Diseases* (Collingridge, 1966). Some of his recommendations for treatment are a little savage and involve chemicals of doubtful safety, but his hints for diagnosing the causes of damage are excellent.

Choice of weapons

When you know your enemy, try to select a weapon that will do the maximum damage to it, and the minimum to yourself and the friendly creatures that share your garden. The following is a rough guide to the various techniques for getting rid of pests without using dangerous materials, and at the least cost. You may occasionally need something more drastic, but if you try to spot troubles as they develop, these homely methods will keep you out of difficulties most of the time.

Biting pests

The easiest pests to spot are those that actually eat holes in the leaves, stems and fruit of plants: caterpillars and maggots of all kinds, beetles, flies and so on. Sometimes, if the infestation has not gone too far, you can pick or brush most of the pests off the plants by hand, dropping them into a basin of salt and water or diluted household bleach to kill them. Beyond this, the main treatments are as follows:

Traps can be used for earwigs, woodlice, chafers, and other similar scavengers, which mainly live on dead vegetation but are not averse to the occasional seedling. Flower pots stuffed with straw or newspaper and inverted on the ground or on short sticks or canes will catch a lot of these pests in dry weather. Shake out the straw or paper over a hard surface so that you can tread on the insects before they escape. Vine weevils—dull black beetle-like creatures with long snouts—can be caught with rolls of paper or sacking placed at the foot of vines.

Borax powder will discourage ants and cockroaches: a mixture of borax with sugar or old beer as bait can be used as a poisonous trap. Ants not only loosen the earth round seedlings but, through their intensive farming of aphids, increase the numbers of these pests. If cockroaches become a pest in the greenhouse or frames (you may have to go out with a torch to spot them moving), sink a number of jam jars in the ground up to their rims, and pour a little beer or molasses in each one. The creatures fall for this simple trick, literally.

Naphthalene or *paraffin* can be used to repel celery fly, chafers, mushroom mites, onion fly and vine weevils. Either fork a few naphthalene crystals into the soil round the affected plants, or spread rags soaked in paraffin. You may have to renew these treatments every week or two during the summer growing season.

Metaldehyde pellets will kill slugs and snails, which account for tremendous losses in young plants. Sprinkle the pellets round any young plants, taking care not to let them touch the leaves. If you buy water-repellent pellets they will last longer.

Lime-sulphur (see page 215) can be used against leaf blister mite, which makes yellowish blisters on the leaves of pear trees. Spray the trees with 5-per-cent lime-sulphur just before the buds open.

Derris (rotenone, an extract of the roots of several plants) is probably the safest of the general insecticides, and can be used for apple blossom weevil, asparagus beetle, cabbage butterfly and moth caterpillars, clearwing moth, codlin moth, flea beetle, pea moth maggots, pear midge maggots, raspberry beetle, red plum maggot, sawfly caterpillars and slugworms. Take care not to use derris near water as it kills fish at quite low concentrations. Even with derris, do not be tempted to spray just 'in case'—only attack definite infestations.

Nicotine can be used in cases of necessity against any of the above insects, and also for leaf miners, whose larvae make tunnels in the leaves of many plants. The larvae can sometimes be killed with a sharp point, but nicotine will clear up a serious infestation. Nicotine is extremely poisonous to you and your animals; it can be absorbed through the skin (so wear PVC gloves with gauntlets when handling it), and at least a month should be allowed for it to evaporate before any treated produce is picked—longer in an enclosed place like a greenhouse or frame. If in doubt, don't use nicotine.

Sucking pests

Aphids, mealy bugs, and so on, may be a little more difficult to spot because they creep under leaves, and are often protectively coloured to match the plants they are destroying. The ideal weapon against them is the ladybird, so any treatment should do no harm to this useful insect.

Soap or washing-up *detergent* will induce many suckers to loosen their hold on plants, and can be used against blackfly, greenfly, mealy bugs, red spider mite and whitefly. Either use washing-up water or make up a solution of similar strength. More concentrated solutions may interfere with the respiration of the plant leaves, giving brown or black 'scorch' marks.

Derris can be used for worse infestations; as it affects ladybirds, it should only be used if simple detergent solutions have failed.

Quassia (see page 216), if you can get it, makes a very good spray for aphids without harming ladybirds. It is intensely bitter, so allow at least three weeks after treatment before you pick any treated produce.

Nicotine can also be used for suckers, with the same reservations as above. It is excellent for thrips on peas, as it is unlikely to penetrate to the pods unless very wastefully applied.

Lime-sulphur (see page 215) is useful against big bud, a mite that infests black and red currants, and occasionally gooseberries, causing great loss of fruit. Lime-sulphur should be sprayed over these soft fruits in spring when the forward leaves are about 1in (2.5cm) across.

Blackfly on broad beans, a very common infestation, can often be prevented altogether by pinching out the growing tops of the beans as soon as the lower pods have started to form.

Woolly aphis, which attacks the woody parts of apple trees, can be killed off by brushing the white woolly covering of the insects with methylated spirit on a paintbrush—treatment not suitable for more fleshy plants. Treat this pest as soon as it is observed, otherwise the wood of the tree will crack at the attacked areas and fungus diseases can get a hold.

Creeping pests

Those that attack roots and tubers, or the base of stems, may not be noticed at all until the crop is lifted and found holey, or a plant falls over. Most of these pests can be discouraged by strong-smelling substances: naphthalene or paradichlorobenzene crystals forked into the soil round plants will usually keep away carrot fly grubs, cutworms, eelworms, gall weevils, leather jackets, millipedes, root aphis and root maggots. Cabbage root fly, and similar insects that lay their eggs near their target plant, can be frustrated by cutting circles of roofing felt or similar bituminised material and placing these round the stems of the plants (Figure 54).

54 Brassica seedling with roofing felt collar to repel cabbage root fly.

Natural 'smelly' materials also discourage creeping pests; garlic, shallots and others of the onion tribe can be planted in between root vegetables for this purpose. Various members of the spurge family also have this effect, although they are not so useful as food, of course. Some people say that spurges have such a strong smell underground that they deter moles, but we have not been able to confirm this. It would be rather a pity to drive moles away as they are great eaters of creeping insects, and only rarely knock over a plant by being clumsy in their digging.

Fungus diseases

These affect a good many varieties of plant, which is not surprising, as thousands of fungi exist and are widely spread. Some can be avoided simply by setting up conditions which are good for the plants and bad for fungi: mildew, for example, will never develop in a well-ventilated greenhouse or frame, but in a neglected one it may get all over plants. Ring spot, which makes brown spots in brassica leaves and eventually kills them, can be avoided if the soil is not over-treated with nitrogenous fertiliser—a good thing anyway for most brassicas.

Among the other fungus diseases, the two most effective treatments, and certainly the safest in the long term, are based on sulphur and copper. Various tricks are used to get these two insoluble elements into solution so that they can be sprayed, but the fundamental action is the same.

Powdered sulphur or flowers of sulphur can be used as a dust, and is good for botrytis, a grey mould that attacks the stems, leaves and fruits of tomatoes, cucumbers, vines, lettuces and many other food crops. Here again the mould is more likely in a damp, stuffy frame than in a well-ventilated area; if it occurs, sulphur is usually effective and quite safe to use. On soft fruit, avoid using sulphur within three weeks of harvesting, as it may affect the flavour.

Lime-sulphur is in fact not a mixture, but a complex sulphur compound made by boiling lime water and sulphur together (see page 215). It has the same properties as flowers of sulphur, but is easier to get into awkward corners, as it can be sprayed. Use lime-sulphur for anthracnose (dark, soft spots on French and runner beans, cucumbers, and melons) and cane spot (purple spots that develop into rotted areas on the leaves of raspberries and other cane fruit).

Bordeaux mixture is the oldest and best-tested of the copper compounds (see instructions for making it yourself, page 214). Use it for mildew, if it develops; leaf spot in celery and soft fruits; potato blight (black rotting patches on the leaves, spreading down to the tubers), and white tip in leeks.

Cheshunt compound is chemically a similar copper compound, but easier to dissolve in water. It can be used for the same purposes as Bordeaux mixture, and is very good for preventing leaf curl in peaches and nectarines, and sclerotinia rot (collar rot) that attacks the crowns of carrots, parsnips, Jerusalem artichokes, etc. You can make this material yourself (see page 215) or buy it ready-made at a far greater cost. Many of the branded copper-based fungicides are either plain Cheshunt compound or simple variants of it.

Lime alone will discourage the growth of the moulds that cause club-root in brassicas, and mycogone, a rather disgusting soft rot in mushrooms that turns the crowns slimy. If you move your brassica patch around in a proper rotation system, and make sure that the soil is adequately limed, but not excessively so, you should avoid club-root; and mycogone is hardly ever seen in a well-made mushroom bed.

Bacterial diseases

Such diseases in plants are rare, but are seen mainly as soft rots. They affect root crops like carrots and potatoes, and sometimes the centres of cauliflowers and broccoli, usually where previous damage has occurred because of careless handling or holes made by slugs, snails or leatherjackets. Copper sprays, such as Cheshunt compound, will sometimes stop the spread of bacteria, but the real answer is to avoid the initial damage.

Virus diseases

In plants, as in humans, viruses tend to be blamed whenever the experts are baffled. Potatoes and tomatoes seem to suffer most, becoming weakened rather than killed, but most other plants have been reported as suffering from virus diseases at some time or other. Nobody knows what to do about any of them, except to breed resistant varieties—such as the well-known Scottish seed potatoes— but there is little doubt that they are spread by sucking insects, like thrips, aphids, capsid bugs and mites of various kinds, so the more you can do to discourage these, the better your chances of avoiding viruses.

Fumigation

These lists of pests and plant ills may give the impression that every garden is a seething mass of corruption, but with luck and good management your plot will never know half of them. If you keep your eyes open for any odd colours in leaves, lumps and bumps in stalks, and bits missing from plants generally, you can usually catch those that do occur before they have done much damage.

One area that encourages pests and moulds, however, is that under glass: your greenhouse and frames. The combination of warmth, damp atmosphere, and plenty of dim holes and corners in which to hide, especially in wooden structures, tends to attract unwelcome visitors. Fumigating the greenhouse and frames once a year will help to get rid of these, or at least keep them under control.

You can buy fumigating cones that just need to be lighted and left to smoulder in a closed greenhouse—but most of these commercial products contain BHC, which will taint food crops for a long time. A simpler, cheaper and less unpleasantly persistent treatment is to burn sulphur.

Roll sulphur is most suitable—if your garden supplier does not have it, you may find it at an aquaria stockist, in lumps like yellow seaside rock—but flowers of sulphur will do. For a 12 × 8ft (3.5 × 2.5m) greenhouse, use 10z (30g) of sulphur —more for a larger building, less for a frame Put it on an old tin or earthenware plate (*not* an aluminium freezer tray, which will melt and react with the sulphur). Place this in the middle of the greenhouse or frame, well away from glass or wood; close any ventilators, then light the sulphur and retire immediately, closing the door or frame lights. The sulphur does not burn fiercely, just a gentle blue flame, but the fumes are extremely bad for your throat. When all of it has burned away, leave the house or frame closed for an hour or two, or preferably overnight, until the worst of the fumes have dissipated.

Fumigation of this kind will get rid of most insects and moulds above ground, but will have far less effect on creeping pests in the soil itself. The only way to deal with these satisfactorily is to change the soil regularly (see page 80).

Home-made remedies

Bordeaux mixture

You will need blue copper sulphate crystals from a garden supplier or chemist; they should be fairly cheap. Be careful how you handle and store this material; although it is not a deadly poison, anyone who swallows it will be very sick. More to the point, if the crystals or solution are in contact with your hands for very long, they will taste and smell of old pennies for hours after, and so will everything you eat.

Use a 5gal (22.5l) plastic or wooden (not metal) bucket and pour in 2½gal of hot water; then add 3oz of copper sulphate crystals and 4oz of hydrated garden lime

(70g copper sulphate and 100g lime to 10l water). Stir with a stick until the sludge at the bottom has dispersed—the liquid never gets really clear.

This mixture is most effective when it is freshly made, but you can in fact keep it for a few days if you stir it well before use. A stronger and more effective spray can be made by using $1\frac{1}{2}$ times the quantities above in the same amounts of water, but this may cause scorching on the leaves of some plants.

Cheshunt compound

A concentrate of this will keep very well; dilute it for use when required. Mix 2oz of copper sulphate crystals and 11oz of ammonium carbonate (50g copper sulphate to 275g ammonium carbonate) and put them in a stoppered jar. Don't breathe in the air at the top of the jar or you may get a shock—ammonium carbonate is the stuff used for smelling salts. When you want to spray, use the mixture at 1oz per 2 gal of water (30g in 10l).

If you cannot easily get hold of ammonium carbonate, a copper fungicide mixture that works just as well can be made as follows: into a large bottle that will hold at least $1\frac{1}{2}$ pts, put $\frac{1}{2}$ pt of hot water and 2oz of copper sulphate (50g in .25l water). If you stopper the bottle and shake, the crystals will dissolve more quickly. When you have a clear mid-blue solution, add about $\frac{3}{4}$pt (375cc) of household ammonia, a little at a time, and shake or swirl the liquid around to mix it. You will see the copper solution throw down a heavy greenish deposit; then, with more ammonia, this will suddenly dissolve to give a beautiful deep blue solution. Stop adding ammonia when this has happened, and stopper the container for future use.

For spraying, add 1 fl oz of the solution to every 1 gal of water (60 cc per 10l).

Lime-sulphur

The process is rather smelly, so an old saucepan on a camp stove out of doors makes the best manufacturing unit.

Add 4oz of hydrated garden lime to 3 pts of water in the saucepan (65g lime to 1l water), and bring the mixture near to the boil, with stirring. Now add 6 oz of flowers of sulphur (100g) a little at a time, while keeping the mixture hot. The sulphur will float on the surface at first, then begin to dissolve, and eventually all the sulphur will disappear to leave a yellowish brown rather evil-smelling solution. It is important that the sulphur actually dissolves; a simple mixture of lime and sulphur is not nearly as effective.

This liquid will keep in a bottle for several months; when needed for use, dilute it at the rate of 2 fl oz per gallon (125cc per 10l) of water. Some diseases, such as raspberry cane spot, really need a stronger solution: anything up to 5oz per gallon.

Nicotine

Collect as many cigarette ends as you can; keep a tin for this purpose. When you have about 4oz (100g) of non-tipped ends, or 8oz (200g) if they are mostly filter-tipped, drop the mess into 2pts (1l) of water in an old saucepan, and bring it to the boil for about 20 minutes. Strain the brown solution through an old pair of tights or a stocking, then burn the nylon filter. Bottle up the filtered solution, but put a 'POISON' label on it and keep it in a safe place. This solution should be diluted at about 1pt to 1gal (125cc to 1l) of water for use. *Wear rubber gloves.*

Quassia

Simmer 4oz of quassia chips in 1gal of water, for about 2 hours, then add a teaspoonful of bicarbonate of soda. Let the solution cool, strain off the chips, add a little washing-up detergent to the solution, and dilute it to 5gal total for use (50g quassia boiled in 2l water; add about 5g bicarbonate; make up to 10l total for use).

Total War: Weedkillers

The harassed farmer, short of labour, and under pressure to produce a 'clean' crop that can be harvested mechanically, may be forgiven for his dependence on weedkillers, but the smaller grower will find that they have several disadvantages, apart from their considerable cost.

First, the ideal commercial weedkiller is one that does not affect the actual crop but kills everything else. While this is rarely achieved in practice, *selective* weed-killers have been developed that can at least kill all the broad-leaved weeds in a field of cereals, or even wild oats in among wheat and barley. The trouble comes the following year. Most of these herbicides are quite long-lived in the soil, so rotation of crops becomes impossible—it is useless to plant, say, beans or swedes after wheat if the soil is full of the broad-leaved herbicide 2,4,5-*T*. Many gardeners use products of this kind to kill plantains and so on in their lawns, but even this can be dangerous—the lawn cuttings cannot be used in compost or for mulching for months afterwards, because they would kill off broad-leaved plants near them.

There are, of course, the general herbicides, used to clear paths and so on. Of these, the simple ones, like sodium chlorate, tend to spread through the soil to places where they are not wanted, and the more sophisticated ones, like simazine, are very expensive. The same applies to paraquat and the products made from it—such as Weedol. Paraquat has the advantage that it is destroyed when it touches the soil, so it cannot kill crops planted subsequently, but it works out very costly if used over any substantial area. It is also very poisonous, and there is at the moment no effective antidote.

The real weedkillers for any cost-conscious gardener or grower must be the hoe and the fingers. Regular hoeing will catch the young weeds almost as soon as they appear, and really takes no longer than the fiddly job of sprinkling paraquat or similar materials round each plant in a row. If you compost any weeds that get beyond the baby stage, you will get back most of the nutrients they have taken from the soil—though not the water, a point to consider in times of drought—and with none of the risk of side-reactions that can occur with chemical herbicides.

If you are faced with a patch that has really got out of hand, or has to be cleared from scratch, you can either use a flame-gun, which is messy but has no long-term side effects, or you can use ammonium sulphamate—at about $1\frac{1}{2}$ oz per sq yd (50g per sq m). This is a general herbicide, and will kill all vegetation, but after about three weeks in the soil it is converted to ammonium *sulphate*—quite a useful nitrogenous fertiliser (see page 189).

The Protection Racket

Even the minimum of protection for your plants against the dire effects of the weather will extend the growing season and markedly increase productivity. The amount you invest in providing shelter and warmth depends on how keen you are and how long term you intend your involvement with gardening to be.

The very simplest type of protection is polythene film, in sheet or bag form. A seedling in a pot can be covered with a transparent bag—the wrapper in which tights are sold, for example—propped up on a couple of lolly sticks, to make a mini-greenhouse. For a box of seedlings use a shirt-size bag and four to six lolly sticks (Figure 55).

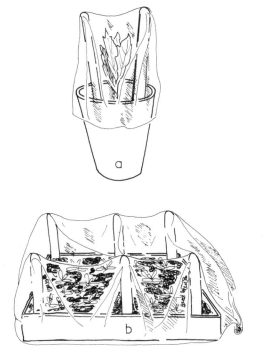

55 (a) polythene tights-bag over pot (b) larger bag over tray. Support on blunt sticks or plant labels.

Cloches

A length of polythene sheeting can be used to construct an outdoor tunnel cloche to protect seedlings until the weather warms up. This sheet is propped up on sticks and supported at intervals by wire hoops stuck into the ground. Pull the ends of the sheet tight and anchor them with a heavy stone. A second set of hoops—over the top—may be necessary to prevent the tunnel being blown away by the wind (Figure 56). A cloche just like this, sold commercially, costs about £3 for 30ft (9m) film plus single wires; you could buy the polythene sheet for around 60p and provide the wires yourself for £1 or less.

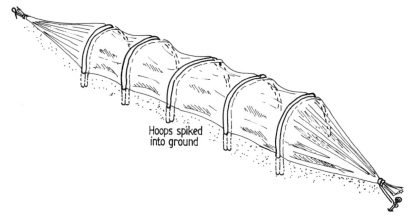

Hoops spiked
into ground

56 Plastic tunnel cloche on wires.

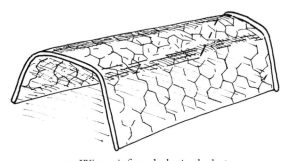

57 Wire-reinforced plastic cloche.

Thin polythene isn't very durable or stable, and high winds may strip it off. The popular trend is to use reinforced or rigid plastic. The reinforced type is wire netting covered with plastic sheet, which can be formed into any shape of cloche and holds itself up pretty well, though it can have a wire hoop added at the ends. Bought as a roll, it costs between £4.50 and £5 for 20ft (6m), and rather more if cut into cloche lengths and supplied with shaped ends. It is a lot more sturdy than plain film, but the wires cut out a certain amount of light from the plants (Figure 57).

Rigid plastic is pre-formed into a sheet or shaped as a cloche. Some of it isn't all that rigid—vacuum formed, like the transparent egg-boxes in shops, it is about as flimsy. This is useless out of doors, because it blows away with the slightest breeze; but it can be used in a greenhouse to cover a seed tray without the need to prop up the plastic. At the moment it is overpriced for what it is—£4 for a thin tray and one of these flimsy covers, for example.

Thicker plastics may be had in a semi-rigid sheet, which can be bent to a curve, or a ridge-tent shape, or shaped permanently as a cloche or tray cover. The thicker the plastic, the more expensive it is, but the better the protection given and the longer the article lasts.

A simple outdoor cloche of semi-rigid transparent plastic with anchoring wires is obtainable by mail order; it arrives flat and makes up into a tunnel 3ft (90cm) long. This costs about £2, and a pack of four nearly £8—plus £1 postage. You could make the same thing out of a sheet of the clear plastic corrugated material sold for roofing carports; this is obtainable in shops locally, so there would be no postal charge. A 6ft. (1.8m) sheet costing about £3.50 would make two cloches. You would need wire or metal pegs to hold the sides in place, and plastic ends to prevent the thing turning into an icy wind-tunnel (Figure 58).

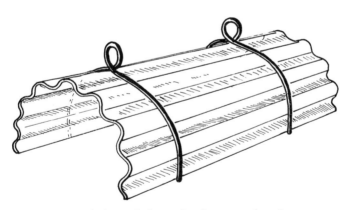

58 Rigid plastic cloche made of corrugated roofing.

Permanently shaped propagators, which act like a small greenhouse, consist of a clear hard plastic cover over a double-sized seed tray, and cost about £5–£6. You can make a similar propagating cover from the very thick, glass-clear plastic used in double glazing (Figure 59). Tape the cut corners or, if you have a very steady hand, try heat-sealing them. This size will take two standard seedtrays. The material costs about 25–30p per foot, but cheaper offcuts are often available in DIY shops.

Anything under cloches has to be watered artificially. This is easy enough with

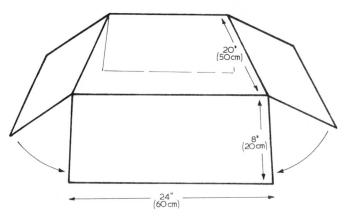

59 Propagator top. Seal edges with heat sealer or heavy duty tape.

small propagators, which retain moisture if they fit closely. Lifting a rigid cloche means loosening the wires and moving the plastic aside. Opening a sheeting tunnel is really awkward, since all the anchorages must be moved. Some of the semi-rigid cloches are therefore sold as 'self-watering', which may mean just having a few holes punched in the top, or an elaborate system of gutters and ribs to deflect the rain back to the plants. These will cost more, but may be worth it if you are likely to lack time for watering. You could punch holes in your DIY film tunnels, but not so many as to allow the cold air to get in too.

When buying plastic material the effect of the sun has to be considered. Ordinary plastic becomes brittle and will shatter after about six months outside. Nowadays, plastic sold for outdoor use should be ultra violet inhibited (UVI)—any rigid plastic cloche you buy should state this on its label. However, with thin sheeting for tunnel cloches, this may not be so important—these get very muddy and creased in use, and need very thorough washing and drying to restore them. As UVI sheeting costs over two and a half times as much as ordinary film, you might settle for buying the cheaper sort and using a new bit each year. After all, there is always another use in the garden for slightly grubby plastic.

No sort of plastic gives as much protection as glass. There has been an effort to improve the situation by making a double-walled polystyrene material, sold as Correx. This is always shown in illustrations as striped vertically. Although early complaints that it shattered within a few weeks have been overcome, it still has the disadvantage of being translucent—as distinct from transparent—and far too much light is cut off from the growing plants when they most need it. It does well for ends of a row of cloches in clear material.

Glass

Glass is still used by traditional gardeners because of its greater thermal insulation. A cloche can be simply two panes of glass held together by a wire or rubber clip

60 Rubber cloche clip.

at right angles (Figure 60). This gives excellent protection to growing seeds for the first few weeks of their lives. This kind of cloche is stable against the wind, but awkward to move aside for weeding or watering. However, if you have weeded the spot first, it should stay reasonably clear for a short time, and glass cloches will stand being hosed over or under better than plastic ones.

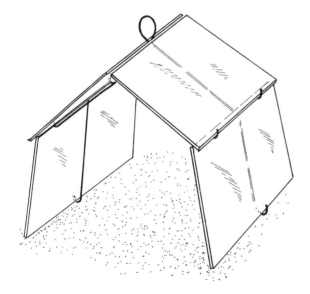

61 Barn cloche.

Where protection is needed for growing tender plants to an advanced stage, a tall, barn cloche is necessary (Figure 61). This has high sides and a mansard roof, held by a complicated system of wire hooks and clips. It is quite heavy and very awkward to move—the roof section tends to slide off if the clips are at all loose. An old method of correcting this was to fill in the top section with wire netting, from which the roof glass could be lifted for watering. A modern version of the triangular cloche, with wire sides which double as pea-guards, or glass supports, is marketed as Wupps-Westray at £7 for about 10ft (3m) of cloche. A barn cloche constructed on the same lines, would be much easier to move for weeding (Figure 62). Horticultural glass measures a standard 24 × 18in, or 24 × 24in

(60 × 45cm, or 60 × 60cm); two sheets would make a cloche, plus ends of broken glass.

If you have glass cloches, you soon acquire broken glass, either from careless moving or from stones flung by mowers or cultivators. Dogs and argumentative cats take their toll too. If you have children, glass is contra-indicated for cloches: babies fall on them, older children kick things through them; neither cloche nor child does the other any good. Glass is also risky for elderly people with unsteady balance or arthritic hands.

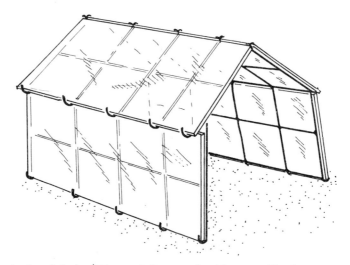

62 Guard cloche. Wire mesh framework with removable glass covers.

Cold frames

The next stage up from a cloche is a cold frame. This is basically a bottomless box, higher at one end than the other, and covered with a glass framework; the lid, or light, lifts off, slides back or hinges open for ventilation. You can make your own frame of scrap wood and an old window-frame—which will determine the size (Figure 63). Or design one to your own specification, tailored to the size of plant you mean to grow, and incorporating a front glass panel as well for extra light. There are commercial versions, with a framework in metal angle or rod, covered with various types of plastic, usually 'glazed' all round, sides as well, since this is cheaper. A simple 4 × 3ft (1.2m × 90cm) frame would cost upwards of £15, and a mini-version about £10. The 'barn' shape is probably best for these light-weight frames, with both sides hinged, since you have to lean on and over them to tend the plants (Figure 64).

A cold frame can be used to hold boxes or trays of seeds for later planting out, but mostly it serves to protect tender crops growing in soil. The base of the frame is filled with fertiliser and fine potting soil—sterilised to remove weed seeds, which

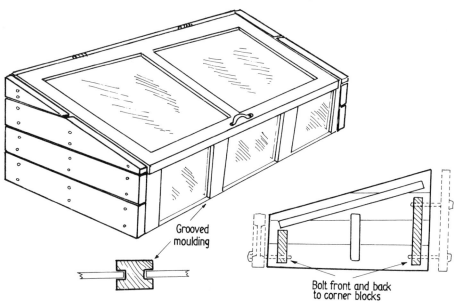

63 Cold frame. Made from old window-frame and scrap wood, with glazed front panel for extra light.

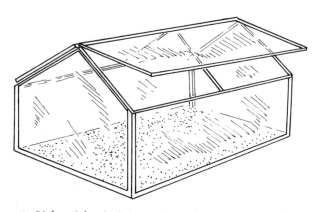

64 Lightweight plastic frame: barn shape, double opening.

saves a lot of trouble later on. Plants are usually started under closed cover; then, in high summer, the top light is opened up or taken off, and replaced when cooler weather comes. In order to close the light, any tallish-growing plants have to be laid down on straw. A small, portable frame can be stood over a crop in the open ground and moved along to shelter a later one.

Vertical cold frames, or wall greenhouses, are popular for growing tender, tall plants—like tomatoes—against the wall of the house. Generally a metal framework, about 5ft (1.5m) square and under 2ft (60cm) deep, it is hooked to the wall and covered with plastic. In this frame, you can start seeds in trays or pots; grow about two levels of bushy plants, like peppers, or shelves on staging, or around four tall plants, like tomatoes, in pots or bags on the ground. The house wall acts as a radiator and plastic covers are quite adequate for wind shelter; the frames are pretty stable, with the house to steady them. Typical prices for the framework plus cover start at £15 and, with shelves or staging provided, cost from £20.

Greenhouses

Greenhouses come in all shapes and sizes, from the small lean-to, which is a walk-in version of the vertical cold frame, to the 40ft (1.2m) free-standing palace. The minimum width is 4ft (1.2m) which allows one thin person to tend one line of plants or shelf of pots; 6ft (1.8m), two sets of shelves (staging); while 8ft (2.4m) is best for serious greenhouse work, leaving room for double rows in beds on either side and space to manoeuvre in the middle.

   In old-style greenhouses, the bottom half or third of the walls were generally panelled in cedar, with only the top part glazed. They were intended to be heated by large-diameter pipes along those walls, which is far too expensive for amateurs these days. In a cold greenhouse, that obscured area is not much use, except for

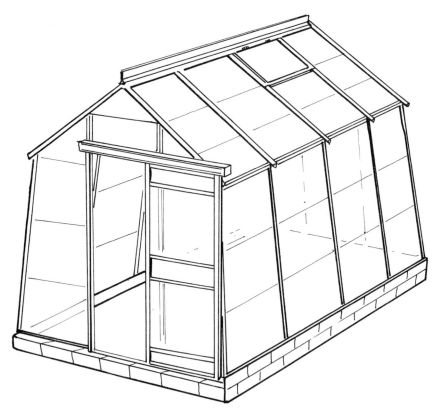

65 Dutch light greenhouse: best for unheated growing.

forcing rhubarb, storing pots and sheltering families of toads. In the modern 'Dutch light' greenhouse, with glass to ground-level, plants can be grown directly in the borders or in pots on the three-deck staging (Figure 65).

Traditional greenhouses, made of wood or aluminium with glass, are best from the point of view of temperature, stability and durability. They cost upwards of £100 new and are usually sold in a kit form which you erect yourself. Aluminium ones mostly bolt together, with patent clips for the glass, which makes glazing and replacement a much simpler and less messy business than using putty. Sometimes a second-hand greenhouse is advertised locally, but allow yourself most of the weekend to take it down and re-erect it.

Plastic greenhouses—metal-rod frameworks with covers of various plastics—are much cheaper. A typical polythene-covered house 8ft × 6ft × 6ft 3in (2.4m × 1.8m × 1.87m) costs about £30, compared with £110–£140 for a similar-sized glass house. The polythene is UVI, but any plastic sheeting used in a greenhouse is fearfully easy to rip and tends to take off in a high wind, leaving your plants naked to the elements. You must reckon on replacing the cover every third year, unless you are unlucky from the outset. This cover forms a very high proportion of the total cost—say, £15 at present prices—so over the years you will pay as much for a plastic house as for a glass one, and with more trouble attached.

Rigid or semi-rigid plastic is better, but for a similar size of house a PVC roofing-type sheet costs about £70. With any plastic house, make sure that adequate ventilators are provided. A greenhouse is like an oven in summer and plants must have plenty of moving air to survive. It is simple to put windows in a glass house, but not nearly as easy in plastic. The rigid house has no roof ventilator to let the hot air out; it has doors at both ends, but these complicate planting across the back as well as the sides, so reducing the productive area.

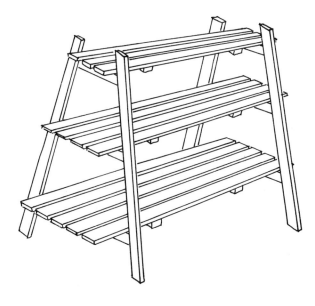

66 Slatted wooden staging:
paint or ship-varnish annually.

We would vote for a glass greenhouse, if you can possibly afford it, with a rigid plastic one as second choice. Although its maintenance problems are infinitely less, a glass greenhouse probably counts as a fixture, should you have to move in a year or two; it is certainly more trouble to dismantle than a plastic one, which is rather like a frame tent.

The traditional type of staging used in a greenhouse consists of triangular framing supporting three decks of slatted shelves in reducing widths (Figure 66). Painted annually or varnished with polyurethane ship varnish, wooden staging lasts for years. It is simple to make yourself, or you can buy it from about £15 for an 8ft (2.4m)-long house. Metal triangular supports are also available—a pair of two-deck trestles cost around £6, for example. Modern aluminium narrow shelves for hanging on the wall bars can be bought for about £2.50 per 3ft (90cm) shelf, and two-deck tables complete with shallow trays for around £35 for an 8ft (2.4m) house (Figure 67).

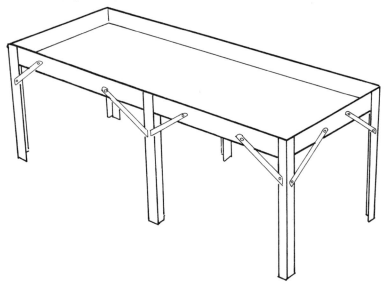

67 Metal staging with tray top: one or two layers available.

The trays are filled with sand or gravel on which the pots stand. If the sand is kept wet, the plant roots can draw up moisture and the air in the greenhouse is kept humid. The trays can also be used for ring culture of tomatoes (page 79). On ordinary staging, cheap plastic tea-trays will serve the same purpose, but painted metal ones will rust in a season in the damp atmosphere.

Any old, narrow table can be used in the greenhouse, but first paint or varnish the wood and wrap polythene bags round the feet where they touch the earth. The standard width for staging along the sides is a maximum 24in (60cm) and across the back about 3ft (90cm) or your own convenient stretch. If you use a table wider than the door, a clear area will be needed nearby to shift it in and out.

In high summer, the roof will need shading; this can be done by painting it with a thin whitewash or cheap emulsion, which can be scraped off again in autumn (fairly cheap but nasty to remove); by rigging up old curtains or nylon shading net inside or out (costing little or nothing), or by fitting automatic blinds which raise and lower themselves according to the amount of light (very efficient, very smart and very expensive).

Advantages of protected growing

Any form of protected sowing means extra work, since the natural rainfall cannot easily reach the growing crops, even in the so-called self-watering cloches. The actual equipment costs more than plain sowing in the garden, and this reduces the apparent return in the first year. It is all the more important to choose durable materials, which will last long enough for the initial costs to be absorbed. Cloches unused in mid-winter and mid-summer have to be stored somewhere out of harm's way, while frames and greenhouses are a permanent feature of the garden.

The advantages of protected growing are: 1, the opportunity to extend the normal cropping season by at least two months and probably more; 2, tender plants can be grown which are not normally practical for outdoor sowings because these leave too little development time before the frost; 3, it is possible with a cold greenhouse, and with careful management with lesser protection, to have something fresh growing all the year round; 4, a greenhouse gives somewhere sheltered to work on gardening operations when the temperature out of doors is uninviting; 5, early cash crops can be raised for market; and 6, the more you can grow in the colder times of the year, the less you have to buy at top prices.

Siting your greenhouse

Because you will want to work in your greenhouse when the weather is bad, and attend to it possibly late at night if conditions suddenly change for the worse, it should be sited near the house—not at the bottom of the garden, as indicated in so many landscape plans. Set it just beyond the area shaded by the house and run a path to it, so you do not have to wade through wet grass to reach it. The nearer it is, the easier it will be to connect electricity or carry water. Try not to let the door opening face the prevailing wind, so the plants are not assaulted every time you go in. Leave room outside the door for getting staging in and out, if you want to plant into the greenhouse borders in summer, and for bringing up the wheelbarrow when you need to change the soil each year.

If the site faces south or west, the greenhouse may get too much sun in high summer, which would wilt the plants. A deciduous tree, carefully sited to serve as a screen, will put on foliage in summer to give dappled shade, while in winter the bare branches do not obstruct light at all.

What about heating?

An entirely heated greenhouse is probably out of the question for anyone but the commercial grower or the fabulously rich. A lot of the heat from a glass-walled house, and practically all the heat from a plastic greenhouse, would escape into the air, which might improve the local temperature but is hardly economic. You might be able to set up a solar panel for greenhouse use (page 237); or, in the few cases where it is practical, tap the resources of a methane digester or a wood/rubbish-burning stove.

To prevent some heat loss, it may be possible to 'double-glaze' the greenhouse with bubble plastic, or line it with polythene sheeting; in wooden houses, this can be pinned on, but for aluminium you will need plastic 'suckers'. You could curtain off one end of the greenhouse, or drape plastic over the staging to make a small tent. Place a small heater underneath, taking great care that the plastic cannot flap on to it. The lining will reduce the amount of available light, possibly to unacceptable levels, and watering must be very cautiously done. Too little and the plants will dry out; too much and mould will develop.

Heated propagators

On the small scale, a heated propagator will ensure that, even in the north, early crops can be raised. The standard unit comprises an electrically heated base, with thermostatic control, over which the seed trays or pots are balanced. This is often topped with a shaped plastic cover to keep in the heated air. Propagators are not cheap: a single tray-unit with cover costs about £8; a base unit for three to four trays around £15. They certainly work; but when the seedlings have outgrown them, more spacious protected accommodation will be needed.

You could make your own propagator in various ways. Tubular heaters—giving 60 watts and costing just over £1 a foot run, obtainable from an electrical wholesaler—could be clipped to brackets under the staging which holds your trays and boxes. A soil cable kit—costing about £9, sometimes less—could be used to make a heated base unit, taking six trays: lay a bed of sand or pea gravel in a large flat tray, set out the cable in a grid pattern, with no part touching another, cover with more sand and sit the trays on top (Figure 68). A thermostat, if you want one, costs under £2 from the same source. Study the small ads before buying, as any equipment like this is a lot more expensive in a local store.

Longer soil cables can be used directly in the earth either in greenhouse beds or in the open garden. The cables are set out in grids or long rows, up and down, in freshly dug soil. It is important not to forget just where they run, or adjacent digging may spear them. Obviously, the heat so generated should not be allowed to dissipate—cover the area with a line of cloches or a cold frame.

All these heated propagators have to be powered by electricity, which is far too expensive to be used casually. However, there is a natural form of under-soil heating—the hot bed—for which a supply of fresh manure, from horses, cows, pigs, or sheep, is the main requisite.

A hot bed

Build a box with the cheapest sort of building block, or from old bricks—which takes longer. Make it 3ft (90cm) deep and cover it with an old window-frame; if you are using a 4 × 3ft (1.2 × .9m) frame, construct it as shown in Figure 69. Fill the box with layers of decomposing leaves, manure, grass cuttings, old compost, more manure—and sprinkle all the non-manure layers with ammonium sulphate. Press the lot well down—tread it, if you dare, wearing long wellies. Top it with at least 6in (15cm) of good quality earth and cover the whole lot with your frame, tightly closed.

The whole thing will heat up to a very high temperature, and will smell indescribable for a day or two. Let it heat as much as it will, testing the temperature now and then. Wait until the reading starts to fall before planting; when it registers 80°F (27°C) or less, the bed is ready for use. The soil on top will have been automatically sterilised by the heat. Plant your seeds and ventilate the bed a little from time to time. A bed made in winter will stay warm right through until spring or early summer, by which time cold-frame protection will be adequate.

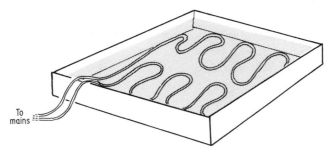

68 Propagator base: soil-heating cable buried in sand and topped with soil compost. Don't let loops of wire touch each other.

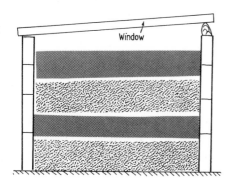

69 Hot bed: layers of compost, manure, etc covered with cold frame or old window sloped for drainage.

Harnessing the Elements –
Alternative Energy

If food is the main priority, and the main expense, for most families, energy runs it a close second. Fuel costs are rising all the time, and we have to pay an even heavier price because of the way we have squandered it—in uninsulated homes, thirsty car engines and an agriculture tied to mechanisation and oil-based chemicals.

While we can reverse some of these trends and get back to more economical ways of living and working, it is important to develop alternative sources for the essential energy requirements. Few people want to return to a life-style of constant discomfort and back-breaking work, and there is no reason why we should have to. There is no real shortage of energy, it is simply that we have tied all our equipment to the wasting resources of the oil-well and the coal-mine, and largely ignored the almost limitless supplies of solar and wind power.

Solar energy

The sun radiates a colossal amount of heat and light into space. Only a tiny fraction of it reaches the earth, and of this only a fraction again actually penetrates to ground level, but even in Britain this accessible energy averages more than 10 watts per square foot (over 100 W per sq m). This means that a normal-sized family house could pick up power at an average rate of 5 kW—more than the average domestic electricity demand even in winter. Over the whole area of the British Isles, solar power, if collected properly, could amount to 400 times the output of all our power stations put together.

So why do so few people actually use this energy? Apart from sheer lethargy, and the legacy of 'cheap fuel', there are two main reasons. One is that, while the *average* amount of solar power received is more than most people's requirements, the quantity we get in the winter is far lower, as little as 1 W/sq ft (10 W/sq m) in some northerly places. Unless you have a very large solar installation, therefore, you need some kind of conventional heating to back it up, and this works out expensive in capital equipment costs whichever way you do it.

The second reason for the neglect of solar power is that any collector obviously has to be set up where it can receive the most sun, usually on a south-facing roof of a house. This entails a lot more structural alteration than, say, putting in a conventional boiler. However, if you do most of the work yourself, the expense of the equipment and installation need not be crippling, and you should reckon to get your money back, in terms of saved fuel bills, in a few years.

70 Solar panel: typical design; the inlet and outlet pipes should be lagged.

Solar panels

The most popular type of collector is a solar panel with circulated water (Figure 70). It works basically as a radiator in reverse, picking up heat from the sun and transferring this to water that circulates through the panel. To achieve maximum absorption, the surface is painted matt black. Special paints, usually based on copper oxide, are available, but blackboard paint does quite well. There are several quite good solar panels on the market, made up complete with channels for the water, black finish, and plumbing outlets to connect up to the water system. Alternatively, you could use some second-hand panel-type radiators—although it is fair to say that these are not really intended to be exposed to the weather, and may corrode externally—or clip a labyrinth of $\frac{1}{4}$in (6mm) microbore copper piping to a metal backing plate (Figure 71), if you are good at handling this material and can make tidy bends.

Whatever the material of the panel, it should be mounted in an insulated box (fibreglass insulation is ideal), and covered in with a sheet of glass tightly sealed to the box, so that there is no loss of heat through air escaping. A few panels use transparent plastic sheets, which are obviously less liable to break, but so far

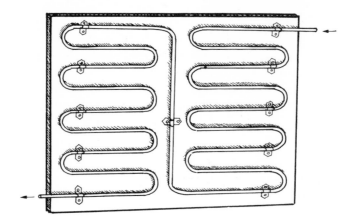

71 Solar panel made from microbore piping on a metal backing sheet. This should be enclosed as in figure 70.

nobody has made a plastic that stands more than two to three years in sunlight without cracking or discolouring, so it is not really a satisfactory covering. If you are making your own panels, you can design the outer cases so that they fit horticultural glass, which comes in standard sizes of 24 × 24in (60 × 60cm), 24 × 18in (60 × 45cm) or 18 × 18in (45 × 45cm). When buying commercial

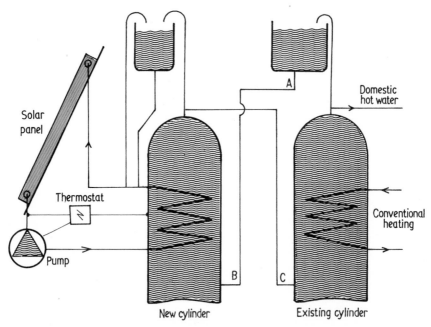

72 Fitting an auxiliary cylinder for solar heating. The existing cold-water inlet (AC) is redirected to form AB, while C is connected to the outlet of the new cylinder.

panels, check whether the price includes the glass—if not, 45 sq ft (4 sq m) of it will cost you at least another £15.

To get the heated water from the panel to your existing hot-water system, you will need connecting pipes running to a cylinder. If you have the space, you can fit another indirect cylinder next to your existing one (Figure 72). Alternatively, you can fit a dual-purpose cylinder in place of your existing one; water from the solar panel runs through one internal coil and your conventional heating boiler is connected to the other (Figure 73). The main reasons for isolating your solar panel from the rest of the water in the system are: 1, so that a leakage or burst in the panel will not empty your whole hot-water supply over the roof; and, 2, to avoid such bursts, it is best to add anti-freeze to the water circulating through the panel, and you do not want this mixed up with the rest of the water.

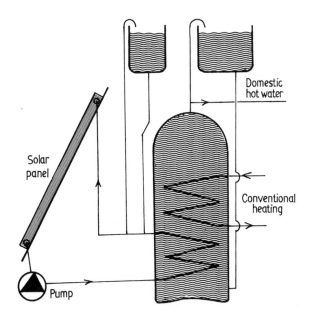

Solar panel

Domestic hot water

Conventional heating

Pump

73 Using a dual purpose cylinder for solar heating. An auxiliary header tank must be fitted into the solar-heated circuit.

You should also have a pump, of the conventional central-heating type, so that water is circulated when you want it. There are gravity arrangements in use for some solar-heating systems, but they put severe restrictions on the placing of the panel and cylinder, and even the type of piping you can use for connections. The pump can be controlled by a thermostat that measures the temperature of the water in the main cylinder and that in the panel; it switches on the pump only when the water in the panel is hotter than the inside, thus ensuring that you do not circulate hot water from inside the house to warm the night air outside. Suitable thermostats can be obtained from mail-order electrical suppliers.

Economics of solar heating

It is not really worth while thinking about solar heating for the average house—at least in Britain—unless you are prepared to fit a minimum of 45 sq ft (5 sq m) of collector surface. You have to buy all the ancillaries—the new cylinder, the pump, the thermostat and so on—whatever size your installation; many people have been disappointed with commercial systems merely because the panel area was far too small to give them any reasonable return on their outlay. If someone tries to sell you a solar-heating system with one panel about as big as an average window, forget it.

If you shop around, you should be able to get commercial panels adding up to this area for about £300; if you build them yourself, or use radiators and build your own casing, you could probably do it for £100. The pump, thermostat control and extra cylinder—or replacing your present one with a dual-purpose pattern—will cost a further £50, and piping, plumbing joints and so on about £25 more. All these prices assume that you study the market thoroughly and make full use of discounts and special offers. Central heating is a cut-throat trade, and you can always find someone anxious to undercut the others. The total outlay should thus be about £375 for commercial panels; £175 for an entirely do-it-yourself job.

Labour is a more tricky thing to cost. Can you do simple plumbing? In our opinion, all plumbing is simple these days, with ready-made joints, micro-bore piping, and PTFE jointing compounds, but it really depends whether you have had any practice. You don't want to learn the job when balanced on one foot at the top of your roof—but, if you know enough to install another radiator in your central heating system, you know enough to plumb in a solar panel. The same applies to the electrical work: it is all elementary, except perhaps setting up the thermostat control. Maybe you could find a friend who does electronics as a hobby, and drag him away from his synthesisers and computerised noughts-and-crosses to do something useful for a change. To get up to the roof for installation, you will need a good ladder or maybe a tower-scaffold, which you could hire for a week for about £15—it won't take you a week to get your panels up, but it will probably take more than one day, so you might as well hire for a week and use the rest of the time repairing broken tiles or clearing out the gutters.

You ought to be able to cover labour and hire of equipment for a further £20, making the total installed costs £395 for commercial panels, £195 for home-made ones.

For this outlay you can expect to collect (in the UK) usable heat equivalent to about 2,000 kW-hours (units) per year. If you used electricity to heat water, this would cost you at least £45. Deduct about £5 for electricity for running the pump, etc, and your solar heater saves £40 per year. The pay-back period for a commercial installation thus becomes about ten years, and for the home-made variety five years.

If you heated your water with solid fuel, the solar panel might save you about

£22 per year, so the pay-back periods expand to eighteen and nine years respectively. For the commercial-panel model, this is about the same pay-back period as double-glazing; but, on the other hand, every rise in the price of fuel is going to make the costing look more favourable.

Siting the panels
Obviously the panels have to go where they can catch most sun, which means facing south and at an angle to receive as much of the winter sun as possible. The best angle for this is given by the simple formula $L + 13\frac{1}{2}°$ to the horizontal, where L is the latitude of your site in degrees. Thus, in Bedford, at latitude 52°, you should set up your panels at $65\frac{1}{2}°$; in Inverness ($57\frac{1}{2}°N$), they should be at 71°.

If the panels have to go on your front roof, or anywhere at the front of the house that shows from the road, you will need planning permission to install them. Planning officers vary enormously in their attitudes to wild ideas like saving fuel, so it may be as well to collect some photographs of existing installations to show your local officer what the panels will look like. If you buy commercial panels, you will often get an illustrated brochure showing incredibly elegant installations.

An alternative to the roof might be a sunny site in the garden; here you will need to lag the pipe runs very thoroughly, but at least this does not need planning permission.

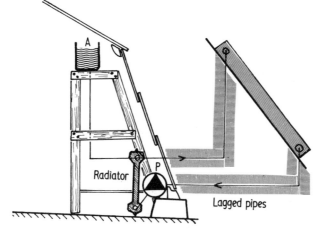

74 Greenhouse heating with a solar panel. Auxiliary header tank (A) can be mounted on the top staging or anywhere higher than the panel.

Solar panels in the garden can also be used very effectively to increase the heating in a greenhouse. Set up a line of panels, facing south (Figure 74), with a pump and thermostat control as for the house installation, and use these to supply hot water to a radiator under the staging in the greenhouse. If you have room to fit a well-lagged hot-water cylinder beside the house, this could conserve the heat overnight (Figure 75).

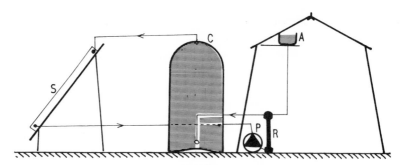

75 Greenhouse heating with a solar panel and storage. P = pump; R = radiator; A = header tank; C = cylinder, which should be heavily lagged.

A solar dryer

The sun can be used to provide hot air, of course, instead of hot water, and this means that the collector can be of much lighter construction, and there is no plumbing to do. You can try your hand at such a collector to make a solar dryer, which is very useful for preparing stores like prunes and apple rings.

The drying chamber is basically a box with perforated shelves, to let the hot air through—peg-board would be suitable, if you give it a couple of coats of gloss paint—while the solar collector (Figure 76) is made like a drawer, except that it has an openable flap at the lower end, to let air in, and is covered with glass. The inner surface should be painted black with a matt surface—blackboard paint is

76 Solar dryer. The flap at the bottom of the collector can be opened or closed to control air flow. The roof should not fit too closely to the walls, as air has to escape under the eaves.

suitable, or you can stir some fine pumice or other abrasive into ordinary black paint to give a matt finish.

In action, the flap at the bottom is set so as to control the flow of air, to allow for the strength of the sun and the temperature that you require for drying. You could, if you wanted to be more elaborate, fit a small cylindrical fan—as used in fan-heaters—at the lower end, and control this with a thermostat in the drying chamber. This does mean, however, that you have to be able to get electricity to your dryer.

Incidentally, when your dryer is not in use for food, it is the ideal arrangement for sterilising soil for the greenhouse, etc (see page 65).

Solar stills

Except in really desert areas, there is usually some water in the soil, even during a drought. The trouble is that it is rarely where you want it; established trees get plenty, but thirsty new seedlings find none. You can get over this to some extent by setting up simple solar stills on any unplanted piece of ground—even between rows—to catch every drop of the moisture that is constantly being sucked up by the sun (Figure 77).

A polythene cloche is set up to condense the moisture rising from the ground, with its edges arranged so that the water collected will not run back on to the soil

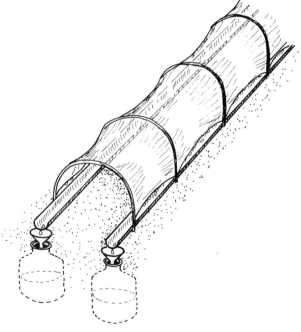

77 Simple solar still. Moisture from the ground condenses on the plastic cloche and runs via gutters to collecting bottles sunk in the ground.

but drips into lengths of plastic guttering. These are slightly sloped so that the water eventually runs into a storage tank set into the ground—this could be something as simple as a large plastic bottle with a funnel in the top. You can lift this out when full, or pump the water out of it *in situ* by fixing a piece of plastic tube through to the bottom of the bottle before you sink it into the ground.

You can also use a simple still of this kind to get (fairly) clean water from brackish or even salt supplies. Simply place another piece of gutter (Figure 78 down the middle of the polythene cloche, and allow a slow stream of your contaminated water to flow down it. As the sun evaporates it, clean water will collect in the still reservoir.

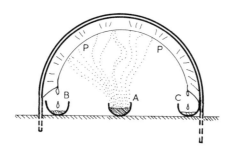

78 Solar still for brackish or salt water. This trickles down central gutter (A), condenses on plastic (P) and runs via gutters (CC) to collecting bottles.

Such a device could also purify waste water for drinking, but it is difficult to keep the surface of the plastic free from dirt and bacteria, and it would be necessary to boil any water collected this way before drinking it.

Wind power

We tend to associate wind power with two jobs: grinding corn and pumping water, but windmills can be used for any heavy work, and have successfully ground cement, broken stones, worked saw-benches and run electric generators— *Make Your Own Electricity* by Terence McLaughlin (David and Charles, 1977) gives details of wind-generator construction.

Savonius rotor

A very simple type of windmill, useful for such purposes as pumping water, is the Savonius rotor (Figure 79). You can make one very easily and cheaply. Cut an old 50gal (225l) oil-drum down the middle, so that you get two half-cylinders; bolt these to two discs cut from $\frac{1}{2}$in (12.5mm) plywood, 3ft (90cm) in diameter, as illustrated. Large washers will be needed to spread the load on the bolts, as the metal used for these drums is not very thick.

The discs will need bearings; the lower one can be made from a salvaged wheel-bearing from a small car—you can pick one of these up very cheaply at a car-breaker's yard—using the wheel studs to bolt the bearing to the disc. The upper

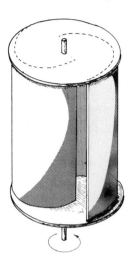

79 Savonius rotor. Two half-cylinders are fixed offset from the centre of circular mountings.

bearing takes only a light load, so you should be able to use a medium-duty ball bearing from a scrap car, old lawnmower or some similar piece of machinery. Fix a pulley wheel to the upper disc so that you can run a belt drive to the pump or whatever it is you want to operate.

Now make a framework (Figure 80) in 4in (10cm) sq timber. This may sound heavy, but there are many strains on the structure, particularly when the wind is high and the rotor spinning well. Wire guys, tightened by turnbuckles, are set at each corner and connected to iron stakes or heavy stones buried in the ground. This will help to ensure that the framework cannot lean out of true and get in the way of the rotor.

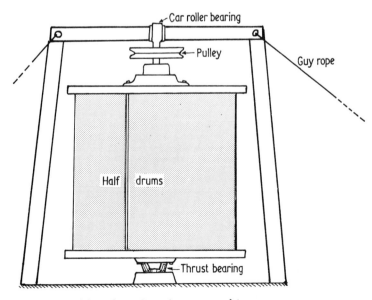

80 Mounting a Savonius rotor to drive a pump, etc.

A Savonius rotor of these dimensions should give about 0.13 horse-power (100 watts) in a wind of 20mph (32km/h); 0.45hp (335 watts) in a 30mph (48km/h) wind. This may not sound spectacular but it will pump a lot of water—say, from your rainwater butt to greenhouse, or for a simple irrigation scheme. Built from scrap parts and second-hand timber, the rotor should cost you under £10, which is less than a 'half-horse' electric motor, irrespective of the running costs.

A slat-mill

The conventional type of slat-mill (Figure 81) is also simple to make on the small scale. It will provide a very useful source of power in the garden and looks a great deal more interesting than concrete gnomes. The diagram shows the dimensions for a 6ft (1.8m) diameter mill: this is quite a good size, as suitable pieces of timber can easily be found. Its output will be about 0.45hp (335 watts) in a 20mph (32km/h) wind; 1.5hp (1150 watts) in a 30mph (48 km/h) wind—so you could use it to drive, say, a 10in (25cm) circular saw.

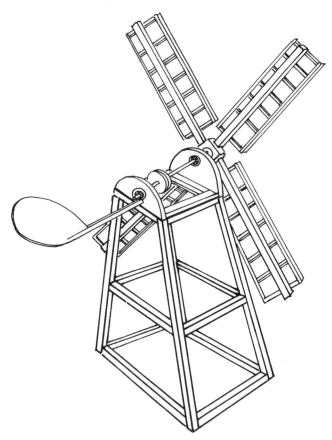

81 Simple slat-mill for driving garden machinery.

The sails are what are called warped sails; the sail-bars which cross the sail-stock —the centre spine of the sail—are set at an angle to the plane of the sail, and this, the weather-angle, decreases from about 18° near the centre of the sail to 7° at the outer end. This variation is to allow for the fact that the sail-tips have to travel much faster through the air than the portions near the centre, and therefore encounter more pressure.

The main shaft—the sail-stock—takes a lot of strain and should, if possible, be made from hardwood, like ash or hickory, about 1½in (37.5m) square. You can sometimes find suitable pieces of hardwood in the framing of old furniture or, if you are lucky, in an old house that is being demolished.

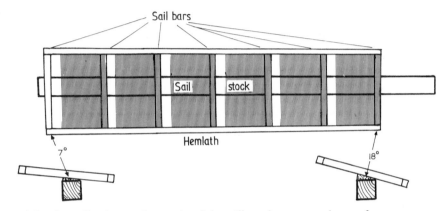

82 Sail for slat-mill. The weather angle of the sailbars decreases as shown, from centre to top. Cladding can be canvas or pieces of marine plywood, as illustrated.

83 Setting back the shaft of a windmill, to relieve strain on mounting.

Finish off the sails by nailing the edge—the hemlath—to the sail-bars. You can cover the sails with canvas, as in the traditional windmill, or alternatively use marine plywood to make fixed slats to catch the wind (Figure 82).

Four sails like this have to be fitted into a large central boss—called the poll-head in real windmills—which carries the shaft. An iron rod is suitable for the shaft, which is best set back at an angle of about 15° (Figure 83) rather than horizontal; this saves strain on the bearings. Fit a pulley to the shaft, and you have a power unit that will work very well when pointing into the wind.

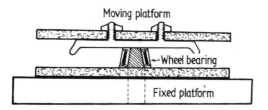

84 Bearings for windmill. The mill mountings are fixed to the upper (moving) platform, which is fastened by wheelstuds on the hub.

The traditional mill has to be able to point into the wind from any direction, which means that it must be mouned on a rotatable platform. Figure 84 shows how this is achieved for your small slat-mill. The mill and its shaft are set up on a round platform made from $\frac{1}{2}$in (12.5mm) plywood; this itself is fixed to a salvaged wheel hub and bearing—obtained from a car-breaker's yard. The wheel studs serve to bolt the plywood to the hub, and the fixed part of the bearing is fastened to the pole or other mounting on which the mill is set up. All that needs to be added is a tail that will turn the mill into the wind (Figure 85).

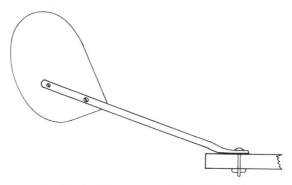

85 Simple tail to turn a mill into the wind.

One very useful occupation for such a wind-powered unit is to drive a small hammer-mill or compost shredder. You may have to look around for a while to find a shredder in Britain, at least on the second-hand market, though they are obtainable in the United States. When there is a good wind blowing, you can toss in all your awkward bits of garden waste that would otherwise take a long time to compost down—cabbage stalks, sweet-corn stems, tough weeds like cow-parsley and docks, hedge trimmings, even old newspapers—and they will be shredded to a compact mass that composts quickly.

Meanwhile, Back at the Ranch...

Keeping livestock

There was a time when the ambition of all true Britons was to own three acres and a cow. This is no longer a practical proposition, with the rising price of land, or viable as an agricultural unit. You could, theoretically, run a cow on an acre of land, devoting half of it to the animal and part of the fodder for it. Even so, the cow would have to come inside in the winter—it would need a strong, weather-proof shed—and concentrates, very expensive now, would have to be bought in. Cows are not cheap, and need skilled care to remain healthy. They also require servicing (fee for bull) and some help with calving (fee for vet). For the ordinary garden-owner, cows are definitely 'out'.

So are sheep, which need to be in multiples and require the same area as a cow. Very strong fencing is essential, for the urge to escape is born in them. They follow their chosen leader anywhere—into your garden, into the neighbour's garden, out into traffic. They eat roots and brassicas and dance on cloches and frames. They give you meat and wool—and a lot of headaches.

Pigs were traditionally kept in cottage gardens, where they fattened up happily on left-overs, with a bit of grain thrown in at gleaning time. They will eat any-thing, but need a lot of it, which means that, unless you have a large garden and a wasteful family to match, you will have to collect swill from pubs or buy in food. Modern pigs pick up nasty, notifiable diseases from strange swill, and have to be slaughtered.

They need grazing space in summer, and unless securely fenced off, they will graze on, and dig up completely, any garden plot and its produce. They must have a sty to live in, and sows want a low hutch to farrow in, when you have paid to have them mated. You could build a sty of any old sturdy scrap, but this would look a mess—and a messy sty in a back garden attracts unfavourable attention from the neighbours. Pigs are, in fact, as clean as their owners let them be. They have a very rapid throughput, and must be mucked out frequently. Their manure is rich, and stinks after about six hours. Unless it is shifted, they slip around in it, and get plastered from top to toe.

245

An earth-floored sty cannot be cleaned out properly, so you must either build a floor of proper concrete or indented tile, which can be raked out and swilled down with water, or learn to live with an increasing aroma. This is when your neighbours will call in the public health inspector and raise an action for nuisance. Either way, pigs aren't going to be easy to live with.

Goats

Goats are not so piggish about food. They eat rough vegetation which no cow would even look at. Theoretically, goats could exist on wayside verges and common land, but in practice verges tend to be sprayed with weedkiller and commons are strewn with broken glass. Goats cannot be run in an orchard, because they strip every bit of growth from the trees. This means strong fencing, but as they can jump incredibly high it is best to tether them by long ropes. They need dry housing to sleep in, and concentrates must be bought in for nanny goats in milk. Mating, too, costs money. Goats produce a lot of milk, which is excellent for babies and people allergic to cow's milk. It tastes rather odd, so try some before you start keeping goats. An interesting cheese can be made from it; this is admirable when washed down with brandy in France, but is not quite the same with tea.

Further information can be obtained from The British Goat Society, Rougham, Bury St Edmunds, Suffolk, and from *The Goatkeeper's Guide* by Jill Salmon (David and Charles).

Poultry

Geese, ducks and chickens are the common sorts. Ducks need water to root around in and soon get distressed if they have no access to it. Geese are admirable security guards—even against their owner's family—but should not be kept where they can get into the road, because they attack passers-by, and can injure children, whose mothers do not like this. Geese also cover any grass with their huge squashy droppings.

Hens are, with certain reservations, a practical proposition on a small scale. They need grass, but they are improvident and rip it to pieces with their claws. When they are laying, they must have grain—some of this can come from wheat straw. Check the cost of local straw and grain before you buy chickens. Both commodities are more easily and cheaply found in the country than in town.

A chicken house, preferably of wood, will be needed, with nesting boxes accessible from outside and a food hopper for expectant hens; also a wire run of small mesh, so that baby chicks can't get out or strangle themselves in the attempt. A second-hand chicken house can often be bought locally, or obtained through *Exchange and Mart* or advertisements in *The Poultry World*.

In theory, chickens can run free round the orchard, picking up scraps hurled out there. In practice, they need to be fenced in, because they are incredibly stupid and will wander off for miles and forget their way home. They are totally vulnerable to attack by foxes—even in the suburbs; they don't run to safety, even if the house is a few feet away, but sit there squawking until they are eaten.

Half a dozen birds is about the smallest number to maintain a reasonable supply of eggs. Hens don't need a cockerel to produce eggs, though they do to fertilise them, if you want to increase your stocks. But don't keep a rooster in the suburbs; it will wake up early—and so will everyone else within earshot.

Birds can be bought very cheaply as day-old chicks, which are pretty but fragile; as eight-week pullets, for just over £1, or at point-of-lay for about £2–£3—the most practical choice. Read up the subject first—public libraries have dozens of books on poultry keeping. If you decide to go in for it, you should buy a copy of your own to fly to in time of trouble.

Rabbits

Easy to keep in a garden, rabbits need strong cages of adequate size, with sleeping and living compartments. A suitable hutch can be adapted from an old orange box or the base drawer of an old-fashioned wardrobe. The dimensions vary according to the size of the rabbit, which must have room to stretch and turn without hitting the sides.

Rabbits like an outdoor run in summer, but must be confined in a netting cage, or they will eat every vegetable in sight. The cage will also protect them from predators, which they are not clever enough to do for themselves.

They should be given hay or straw for sleeping; and fed with vegetable scraps and ends, plus a daily meal of bought-in oats, bran or other cereal.

In return, rabbits provide you with a good supply of meat, which mixes well with vegetables in casseroles and stews. Their skins can be tanned and made into rugs or garments, with some sales potential. Flemish Giants are best for meat, Rexes and chinchillas for their skins. The Angora rabbit's long fur can be stripped and spun into wool; each produces about 1lb a year, but brushing and combing the coat regularly is essential so that it does not get matted.

Rabbits breed like rabbits—thirty days from mating to birth, then off again as soon as the buck sees the doe. This will necessitate a lot of cages and room to stack them. Rabbits need an awful lot of straw and hay to keep warm and dry, and they eat their bedding—which can be pricy. Straw costs 35–50p a bale off the farm, hay twice that. In a pet shop in town, the cost may be ten times as much, so check your source of supply before you embark on the enterprise.

Get a book on rabbit keeping and make the cages before you buy the stock. Good does cost at least £6, though younger and possibly weaker stock can be bought in markets for less. A good local breeder would be the best source of supply and could give advice on cage sizes and eating habits.

Caring for your stock

The most important consideration is that animals and birds are a tie. You must deal with them at least twice a day—letting them out, shutting them in, preparing food and feeding, mucking out, providing cages and bedding, coping with childbirth, checking on their welfare in the worst of weather and being alert to the first sound of fox attack in the night.

Making arrangements to cover a garden's needs, if you are away for a few days or a long holiday, is not too difficult. But for stock, you must have experienced care. An ignorant neighbour or a casual teenager won't do. Animals left unattended or treated wrongly die. This isn't just upsetting for the owner, it could lead to legal prosecution. So, unless you are able to give your stock 365-day care, don't keep any.

There is also the question of what happens when they reach the end of their useful lives. You keep hens for their eggs and when they stop laying they will do for the pot. Goats give milk but, when they are old, they are meat—so are all billy kids. Ducks, geese and turkeys are mostly destined for the table, pigs completely so. But before they can be eaten, they must be killed. Some animals must be slaughtered by licensed persons anyway—this adds to the cost of rearing pigs. Can you see yourself killing the rest? It would look odd taking rabbits or chickens to the butcher or farmer to be killed, apart from the cost. The alternative is physically picking up a creature and breaking its neck or cutting its throat—and seeing it jerk about *after* you have done that.

Even if you are sure you could carry out this necessary task quite unemotionally, will you feel the same after you have got to know an animal over weeks or months of protecting it from danger? Your children certainly won't. A daddy who slays Henrietta Hen or Benjamin Bunny is a loathsome creature not fit to be spoken to for at least a week. The more sensitive child will refuse to eat the cooked corpse or will sick it up over the table. This is silly, weak and sentimental—and thoroughly understandable.

One way round this is to arrange with another animal-keeping family that you eat theirs and they eat yours. Your Henrietta becomes their *poule au pot*, and their Mary Ann is your *pollo diavolo*. But if your children are bosom friends of the other children, or even attend the same school, you have double trouble.

A better alternative is to depersonalise any animals destined for the pot. Number them for statistical purposes and from time to time harp on the quantity of meals they represent. This is rather difficult with pigs, who are bright, affectionate creatures, but you could give the children one of the litter to keep as a pet—with a promise that it will never be killed.

Fish farming

If you have a swimming pool, minus chlorine, or a very large tank, you could heat it with a solar panel and keep tilapia fish. They breed easily, live on any waste vegetable matter, provide a good source of protein—and apparently have no personalities whatsoever. The magazine, *Fish Farming International*, will give you further details of costs and methods.

Bee-keeping

Bees provide honey, which was our natural sweetener long before this new-fangled stuff, sugar, came to Europe, and many folk claim that eating honey has far fewer attendant health risks. It certainly tastes delightful and, when you get tired of it, you can use it to make mead.

Bees take up very little room and can be kept in quite a small garden. They look after themselves, feeding from your plants and flowers, or any others in the neighbourhood. They need very little attention and can be left alone while you are away on holiday without any worries. You might be able to acquire them free of charge—if you find a swarm on public land and have the nerve and the very simple know-how to collect it. Once you have them—provided you don't take all their honey in summer—they stay with you for years, recreating colonies all the time.

If they are not interfered with, bees are not normally dangerous. Only when you disturb the hives for honey gathering will they get upset, and maybe sting; you should therefore wear impervious garments and a face veil for the purpose. Just a few people are allergic to bee-stings, so it might be sensible for the whole family to experience being stung before you start—if anyone is more than mildly irritated, consult a doctor to check if this is an allergic reaction.

Although bees can be kept in any old box or rough hive, it is a lot simpler to use a purpose-built sectional hive, in which the honey layer can be separated from the bee-grub layer, without killing the bees or going through a rather messy process. These sectional hives cost £50 or £60 new, but secondhand ones, complete with a stock of bees, can often be picked up for half that price if you study local advertisements, *Exchange and Mart* or any bee-keeping magazine.

The Ministry of Agriculture publishes a series of pamphlets on bee-keeping, beehives and allied subjects; and a useful book by Ted Hooper is *Guide to Bees and Honey* (Blandford Press). There are often local classes in bee-keeping, and it is useful to join a bee-keepers' club, for contacts with experienced handlers and possible sources of stock and hives.

Does It Pay?

The whole enterprise of running a self-sufficient garden is intended to be cost-effective. You will want to check if your personal effort is economically viable, if only to have an answer for idle friends and armchair critics. The only way to do this is to keep a detailed account of profit and loss, under various heads. The first year's expenditure is going to make the accounts look pretty silly if it includes the whole of the outlay on items which are going to last for years. The answer is to spread the costs in a logical way.

First, extract the annual running expenses. These will be very similar every year and include the cost of the following: packets of seeds, onion sets, seed potatoes, and any annual plants bought in; peat, sand, potting composts, growing bags; fertiliser, insecticides, any other chemicals or treatments; peat and plastic-film pots, fillis, plant ties, natural fibre nets and anything else which doesn't last more than one season; hire of cultivator or other machinery; rent of allotment; charge for metered water there or additional hose rate above the ordinary house water rates; any paid labour for holiday periods; cost of advertisements, hire of stall, packaging etc, for selling surplus produce. In later years, repairs and replacements will also figure in running costs—these are dealt with below. Against this, set the value of any assets in hand other than produce. You will have quite a lot of seeds and probably some peat or fertiliser which can be costed, for example.

Small equipment and accessories bought in the first year will last, with luck, for other years. In the case of single items, assess their life-span realistically: thick bendy polythene will probably last three years, hard plastic two; galvanised wire netting seven years, plastic-covered wire nine or ten. Items which get a lot of handling, like seed trays, deteriorate faster than static equipment like water butts. Having estimated the life expectation, divide the initial cost by two, three, eight, or whatever, and include it in your account each year, plus the whole cost of any item damaged during the period. For instance, if you buy ten seed trays at 15p each and you still have ten at the end of the season, charge 75p to the first account. If four of them get broken in the first year, charge 4 × 15p (60p) plus half of 6 × 15p (45p): total £1.05. In the case of an item intended to last three years which is smashed in the second, one-third of the cost has already been written off in the first year, so include the whole of the balance—two-thirds. For example, a watering can costing £2.10 should last three years. In the first year, the written-down cost is 70p. But little Jimmy uses it as a football in year two, resulting in a nasty split, so the second-year figure is £1.40.

Larger equipment is difficult to assess. It costs more, so in theory it should last longer, but some expensive plastic items are fragile. Judge the article on whether it can be simply repaired. When a one-piece, shaped, propagator top breaks, it is useless. Rate it at two years. A glass barn cloche, on the other hand, is made of several pieces of glass and a wire framework. The glass may break, but can easily and cheaply be replaced to make the cloche as good as new. Rate it at about seven years—the probable life of the most durable component—and add in the whole cost of replacing panes of glass as and when they occur.

A glass and aluminium greenhouse ought to last twenty years or more, with no more than an occasional glass replacement; and a wooden one easily the same, if the wood is regularly treated with preservative (cost of this to be included in running expenses). The framework of a plastic house might last as long, depending on the metal used, but the plastic cover will need replacing at regular intervals. In the case of a soft-plastic-covered house costing, say, £30, you might have to replace the cover every third year and this would cost £15 a time. This is such a high proportion of the initial outlay that you might prefer to assess the annual cost differently. Take the prime cost (£30) and add on the cost of the minimum six covers at £15 (£90)—assuming the price stays the same over the years, which is doubtful. Divide this £120 by 20, for the expected frame life, and charge £6 each year. Incidentally, the total outlay on your plastic greenhouse will work out over the years as the same as, or more than, a glass one would have cost, but with greater maintenance problems.

Tools, which are a big expense at the beginning of your gardening career, will last an average of ten years, given reasonable care; so charge one-tenth of the cost each year, plus the total cost of anything damaged or rusted beyond repair. Add the total cost of repairs as running costs, but if you buy new tools as replacements or additions, include one-tenth of the cost from the year of purchase.

Perennial plants, like asparagus, fruit trees, etc, will last for many years and increase in value over most of the period. Fruit trees last thirty-odd years (less for dwarfed types); bushes for twenty, asparagus for over fifteen, artichokes four and strawberries three years. However, it may be best to amortise them over half the expected life period, since they are liable to loss at any time, in theory. If they die, the whole balance must go down in that year and, if you move house, they count as fixtures and should be left behind, which means writing off the whole cost.

Any bulk-purchased goods, like a whole roll of polythene or wire, last for many years, and the best way of costing is probably to measure the length used in any year, making an allowance for any part of it which is as good as new at the end of the season.

Against all this expenditure, reduced to an annual figure, you should set the value of your produce. This can be worked out quite simply by weighing it as it is harvested and checking the current prices in local shops. Early produce is worth more than main crops, because you would have had to pay more for it at the time.

When you have a surplus of produce, don't include it in the normal accounts at its shop value, if you mean to sell it. You won't get the shop price for it, unless you are a remarkable salesman. Regard what you make, less expenses, as profit, since the produce would otherwise have gone to waste. Keep a record of the weight of this produce, and any you give away, so as to judge yields of any type of plant.

Where food is stored in its natural state, it would be strictly fair to deduct the price of anything which goes bad before use. When it is treated before storage, charge the cost of any materials—like salt, sugar, containers and fuel used in the treatment. Re-usable containers, bottles, crocks and boxes can be written down in value over a period of years—quite a long one in most cases.

When freezing produce, you should charge the cost of wrappings, boxes (re-usable), salt, sugar and the small amounts of fuel used for blanching. Include the actual running costs for the freezer, which will probably average around £50 a year for a sizeable cabinet. The total cost of the operation will be more than wiped out by the amount you would have lost by almost any other method of storage.

Include the amortised cost of the freezer over about twenty years (see page 181) and any amounts spent on repairs, servicing or insurance. Some so-called economists insist on including in the cost of having a freezer the theoretical loss of income you might have incurred had you invested the money elsewhere. If you are totally sure that you wouldn't otherwise have spent the money on booze or petrol, then include this sum if you wish—though, if you allow the amount as dividends after tax, the end result will be about 2p. On the same principle, the cost of all your kitchen cupboards, larders and shelves ought to be added in—personally, we should ignore this artificial cost.

Food which you process should be valued at the equivalent commercial rate, rather than the cost of fresh food. Don't forget to deduct the same poundage from the unprocessed total, if you have included it already. Pricing frozen food is easy, but it may be hard to find a commercial comparison for your bottled fruit. If necessary, treat it as the equivalent weight of tinned food. Sauces and pickles, sauerkraut etc, can be costed from the nearest similar product. Jam is difficult, since your home-made product is usually all fruit and sugar, whereas the cheaper commercial grades include stretchers, like swede and other cheap vegetables. Compare yours with the best quality stuff in price, and allow a sum for fuel, since the long cooking process does cost more than the few minutes for freezer blanching.

When you have included every item in your accounts, you will be left with the unquantifiables. How do you cost the value of fresh food as against tired shop food? How do you rate your better health, not only from working out of doors but from eating food which has not been processed commercially or exposed to disease through being handled in markets and shops by people who may be carriers of viruses? How much less have you paid in prescription charges because you don't any longer need drugs to sleep or calm down? How much money have you saved by not driving to the shops for food?

Gardening is hard work, done consistently and conscientiously. Some economists insist that you should include in your accounts the cost of your labour. We think this would only be equitable if you were giving up other paid work to do the gardening. The vast majority of folk do it in their spare time—for which they would be covered financially by their monthly salary. Indeed, it might be fair to consider the alternative. If you were not gardening, what would you be doing? Driving around? Golfing? Boozing? All those activities cost money— perhaps the amount you save by *not* doing them should be added to the profit account?

Index

254